THE SERVANT KING

READING MARK TODAY

THE SERVANT KING

Reading Mark Today

Paul Barnett

AQUILA
PRESS

First published December 1991
Reprinted 1997, 1999, 2001

Aquila Press
PO Box A287, Sydney South, NSW 1235

National Library of Australia
ISBN 1 875861 32 7

Cover design by Helen Semmler

Printed in Australia by Southwood Press Pty Limited

For J.B. Geates, physician and friend

CONTENTS

Reading Mark Today I

1	Why should we read Mark?	1
2	Why should *you* read this book?	2
3	Mark's story	3
4	Mark's world	6
5	Who wrote this Gospel?	8
6	Who was John Mark?	11
7	Is Mark a history of Jesus?	13

Reading Mark Today II

8	The beginning of the gospel (1:1-13)	16
9	The kingdom of God is near (1:14-45)	27
10	The Son of Man is revealed (2:1-3:6)	44
11	Jesus calls the Twelve (3:7-4:34)	62
12	The Lord is revealed to the Twelve (4:35-6:6a)	80
13	Two feasts, two kings (6:6b-56)	98
14	Uncleanness (7:1-23)	128
15	Jesus in Gentile regions (7:24-8:26)	139
16	The Christ (8:27-9:1)	162
17	The mountain and the valley (9:2-29)	176
18	Journey through Galilee (9:30-50)	186
19	Journey to Jerusalem (10:1-52)	198
20	Jerusalem: The Lord in his temple (11:1-12:44)	221
21	The end of the temple (13:1-37)	247
22	The night he was betrayed (14:1-72)	259
23	King of the Jews (15:1-47)	284
24	The empty tomb (16:1-8)	303

Maps

1	Perea-Judea: Where John was baptising	20
2	Capernaum and northern Galilee	39
3	The Decapolis	84
4	Nazareth and southern Galilee	99
5	Perea, including Machaerus and Petra	105
6	Jesus' journey through Gentile territory	144
7	The Sea of Galilee	153
8	Bethsaida and Capernaum	157
9	Jerusalem	222

Reading Mark today I

1

Why should we read Mark?

The reason is simple: Mark's Gospel is the closest in time to Jesus and is based on information supplied by Peter. No one knew Jesus better than Peter. In this Gospel we are in touch with the historical Jesus. Christians will read Mark because it lets them see their Lord through the eyes of a contemporary disciple. Those who do not count themselves as believers will be interested in Mark as an early account of the most influential figure of history.

Mark's is the shortest of the Gospels as well as the most action-filled. Mark is more interested to tell us what Jesus did rather than what he said. He tells his story simply, in an understated way, but with great emotional power. For many years the actor Alec McCowen has presented Mark's Gospel as a solo performance to packed houses in London and New York, such is its dramatic intensity.

So do yourself a favour: read the Gospel of Mark!

2

Why should *you* read this book?

Despite Mark's outward simplicity the book runs very deep. Not everything in it will be clear at the first reading.

During the past 30 years I have read Mark many times, as well as quite a number of books about this Gospel. I have written this simple, non-technical commentary on Mark for ordinary readers. Mark's own words will tell his story, with some brief comments from me about the historical background of the Gospel as well as its leading themes.

This book is designed for busy people — including ministers — with brief chapters suitable for reading in short bursts.

There are questions at the end of each chapter, aimed at helping personal reflection, family or group discussion. Ministers will find the text and the questions suitable for a preaching series on Mark, integrated with home Bible study discussion groups.

For further information about Mark's Gospel, readers might like to refer to W.L. Lane's *Commentary on the Gospel of Mark* (Eerdmans, 1974).

The Bible translation generally used is the New International Version.

3

Mark's story

It is now widely recognised that Mark wrote his Gospel to be read aloud, to be listened to as a story or narrative. At the time he was writing, all reading was spoken, even when a reader was alone. As musical notes come to life when the music is played, so Mark's words come to life when heard; try it and you will see the difference it makes.

Mark also cleverly introduces key words near the beginning of his story which keep reappearing as the narrative unfolds. His leading themes are associated with these key words; these will be pointed out along the way. One example is the word 'gospel' which appears in the first sentence and reappears later several times (see 1:1; 1:14-15; 8:35; 10:29; 13:10; 14:9).

There are two interconnected plots in Mark. The first is the *kingdom of God:* how it was announced and when it appeared. With a minimum of warning, Jesus comes on the scene and tells the people of Galilee that God's kingdom will materialise at any moment. He casts out unclean spirits to signal to the people what manner of kingdom it will be. We are surprised to find Mark has his spotlight on Jesus the announcer and not on God. Jesus says striking things about himself and performs amazing miracles like silencing the storm and raising a dead child. Obviously the kingdom of God is about Jesus.

But then, astonishingly, Jesus sets out for Jerusalem with many warnings that he will be killed there and rise again from the dead. Jesus had tried to suppress the fact that he was the Messiah — the people would have rushed to acclaim him as a popular military deliverer — but when he arrives in Jerusalem he deliberately and publicly presents himself as 'the king of the Jews'. Yet Mark still does not say directly that Jesus is the centre of the kingdom of God nor that the kingdom has materialised; the hearers of the gospel work that out for themselves by the numerous references to the similar sounding word 'king', applied to Jesus, of all places, at his execution in Jerusalem. The hour the kingdom comes is when the King is crucified.

The second plot focuses on the *disciples*, whom we meet immediately following the introduction of the kingdom of God. Jesus first calls four men, a fifth and finally twelve altogether. They leave everything to be with him, in preparation for their mission as his representatives to Galilee, which is in turn a preparation for their mission to represent him to all the nations in the world.

Jesus' teaching about discipleship, as he leads the Twelve from Galilee in 'the way' to Jerusalem, lays down the outlines of Christian behaviour for the post-Easter period. As they bring the gospel to all the nations, the followers of Jesus must value him more highly than their own lives or possessions, they are to remain loyal in marriage throughout their lives and they are to imitate Jesus' spirit of sacrificial service in their relationships with others.

Yet despite the great privilege of being with Jesus, the disciples stumble about, struggling to work out who he is. Even when they recognise him as the Christ (= the messiah) they misunderstand entirely the servant nature both of his messiahship and their discipleship. They disgrace themselves on the night of his arrest by deserting him and, in Peter's case, by denying him. But the women at the empty

4

tomb are told that Jesus is risen and that he will lead Peter and the others to Galilee and graciously restore them as his flock.

The heroes of faith, however, are not the Twelve, but the desperate sick and disabled folk who clamour to get near Jesus, and whose faith is rewarded by healing. They point forward to the post-Easter period when faith in Jesus would be rewarded by salvation. The greatest hero of all, paradoxically, is the Roman officer in charge of the execution squad who, at the point of Jesus' death, recognises him to be the *Son of God*. Ironically, this first Christian confessor is a Gentile — to be joined as history unfolds by many millions of Gentiles who discern in the crucified Jesus their king and Lord.

4

Mark's world

The author of the second Gospel can hardly have escaped the influence of the political era in which he grew up. He would have been a boy when, in AD 14, news came of the death of the Roman emperor, Augustus.

Augustus was no ordinary emperor. The poet Virgil wrote about him in messianic terms, as the first of a 'new breed of men come down from heaven'. Under his rule, Rome, which had been a republic for centuries, began a process by which it became a monarchy. After him, Tiberius, Caligula, Claudius and finally Nero — all relatives of Augustus — were appointed in a kind of dynastic succession.

More importantly, ordinary people all round the Mediterranean were conscious that Augustus had brought peace to the Roman world. They were generally glad to allow more power to pass into his hands if it meant continuing peace, a situation he was quick to exploit.

Augustus was not only a clever soldier able to destroy all military opposition; he also set about capturing the minds of the people. As a resourceful politician he skilfully used various familiar media to establish that a new order had come. He made unprecedented use of coins, with special captions and symbols; of public buildings erected in his honour; of carefully stereotyped statues of himself as a man of strength and reliability (statues were believed to be capable of miraculous powers); and of public inscriptions of his achievements; all established in the popular mind that the world now had a kind but powerful master, against whom any opposition would be futile.

The people of Judea could not have been totally unaware of these remarkable developments. Until his death in 4 BC, Herod was Augustus' favourite client-king. The wily Herod was a prolific builder of cities and imposing structures, many of which he named after and dedicated to Augustus: for example, his great new seaport city, *Caesarea* Maritima. And those who lived in Jerusalem were reminded of Augustus every time they passed Herod's imposing palace: one of its two major buildings was the *Caesareion*. Josephus, the Jewish historian, comments, 'I cannot think of any suitable spot in his kingdom that he left without some tribute of esteem for Caesar [Augustus]' (*Jewish War*, i.407). In addition, the coinage which Pontius Pilate introduced into Judea stated that Tiberius was 'son of the deified Augustus'. (At his death, Augustus was deemed to be a god.) This was the coin Jesus pointed to when he said: 'Render to Caesar the things that are Caesar's, and to God the things that are God's' (12:17, RSV).

When, therefore, Mark reflected on the Gospel he would write, he had in mind readers who were part of a society which had been profoundly influenced by Augustus' achievements. He chose to present Jesus Christ to them in such a way as to leave no doubt that the real new age had dawned with one who was 'truly ... the Son of God' (15:39, RSV). Implicitly, in every sentence, Mark rebuts the claims of a very fallible Roman politician who permitted himself to be depicted in god-like terminology. The contrast of figures like Augustus or Nero with Jesus Christ is an underlying theme of Mark's work from its beginning to its conclusion.

5

Who wrote this Gospel?

The author of the second Gospel nowhere identifies himself by name. There was no need: readers and writer apparently already knew one another. Several examples make this clear.

First, when the author is narrating Jesus' prophecy about '"the abomination that causes desolation" standing where it does not belong', he adds the words· 'let *the reader* understand' (13:14). Here is a secret which writer and readers share but which an outsider who happened to read Jesus' words would not. Roman readers loyal to the state would have regarded Jesus' words as treasonable... once they had understood they were directed at *them* for entering the Holy of Holies in the temple!

This familiar understanding between writer and readers is also clear from the reference to two men, Alexander and Rufus, who are known to the readers (15:21). They are sons of Simon 'from Cyrene', the man who 'on his way in from the country' was forced by the Romans to carry Jesus' cross to the site of the crucifixion. The readers do not know Simon personally, hence the details the writer supplies about him; but they do know Simon's sons, since it is enough to refer to them by name.

Another example of shared understanding relates to a small incident at the time of Jesus' arrest: 'A young man, wearing nothing but a linen garment, was following Jesus. When they seized him, he fled naked, leaving his garment behind' (14:51-52). The event in itself is trivial; it has no bearing on the stark tragedy which was enveloping Jesus at that moment. Matthew and Luke, who make use of Mark's text, omit it; it is only found in Mark's account. Why, then, does the author relate it? In all probability he is appealing once again to information, another secret, which he and his readers share. It is likely that they know the name of this 'young man' and that he is, in fact, the writer himself: he was there when Jesus was arrested, and he attempted to follow the Lord but was prevented from doing so by the loss of his garment. This episode is his cryptic signature.

Who, then, wrote this Gospel, and why? Fortunately a fragment of a book written early in the second century has survived which throws light on that question. Its author, Papias, explains how the Gospel of Mark came to be written.

Papias was a bishop in Hierapolis in Asia Minor in the first half of the second century. He had been a disciple of the apostle John, doubtless in Ephesus which was in the same province as Hierapolis (Eusebius, *History of the Church*, iii.39). So Papias is a link to the era of the apostles. He attributes his understanding of the origin of the Gospel of Mark to a man he calls '[John] the Elder', who may have been John Zebedee, 'the beloved disciple' (see John 13:23; 21:20).

Papias writes: 'Mark ... having been the interpreter of Peter ... neither heard the Lord, nor was he a follower of his, but at a later date of Peter' (*History of the Church*, iii.39). Peter, as a Galilean, probably spoke some Greek along with his first language Aramaic; and as this passage suggests, Mark's role may have been to assist the ageing apostle tell the gospel to Greek-speaking audiences.

9

The New Testament links Mark with Peter in a number of ways. After his escape from King Herod Agrippa, Peter went to the house of Mark's mother (Acts 12:12), and Peter had Mark with him when he wrote his first letter, where he refers to him as 'my son' (1 Peter 5:13). Papias' manner of referring to Mark as a non-follower of Jesus, though associated with Peter, is also consistent with the New Testament: Mark was from Jerusalem, not Galilee, so would not have been one of the original followers of Jesus.

But Papias' tone is defensive; evidently Mark was thought to be inferior to Luke and Matthew. If Luke wrote 'accurately', so, too, Papias assures us, 'Mark wrote accurately'. If Matthew 'compiled the oracles [of Jesus]' (*History of the Church,* iii.39), then, says Papias, 'Mark ... did no wrong ... in not compiling the dominical oracles.'

This low opinion of Mark reflected by Papias' defence persisted through centuries of church history. The second Gospel was so brief. It lacked Matthew's portrayal of Jesus as the great teacher, Luke's elegant style and majestic historical sweep, and John's profoundly simple narration of Jesus' signs and sayings. For a long time Mark remained the neglected Gospel, a curiously irrelevant work.

But all that changed last century with the rise of the critical analysis of biblical texts. Now Mark is almost universally regarded as the first Gospel to have been written and the major narrative source on which Matthew and Luke depend. Moreover, it is now widely believed that despite its apparent naivety of style, this Gospel is written with considerable dramatic skill and with profound development of its leading themes.

6

Who was John Mark?

John Mark was from a house in Jerusalem, sufficiently large to accommodate the 'many people' who were gathered together praying for the release of Peter (Acts 12:12); the presence of a servant girl (Acts 12:13) adds to the impression of financially secure circumstances. Affluence in antiquity was usually associated with literacy and some level of education.

Even though Jerusalem was the centre of the Jewish world, it is now well established that many of its inhabitants spoke, read and wrote Greek. The two names, *John* (Hebrew) and *Mark* (Latin or Greek), are consistent with a profile of John Mark as an educated and bilingual Jew. There is, therefore, no good reason to doubt that such a man would have had the level of literacy required to write the Gospel that bears his name.

Further, Mark had strong associations with noted Christian leaders. He was related to Barnabas (Colossians 4:10), whom he accompanied on two missionary tours of Cyprus, in about AD 47 and 50 (Acts 13:4-5; 15:39). Paul was also part of the earlier tour which, however, Mark quit after the group arrived in southern Asia Minor from Cyprus (Acts 13:13). Although Paul was not prepared to have Mark accompany him on his later overland tour of Asia Minor, his letters written in the 60s suggest that by then he and Mark had reconciled their differences (Philemon 24; 2 Timothy 4:11). And, as we have already noted, Mark also knew Peter, who affectionately wrote of him as 'my son', suggesting that he was a kind of surrogate father (1 Peter 5:13).

Finally, an interesting term is applied to Mark by the writer of the Acts of the Apostles. When Barnabas and Paul proclaimed the word of God on Cyprus, 'John [Mark] was with them as their helper' (Acts 13:5). More literally, he was with them as 'catechist'. The original word *hyperetes* was used of the synagogue assistants who, among their other duties to the scribes, taught boys to read and recite the Hebrew Bible. Possibly Mark was an apprentice to Barnabas and Paul in their ministry in a similar manner. Luke also uses this word in the prologue of his Gospel of 'those who from the beginning were ... ministers [Greek *hyperetai*] of the word' (Luke 1:2, RSV). He acknowledges that he had depended on these 'ministers' for the narratives which he incorporated into his own larger 'orderly account' (Luke 1:3). Since Luke depends heavily on Mark's text, it is probable that in referring to *hyperetai* he specifically had John Mark in mind.

7

Is Mark a history of Jesus?

It would be better to say that Mark is *historical* rather than a history. Any history of Jesus would give precise information about his parents, background and temperament, as well as a chronological account of his life and influence within his particular historical and cultural setting. Certainly, there are historical elements to be found within Mark's account (for example, in regard to John the Baptist, Herod Antipas and Pontius Pilate); they are quite accurate as far as they go, and we shall consider some of the many historical and biographical details in the Gospel as we proceed. Nonetheless, these details are fragmentary, incomplete and usually incidental to the dramatic story Mark is telling. Mark says nothing about Jesus' parents, social circumstances, education or early life, nor anything about his age, appearance or the length of his public ministry. Even allowing for less exact standards of history writing in Mark's time, we have to admit that he does not set out to write a history or biography of Jesus.

Mark calls his work 'gospel' (1:1), a word which in his time meant an announcement or proclamation, usually of an official and important kind. Mark's Gospel is about Jesus Christ, the Son of God. It is in the form of a dramatic narrative of part of Jesus' life, from the beginning of his preaching in Galilee of the approaching kingdom of God to his death and resurrection in Jerusalem. Through this narrative we see Jesus' supernatural power over evil and over the elements of nature, as well as his personal struggle to remain faithful to God's will for him. But we also observe many people's reactions to Jesus, their belief and unbelief, culminating with the centurion's confession, 'Surely this man was the Son of God!' (15:39). In other words, this narrative is a vehicle which brings Jesus before us, the readers, so that we might make a faith commitment to him. It is a *Gospel,* not a history or biography; yet it also gives true information about Jesus and others.

Reading Mark today II

8

The beginning of the gospel 1:1-13

The 'beginning of the gospel' tells us that God is active, keeping the promises he made under the old covenant, tearing open the heavens and sending his Spirit on the man he calls 'my Son, whom I love' (1:11). We stand at the threshold of a mighty act of God.

(1)   The gospel about Jesus Christ, the Son of God (1:1)

The word *gospel* in the opening sentence establishes that what follows is an *official proclamation:* that was the meaning of the word at the time Mark wrote. Citizens of the Roman empire were familiar with proclamations or 'gospels' which usually focused on the emperor and conveyed important and joyous messages. An inscription about the Emperor Augustus, dated 29 BC and found at Priene between Ephesus and Miletus on the west coast of Roman Asia, is strikingly similar to the opening of Mark: 'the birthday of the *god* [ie Augustus] marked for the world the *beginning of good tidings* [=gospel] through his coming'. This 'gospel' declared that a new age of peace for the war-torn Roman world had begun with the birth of Augustus. Josephus, the Jewish historian, likewise describes the way news of the appointment of the Emperor Vespasian quickly spread in

AD 69 and how 'every city kept festival for the good news [= gospel] and offered sacrifices on his behalf' (*Jewish War*, iv.618).

God's *gospel* is *about* a person called *the Son of God*. This, too, was a title of honour often bestowed on Roman emperors, so it can hardly be accidental that, as a climax to the Gospel of Mark, a *Roman* centurion declares that Jesus is 'Surely ... the Son of God' (15:39). While the emperors as 'sons of God' were powerful in pomp and procession, this Son of God was powerless, hanging on a cross, at the very moment the Roman soldier recognised his true identity.

Mark was making a highly provocative, even treasonable, claim. It implied that the true and rightful ruler of the empire was not the Roman emperor but Jesus Christ, a crucified Jew. Mark's Gospel will demonstrate beyond doubt that Jesus Christ is the true Son of God. His preferred title for Jesus, *Son of God*, appears repeatedly within the Gospel and is its chief theme.

Jesus is Greek for the Hebrew name 'Joshua', which means 'Yahweh is salvation'. It was a common name at the time: the historian Josephus mentions some 20 persons named Jesus. From the next century, however, Jews would cease to give this name to their sons. *Christ* is Greek for 'Messiah'. Originally Jesus was called 'the Christ' – a title rather than a name – but because non-Jews would not have heard of such a person he came to be known simply as *Jesus Christ*.

While the *gospel* is *about Jesus Christ*, it begins with Jesus' own 'gospelling'; very soon we meet him preaching the gospel of God (1:14-15). The written gospel – Mark's Gospel – originated with Jesus' *verbal* gospel; Jesus, not Mark, is its true author.

17

(2) The gospel: its beginning (1:2-13)

Mark's first word *beginning* (Greek *arche*) reminds us of the first words of the Bible: 'In the *beginning* God created the heavens and the earth' (Genesis 1:1). God is the beginning and initiator of the salvation of humanity as well as of the creation of the universe.

What, then, is *the beginning of the gospel?* Surprisingly it is not Jesus Christ but John the Baptist, who preceded him. 'The beginning' – verses 2-13 – narrates three episodes spanning John's period of ministry: John baptising and prophesying in the desert; John's baptism of Jesus; and Jesus' temptation in the wilderness. Although Jesus is involved in the second and third episodes, they take place during John's time. Not until John is removed from the scene at verse 14 will Jesus step out of John's shadow; only then will the beginning of the gospel come to its end.

(i)   John in the desert (1:2-8)

In the first episode, the voice of a prophet of God – long silent in Israel – is again heard. It is the voice of John the Baptist, whose message is two-pronged: John calls the people of Israel to *repentance –to turn back wholeheartedly to their God – and to accept baptism* as a sign of their new beginning and of God's *forgiveness of sins.*

This was a startling demand, since baptism was a requirement for non-Jews who converted to Judaism. John was saying that, in spite of their sense of superiority as God's people, Jews had to regard themselves as no better than Gentiles, as non-Jews. Yet despite this humiliating message *the whole Judean countryside and all the people of Jerusalem went out* to meet him.

John also spoke of *one more powerful* than himself, who would come after him and who would *baptise ... with the Holy*

Spirit. The prophet Malachi had prophesied that an Elijah-like figure would precede the Day of the Lord (Malachi 3:1; 4:5), and John saw himself as that 'Elijah': he carefully imitated Elijah's distinctive clothing of *camel's hair, with a leather belt around his waist* (2 Kings 1:8). God had called John to be the forerunner of the Lord who was coming to his people.

The historian Josephus confirms John the Baptist as a genuine figure of history, referring to him as one who was attended by large numbers of people and who baptised; though he does not speak of John as a prophet or as a forerunner of the Lord, only as 'a good man' (*Antiquities*, xviii.116-119).

Through his call to repent and be baptised, John fulfilled the prophecies of Malachi 3:1 and Isaiah 40:3. He was indeed the long-awaited *messenger* of God, sent ahead of the Lord, and his was *the voice of one calling in the desert, 'Prepare the way for the Lord'*.

So why is Isaiah's quotation acknowledged by Mark, but not Malachi's? Probably because Malachi was a minor prophet whose book came at the end of the prophetic writings, whereas Isaiah came first, is much longer and was more famous.

Although verses 2-8 focus on John the Baptist, in his shadow we see a greater figure, the Son of God. He is the *more powerful* one who would come after John, the Lord whose way in the desert John was preparing, who *will baptise ... with the Holy Spirit* (a reference to Jesus' sending of the Spirit on the day of Pentecost; see Acts 1:5; 2:4).

John's baptisms, and also Jesus' time of testing, took place in *the desert* (verses 3,4,12,13) – the arid, treeless Jordan valley in southern Perea. John appears to have been based on the eastern, or Perean, side of the Jordan River (which is the modern kingdom of Jordan) within the jurisdiction of

Herod Antipas, under whom he would later be arrested and killed (6:17-29; cf John 1:28; 10:40).

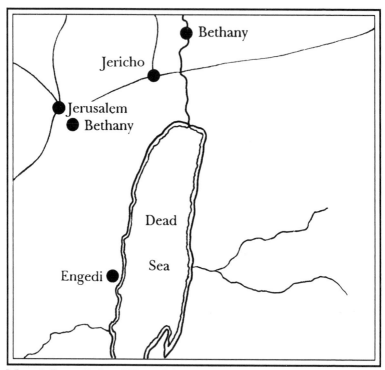

Map 1 *Perea-Judea: Where John was baptising*

(ii)   John baptises Jesus (1:9-11)

The second episode focuses on one of the many people who came to John for baptism in the river Jordan. This individual did not come from Judea but from Nazareth in

Galilee. Few details are given; no conversation between the prophet and Jesus is recorded.

As Jesus was coming up out of the water he saw and heard awesome phenomena from heaven by which God dramatically called him to begin his mission. When *he saw heaven being torn open and the Spirit descending on him like a dove,* he recognised that he was being empowered by the Spirit for a mission such as no other could undertake. When he heard a voice from heaven saying: *'You are my Son, whom I love; with you I am well pleased,'* he was reassured of a relationship with God such as no other could enter into, and of which he was aware from an early age (see Luke 2:49).

These two phenomena from heaven – the Spirit descending and the voice – were God's commission for the task which Jesus had been sent to accomplish and which he is about to begin. Jesus will be locked in battle with the Devil throughout his ministry, from the time of the temptations in the wilderness to his death on the cross; but he will prevail as the Holy One of God, in the power of the Spirit.

Others who came to the Jordan were sinners, seeking the cleansing and renewal of God at the hands of a prophet. But Jesus came as God's beloved – or only – Son, the object of the Father's love and pleasure. Though God's Son, he stands with sinners in the Jordan, as in the future he would be crucified with and for sinners, while being himself without sin.

Later, on the mount of transfiguration, the voice of God would again assure Jesus he was the beloved Son (9:7); and his own teaching confirms that he knew he was the Son loved by God (12:5-6; 13:32). Jesus' filial consciousness was also understood by the apostle Paul, who called Jesus 'the Son [the Father] loves' (Colossians 1:13).

(iii)   Jesus is tempted (1:12-13)

The mission for which the Spirit had come on Jesus was not political or social, but spiritual and cosmic. It would involve terrible conflict with *Satan*, and here Jesus is *tempted* or tested (Greek *peirazomenos*) by him. This is no minor moral skirmish but Satan's full-frontal attack on Jesus to capture his soul.

Jesus had been addressed first by God (1:11), now by Satan. In the baptism, God had reassured Jesus and called him. But now Satan, the enemy of God and his Son, seeks to destroy Jesus before he can begin his assault on the demonic kingdom.

The struggle that begins here will rage throughout the Gospel, reaching its climax when Jesus is on the cross; the cosmic character of that final battle will be symbolised by the day becoming night (see 15:33 — 'when darkness came over the whole land'). The presence of the *wild animals* here signals the grave danger facing Jesus in the loneliness of the desert. At Golgotha he will again be alone, abandoned by his friends and, so it will seem, even by God; then, instead of wild animals, ferocious men will bay at the crucified man (15:29-32; cf Psalm 22:21-22).

Alongside Jesus' temptation, however, is his triumph. The *angels* attend Jesus in the desert, and he does not succumb to Satan or to the wild animals. Jesus is a new Adam. Like Adam, Jesus is Lord over the beasts (cf Genesis 1:26; 2:19-20) or, in the language of Daniel, a 'son of man' who prevails over the evil, beast-like kingdoms (Daniel 7:1-13; cf Revelation 13-14). Unlike Adam, however, Jesus resists temptation, remaining obedient to God. Thus, implicit in Mark but explicit in Paul is the notion that Jesus is the first man of a new race, the leader of a new humanity (see Romans 5:12-21; 1 Corinthians 15:21-24).

In the 'beginning of the gospel' we find *desert* and *Spirit* side by side. In the Exodus God's people had been purified as they passed through the desert to the promised land. Later they knew God's promise that the future blessings of the Spirit would be bestowed in the desert (Isaiah 32:15; 44:3; 63:11-14). God was now keeping these promises: in the desert John spoke of the coming one who would *baptise ... with the Holy Spirit* (verse 8); as Jesus went to the desert to be baptised in the Jordan, the Spirit descended on him (verses 10-11); and the Spirit then took him further into the desert to be tested (verses 12-13).

Jesus is a man of the Spirit, 'powerful in word and deed' (Luke 24:19). Soon we will see him preaching the kingdom of God and confronting a man possessed with an evil, or unclean, spirit (1:21-28). People and demons alike are impressed by him: people by 'his new teaching – and with authority!' (1:27); unclean spirits in their terror that here was at last 'the Holy One of God' who had come to destroy them (1:24).

****

The 'beginning of the gospel' also contains key words which will be repeated throughout the written Gospel. These key words strike a chord with the hearer whenever they are heard during the narration of Mark:

(a) 'Son' and 'Lord'

These two words focus our attention on Jesus. He is addressed as the *Son* (Greek *huios*) by God (1:11; 9:7) and even by the demons (3:11; 5:7; cf 1:24). He knows himself to be the Son (8:38; 12:6; 13:32; 14:36), and when the Roman centurion identifies Jesus as 'the Son of God' it is the climax of the whole story (15:39).

Not so often noticed are Mark's references to Jesus as *Lord* (Greek *kyrios*). This is the name of Yahweh, Israel's God. Jesus is the Lord whose way John the Baptist prepares (1:3). We will also hear of him as 'Lord ... of the Sabbath' (2:28), the Lord who shows mercy to Legion (5:19), the Lord who needs the colt on which to ride into Jerusalem (11:3), and the Lord who according to Psalm 110:1 will sit at Yahweh's right hand (12:36).

(b) 'Way'

Jesus' journey or *way* (Greek *hodos*) is very important in the second half of the Gospel. Jesus' way takes him from Galilee to Jerusalem, where he will meet rejection, betrayal and death at the hands of the temple authorities, followed by resurrection after three days (10:17,32-34). The disciples follow Jesus on the way, symbolising the sacrificial way they must live after Jesus is gone from them. In his second sentence Mark has introduced the word *way*, quoting Malachi 3:1 to show that John the Baptist had come to *prepare the way for the Lord.*

(c) 'Tempted'

The tempting or testing (Greek *peirazein* and *peirasmos*) of Jesus by Satan is also heard throughout the Gospel: the demons discern Jesus' supernatural person and mission in the synagogue of Capernaum (1:24); by the lakeside they offer menacing worship (3:11); when Jesus goes to a lonely place outside Capernaum (literally a 'desert' place), he prays not to be deflected from his God-given mission (1:35-39); solitude on a mountain and in Gethsemane signifies his ongoing struggle with temptation (6:45-46; 14:35); and Peter's opposition to Jesus' sufferings is seen as emanating from Satan (8:33).

24

Jesus viewed the whole of his ministry as a struggle with 'the strong man' Satan (3:27), and the concerted opposition of the Pharisees to Jesus (2:6-7,16-18,24; 3:6; 7:1-5), which is called 'testing' (8:11; 10:2; 12:15), shows that Satan's tempting of Jesus continued throughout his ministry at their hands.

QUESTIONS ON MARK 1:1-13

1. How surprised would Roman readers have been after reading Mark's opening sentence?

2. In your own words, give John's message to the people of Judea as they came out to him at the Jordan River (1:4-5).

3. What did John say about the one who would come after him (1:7-8)?

4. According to Old Testment prophecy (1:2-3), who was John and what would he do? How did John fulfil the prophecy?

5. In his baptism, what supernatural phenomena did Jesus see and hear (1:9-11), and how did they relate to what he was to do?

6. Jesus is addressed first by God then immediately by Satan. What is Satan attempting to do to Jesus?

7. Isaiah prophesied the renewal of God's people in the desert by the Spirit of God. How do the desert and the Spirit figure in Mark's account of the 'beginning of the gospel' (1:2-13), and why is this important?

8. What helpful application can we make to ourselves of facts like:
   a. the coming of John the Baptist as fulfilment of prophecy;
   b. the things Jesus saw and heard from heaven during his baptism;
   c. Jesus' possession by the Spirit and his resistance to temptation?

The kingdom of God is near 1:14-45

The 'beginning of the gospel', which focused on John the Baptist, is ended; the story proper now begins. John the Baptist has been removed from the scene; Jesus comes fully into view.

Mark introduces the two major themes which will run through the Gospel: Jesus and the kingdom of God (1:14-15) and Jesus' call to discipleship (1:16-20).

(1)   The gospel of God (1:14-15)

Up to a year has passed since Jesus went from Nazareth to the desert of southern Perea for baptism and temptation. He returned from Perea to Galilee for a period (John 1:43; 2:1,12) before going to Jerusalem for the Passover (John 2:13-3:21). On his return north, he diverted from his usual route to Galilee via the Jordan valley to visit Samaria (John 4:1-42). This must have been in late spring or early summer (the fields were 'ripe for harvest'; see John 4:35). News of the arrest of John the Baptist (verse 14) might have come to him then (cf John 3:24).

The arrest of John was the signal for Jesus to commence his public ministry. We now meet Jesus in his own right. For the next year and a half, which Mark relates in the next six chapters, Jesus will proclaim the kingdom of God in Galilee.

After his visits to Jerusalem and Samaria, Jesus began his ministry in Galilee, probably in the synagogue of his hometown Nazareth (cf Luke 4:14-30). Mark summarises Jesus' message as *the good news* [= gospel] *of God*. What is this gospel? It is that *'The time has come* [literally 'is filled up']. *The kingdom of God is near.'* And how were his hearers to respond? They were to *repent and believe the good news.* In other words, Jesus' gospel was that:

God's time had now arrived;
God was about to reveal his almighty power in the world;
Everyone is to repent [= return to the Lord their God].

The word 'gospel' was used by Gentile rulers to proclaim important and good news (see comment on 1:1). Gentile readers would have immediately recognised the word and, indeed, the point Mark was making, that Jesus was an emperor-like figure. But for his part Jesus chose the word 'gospel' because of its very pointed use in the Old Testament, in particular by the prophet Isaiah who promised a new exodus to the Jews exiled in Babylon:

How beautiful on the mountains
are the feet of those who bring good news [= gospel],
who proclaim peace,
who bring good tidings,
who proclaim salvation,
who say to Zion,
'Your God reigns!' (Isaiah 52:7)

Jesus is the proclaimer *par excellence* who brings the good news, or gospel, to Israel that her God reigns, that *the kingdom of God* has drawn *near*. Jesus is not teaching the general truth that God is king over history, but rather that *the time has come* for God to fix up the world, as the prophets had said he would. Zechariah, for instance, had prophesied: 'The LORD will be king over the whole earth. On that day there will be one LORD, and his name the only name' (Zechariah 14:9).

When Jesus announced that *the kingdom of God* was *near* he was saying that, at last, God was about to rule in history in a new and perfect way; to set wrongs right, to bring healing, to correct injustice and to establish peace and plenty. Men and women would no longer have to believe through gritted teeth that God was king; soon they would see that he was, with their own eyes. The proof would be before them: God's will would be done on earth as it is in heaven. The Day of the Lord was about to arrive. The passengers on the wharf would be able to see the smoke of the approaching ferry and hear its siren. Soon the vessel would dock, the moorings be fixed, the gangplanks lowered and the travellers welcomed on board.

But, to his hearers, Jesus was external to this rapidly approaching kingdom, a prophet pointing to its coming. What did they expect to happen? They might have replied, 'The kingdom of God will appear when Messiah comes' (cf Luke 19:11). Such a Messiah was, of course, a figure of victory and triumph. But Mark has an incredible surprise in store at the end of his Gospel. His key phrase 'kingdom [Greek *basileia*] of God' will be heard many times, but its climax comes – of all places – in his telling of the crucifixion of Jesus, 'the king [Greek *basileus*] of the Jews' (15:2,9,12,18,26). Contrary to every human expectation that the kingdom of God would come in naked power, its actual appearance is characterised by utter powerlessness. Betrayed, deserted and denied by his friends, the 'king' is subjected to a Jewish 'kangaroo court', handed over to the Romans on the false charge of high treason, and crucified

29

– an unspeakable thing – for a crime he did not commit.
Astonishing as it is, this is precisely Mark's message: the
kingdom of God finally arrives in the shameful crucifixion
of Jesus of Nazareth, the King of the Jews.

What did Jesus ask his hearers to do in response to his
gospel? They were to *repent and believe the good news* (=
gospel). To *repent* (Greek *metanoiein*) means to change our
attitudes so radically that our self-centred behaviour comes
into line with God's will. Jesus' call is similar to the prophets'
demand that Israel 'return' or 'turn back' to Yahweh (eg
Amos 4:6,8-9,10,11). To *believe* the gospel means to welcome
the glad tidings that the kingdom of God will soon come.
To *repent and believe* the gospel means to rejoice that God is
about to rule and to yield our lives to his will gladly.

Jesus' message in Galilee was not about himself, but about
God. It was also similar to and continuous with that of John
the Baptist (cf Matthew 3:1-2). This similarity of message
would not have been lost on Jesus' Galilean hearers. To
them Jesus was not merely a rabbi but a prophet with a
message similar to John's: that the kingdom of God was fast
approaching and it was time to turn back to Yahweh their
God.

(2)   Disciples (1:16-19)

If Jesus and the kingdom of God is Mark's dominant
theme, discipleship – the theme he now introduces – is
second in importance. Jesus' call to the disciples
immediately follows the announcement of his mission
(1:14-15). From this point, disciples and discipleship play a
prominent part in the unfolding story.

Jesus comes to the *Sea of Galilee*, a day's walk down from
the high country of Nazareth. The most direct route would
have been via the trunk road from the coast, which passed
about eight kilometres east of Nazareth en route to

Damascus in the north-east, and also passed close to Capernaum. As Jesus walked by the north-western shore of this beautiful, harp-shaped freshwater lake (20 kilometres north to south and 12 kilometres across), he meets two pairs of brothers, *Simon* and *Andrew* and *James* and *John*, who are partners in a fishing business (cf Luke 5:10).

This was not their first meeting; Jesus' call to these four fishermen to *'Come, follow me'* was based on associations which had begun a year earlier. Andrew and Simon had been disciples of John the Baptist in southern Perea at the time of Jesus' baptism (see John 1:35,40). Being among those devout Jews who had recently returned to Yahweh in response to John's preaching (1:4), they formed the human highway on which the Lord would walk (see 1:2-3). They accompanied Jesus from Perea back to Galilee (cf John 1:43; 2:2,12).

But now, as Jesus becomes fully committed to proclaiming the kingdom of God, they join him in his mission. *'I will make you fishers of men,'* he says to them; and the four fishermen leave their nets and begin to catch men for the kingdom of God.

These boatmen, with rough hands and weather-beaten faces, whom the Jerusalem chief priests later scorn as 'unschooled, ordinary men' (Acts 4:13), within a year are visiting the towns of Galilee calling on the population to repent. And in the years to come they travel the roads of the Roman world proclaiming the gospel of the kingdom of the Messiah Jesus. They do indeed become *fishers of men.*

In particular, what happens to Peter over the next 35 years is evidence that the kingdom of God announced by Jesus did indeed come in his death and resurrection. Would Peter have left the security of Capernaum for danger and ultimately violent death in Rome unless the message about Jesus were true? How else can we explain Peter's remarkable career change from semi-literate fisherman to apostle, re-settling in Jerusalem and then becoming an itinerant 'shepherd' to Christian communities in Syria, Asia Minor, Greece and Italy? Had the kingdom of God not arrived in the death and resurrection of Jesus and in the outpouring of the Spirit of God, Peter would surely have returned to the obscurity from which he had come, sadly disillusioned that Jesus had been just another deluded prophet.

With great authority Jesus first addresses one pair of brothers then the other. The former *left their nets and followed him*; the Zebedees *left their father ... in the boat with the hired men and followed him*. With all four there is no argument, no delay, only immediate compliance with his command. Jesus' call to these men contrasts with the manner in which pupils then attached themselves to a rabbi. Would-be pupils usually applied to the teacher, but in this case Jesus takes the initiative and the pupils do as he commands. Jesus' authority, matched by the disciples' obedience, is another sign that the kingdom, whose gospel Jesus has begun to announce, is indeed close at hand.

The key word in this first discipleship passage, the verb 'to leave' (Greek *aphienai*), will be heard repeatedly throughout the narrative. The disciples *left* their nets and family (18,20). Later Peter tells Jesus, 'We have left everything to follow you' (10:28), to which Jesus replies that to follow him a disciple must leave family, security and possessions (10:29; cf 10:17-22). To follow Jesus means to leave... people and things.

(3)   Capernaum: The synagogue (1:21-28)

Jesus, with the four men, now goes to *Capernaum* on the northern shore of the Sea of Galilee. A town of about 15,000 inhabitants, Capernaum was set in a rich agricultural region. Additionally it was a centre for both catching and preserving fish. Only five kilometres separated Capernaum from the

upper Jordan River to the east, the border of the tetrarchy
of Herod Antipas. Beyond that lay Gaulanitis, the territory
of Herod Philip. An important road passed by Capernaum
linking Alexandria with Damascus and ultimately Babylon.
Travellers on that road were compelled to pay a toll at or
near Capernaum (see 2:13-14). Further indication of the
strategic significance of the city may be seen in the presence
of Roman troops (see Matthew 8:5-13; Luke 7:1-10) and of
the Herodian royal official who lived there (John 4:46).

Jesus probably chose Capernaum as the centre of his
ministry on account of both its strategic location and the
ease with which he could withdraw from there out of reach
of Antipas into Philip's neighbouring tetrarchy.

Capernaum has been subject to continuing
archaeological investigation since 1968, and the remains of
an elegant synagogue there date from the fourth century.
The *synagogue* to which Jesus went on his first *Sabbath* in
Capernaum may have been located on the same site.

Passages from the Law and the Prophets were read aloud
in the synagogue in Hebrew – the language of the scholars
(the equivalent of Latin in the Roman Catholic Church) –
with free translation, commentary and exhortation in the
everyday Aramaic. The ruler of the synagogue, who
controlled the services, would have permitted Jesus to *teach*
on the basis of his competence in reading and translating
the Hebrew text of the Bible. (At that time synagogue
teaching was less regulated than in later centuries.) Jesus
probably chose a passage from the Prophets, as he did in
the synagogue in Nazareth (Luke 4:14-22), and taught from
it that the prophetic promise was now at the edge of
fulfilment, that the kingdom of God was imminent.

Two responses are recorded by Mark (probably based on
the first-hand recollections of Peter). First, the congregation
is amazed at Jesus' teaching, because *he taught them as one
who had authority, not as the teachers of the law*. Unlike the

33

rabbis who quoted other rabbis for their authority, Jesus appealed to no authority higher than his own. He said characteristically, 'I say to you' (see Matthew 5:22, 28, 32,34, 39, RSV) and often prefaced his words with the solemn, 'I tell you the truth' (eg 3:28). The rabbis taught *by* authority but Jesus taught *with* authority, the authority of God.

A second, more dramatic reaction comes from *a man ... possessed by an evil* [= unclean] *spirit* who exclaims *'What do you want with us, Jesus of Nazareth?'* Mark's Greek words reproduce the flavour of this outburst in native Aramaic; literally they are 'what to us and to you?' The spirits continue: *'Have you come to destroy us? I know who you are – the Holy One of God!'* The plural *us* suggests the man is the mouthpiece for a community of unclean spirits who recognise Jesus as their destroyer.

How striking that an unclean spirit is the first to identify Jesus as *the Holy One of God,* the one on whom the Holy Spirit of God had come (cf 1:10), and to discern that Jesus' mission was to *destroy* the power which Satan held over people. The unclean spirits understood that in Jesus the kingdom of God – the new age of the Holy Spirit – was breaking in and that their days were numbered. Mark tells this story at such length because it will be repeated many times as Jesus proclaims the kingdom of God and confronts the strongholds of Satan.

Demon possession has symptoms in common with mental illness yet the two are not identical. Demon possession arises from involvement with spiritual or cosmic evil whereas mental illness may be attributable to organic or social causes, similar to a physical disability. We do not know how this man came under the control of the unclean spirits; perhaps he had been involved in occultic practices or the worship of Satan.

Jesus demands that the man *be quiet* (literally 'be muzzled', like a wild, uncontrollable beast needing its mouth to be restrained) and that the unclean spirit *come out* of him (25).

The congregation is *amazed* when they see the unclean spirit shaking the man violently and coming out of him *with a shriek.* They vigorously question one another about what has happened: *'What is this? A new teaching – and with authority! He even gives orders to evil spirits and they obey him.'*

This *amazement* shown towards Jesus is expressed in key words (Greek *ekplessesthai* and *thambeisthai*) which we will hear many times during the course of the Gospel (cf 2:12; 5:20,42; 7:37). In Jesus' presence the people in the synagogue – and we the readers – stand at the edge of the eschatological abyss, the appearance of the kingdom of God. Such supernatural intervention is greeted by amazement.

The people also immediately recognise Jesus' *teaching* as *new* (Greek *kainos*), so new that even the unclean spirits now submit to him. This new teaching is appropriate to the kingdom which Jesus says is now upon them; and he later tells parables about the kingdom being radical and destructive, like new cloth and new wine (2:21-22). He will also say that the 'new covenant' would come through his death, and that he would 'not again drink from the fruit of the vine' until the new order had come, when he would then 'drink it anew' (14:24-25).

Above all, the people discern in Jesus his *authority.* God was the source of his new teaching and his mastery over the unclean spirits. Jesus' casting out of evil spirits with authority was a sign of his new teaching that the kingdom of God was about to appear. *Authority* (Greek *exousia*) is another of Mark's key words (2:10; 3:15; 6:7; 11:28-29,33).

The immediate obedience of the four fishermen and the amazement of the synagogue congregation show that in Jesus something new and supernatural had come. As a result

news about him spread quickly over the whole region of Galilee.
Mark probably does not mean the entire political or
geographical region so much as the area in the immediate
vicinity of Capernaum, in northern Galilee.

(4)   Capernaum: the home of Simon and Andrew (1:29-34)

Leaving the synagogue, Jesus goes with the four
fishermen (back?) *to the home of Simon and Andrew,* which
they apparently shared and where Simon's mother-in-law
also lived. Since Jesus also now lived in this house we may
be interested to know how so many could occupy one
dwelling.

As it happens, Capernaum is the best-preserved Galilean
village of the period. Through the work of archaeologists
the outline of some of the streets is now established, as well
as the ground plans of several houses. Typically the houses
had an inner courtyard with two depths of rooms on each
of the four sides. It is possible that three or four families
shared the one complex, each enjoying access to a common
internal court and the outside street. It should be
remembered that Simon and Andrew were self-employed
partners in a fishing business, well capable of owning a
house of this size.

Mark now records the first healing miracle of Jesus:
Simon's mother-in-law. She was *in bed with a fever,* no doubt
distressed by the accompanying headaches and discomfort
associated with high temperature. In their helplessness *they*
(the wives of Simon and Andrew?) told Jesus, who went to
her bedside, *took her hand and helped her up,* whereupon *the
fever left her.*

In this first healing miracle, as in many that follow, Jesus'
physical contact with the sick should be noted, in particular,
his hands and the hands of the sick (cf 1:41; 5:41; 7:33; 8:23).
The healing was also immediate and complete, the evidence

of which was that *she began to wait on them* (the five men?) at the Sabbath meal.

Word of these dramatic events in the synagogue and in Simon's home rapidly spread through Capernaum. Many families and friends in their desperation *brought to Jesus all the sick and demon-possessed.* Again, Mark's vivid account suggests an eyewitness's recollection. First, these needy people were not brought until *evening after sunset,* when the Sabbath restrictions on carrying people had passed. Moreover, Mark's expression, *all the sick,* translates an underlying Aramaic phrase (literally 'all who has sick') which may have been Peter's actual words. Again, the sense of expectation, expressed in *the whole town gathered at* [literally 'towards'] *the door* of Simon's house waiting for Jesus to appear, is well explained as Peter's reminiscence.

Jesus demonstrates his complete mastery over the illnesses of these helpless people: he *healed many who had various diseases* and *drove out many demons.* But because the demons know who he is – the Holy One of God (1:24) – Jesus will not let them speak. Galileans might have interpreted such a confession in messianic terms, but the only messiah those volatile people could conceive of was a military one who would defeat the Romans and establish a Jewish world-empire based on Jerusalem. The mere mention of 'messiah' in connection with so dramatic a figure as Jesus would have wrongly typecast him in the eyes of the Galileans. The demons knew who Jesus was and why he had come – ironically their understanding was accurate – but they were not permitted to speak lest Galilee be set ablaze with wild messianic rumours.

(5)   Into the towns of northern Galilee (1:35-45)

The dramatic impact of Jesus on the town of Capernaum is now repeated in the towns of northern Galilee. Just as *the whole town* had converged on Jesus (1:33), so now people *from everywhere* seek him. And the reason for this excited interest - first in Capernaum, then in the whole region - is but one: Jesus' healing of the diseased.

The *morning* after the dramatic sabbath in Capernaum, Jesus got up *while it was still dark, left the house and went off to a solitary place* [literally a 'desert' place] *where he prayed.* Mark's use of the key word 'desert' (Greek *eremos*) could suggest that the temptations of Satan in the wilderness have reappeared. Is Jesus being tempted to welcome the interest of the crowds who were drawn to him for the healing of their diseased relatives and friends? When *Simon and his three companions* eventually *found him* (literally 'persecuted him'), their words, *'Everyone is looking for you!'* would certainly have added to any felt temptation to accept the adulation of the crowds.

Jesus' reply: *'Let us go somewhere else – to the nearby villages'* – villages in the region of Capernaum – leads him to make a very significant statement of the purpose of his coming. We should take careful note whenever Jesus declares, *'I came ...'* or 'I have *come* to ...'; for example, 'have ... *come* to call ... sinners' (2:17) and 'the Son of man ... *came* ... to serve, and to give his life a ransom for many' (10:45, RSV). Such statements take us into the mind of Jesus and allow us to hear from his own lips what his mission was, what he had come to do. Embedded within the words quoted by Mark (verse 38) is Jesus' critical declaration: *'I have come to preach'* [= proclaim].' And if we ask, 'Proclaim what?' the answer (based on verses 14-15) must be that Jesus came to proclaim:

The time has come:
the kingdom of God is near.
Repent and believe the gospel.

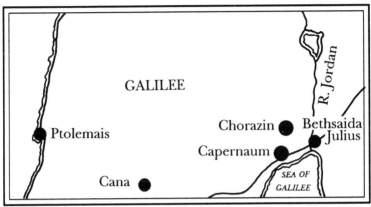

Map 2 *Capernaum and northern Galilee*

But the Galilean onlookers have their own agendas for Jesus: families of the sick want him to heal their relatives, and fiery nationalists want him to conquer for God as a warrior-messiah. Jesus' mission, however, is to announce to Israel that the hour for God's rule has come and that the people must return to their God and welcome his gospel. So, true to his purpose, he left Capernaum and *travelled throughout Galilee, preaching* [= proclaiming the kingdom of God] *in their synagogues and driving out demons.*

Although Jesus performed other kinds of miracle – healing the sick, raising the dead, nature miracles – the casting out of demons was the particular sign of the kingdom of God. He said: 'If I drive out demons by the finger of God, then the kingdom of God has come to you' (Luke 11:20; cf Matthew 12:28).

Mark's account of what transpired in these northern Galilean synagogues is in summary form because he has already described at some length what occurred in the synagogue at Capernaum (1:21-28). That pattern was probably repeated in the other synagogues: Jesus would translate a passage from the Prophets, declaring that God's hour had struck, that the time of fulfilment had now come; and when a demonically inspired reaction occurred, Jesus would cast out the demons as evidence of the nearness of the kingdom.

This section concludes, however, with an incident which is told in some detail. In one of the towns (not identified) *a man with leprosy* came to Jesus and *begged him on his knees,* perhaps expressing homage or worship, 'If you are willing, you can make me clean.'

Clearly the man has heard about Jesus' remarkable powers, no doubt from the reports from Capernaum which had spread from village to village. But his request places Jesus in a difficult position. The casting out of demons was the sign that the kingdom of God was fast approaching. Curing the diseased, however, seemed only to arouse a heightened expectation of healing, with minimal interest in Jesus' call to turn back to God in light of the nearness of his kingdom.

The situation provokes a twofold emotional response from Jesus. On one hand, *filled with compassion,* he says, '*I am willing. Be clean!*' and *immediately the leprosy left* the man *and he was cured.* Jesus did not merely speak these words: he *touched the man* to express compassion for outcasts from society, as lepers were. Notice once more Jesus' physical contact with the sick (cf 1:31), and how, by touching an 'untouchable' man, Jesus transferred the uncleanness to himself, symbolising in advance the nature of his atoning death.

Mark frequently comments that Jesus healed the sick or fed the hungry out of 'compassion' or 'mercy' for their desperate plight (5:19; 8:2; 10:47,48; cf 9:22). Yet this was not what he *came* to do (cf 1:38). Healing was incidental to

Jesus' mission of proclaiming the kingdom, casting out demons and calling the people to return in repentance to Yahweh their God; and many times, as we will see, healing was a hindrance to that mission.

So, on the other hand, Jesus' action towards the man is *stern*, in contrast with his compassionate healing of the disease. He *sent him away* (literally 'threw [him] out', as he would throw out mourners from the house of Jairus, 5:40, and traders from the temple, 11:15) *with a strong warning, 'See that you don't tell this to anyone.'* Except, that is, *the priest*, who was to declare a leper 'clean' in the event of his recovery from the disease (Leviticus 14:4-32). Jesus thus encouraged the keeping of the law.

Jesus' concern about the undesirable publicity of the healings is confirmed. The leper *went out and began to talk freely, spreading the news.* As a result, so many are attracted by the healings that Jesus is now unable to *enter a town openly* and is forced instead to remain *outside in lonely places* (literally 'desert' places; cf 1:12,35).

Once more, this key word 'desert' introduces the idea of Jesus' temptation. He is again under pressure, now the pressure of his own compassion, to abandon his kingdom/demons/repentance mission to become instead a mass healer. As a result of the healed leper's failure to remain silent, the experience of Capernaum is repeated in other towns. And just as the four fisherman came to Jesus in the 'solitary' (= desert) place outside Capernaum (1:35-37), the people from the towns *still came to him from everywhere.*

We have gained further insight into the ongoing testing of Jesus, and thus the first phase of Jesus' Galilean ministry is now complete. In the towns of Galilee, in Nazareth, Capernaum and the northern towns centred on Capernaum, Jesus announced the rapid approach of the kingdom of God and demonstrated it by driving out demons and calling for repentance. He summoned four men to leave everything to follow him, calling them to become fishers of men.

But Jesus' encounters with the sick, first Simon's mother-in-law, then many others in Capernaum and finally the leper, forced him to restrict his healings to those needy individuals who confronted him directly, lest the whole character of his mission be misinterpreted and a messianic fervour erupt. For the same reason, he silenced the demons. Healings attracted crowds of the sick and their relatives, and messianic confessions stirred nationalistic fervour; but neither brought the repentance which was appropriate to the appearing of the kingdom of God.

Running through all these stories, therefore, is Jesus' underlying cosmic struggle with Satan, which begins in the desert of Perea, continues in the 'deserts' outside Capernaum and in the northern region, and will go on until the climactic struggle of the crucifixion. Jesus came to announce and, by his death and resurrection, to activate the kingdom of God, in which the Son of God overpowers 'the strong man'. From beginning to end, however, Satan continually attempts to deflect Jesus from this mission.

But at this earliest stage in his ministry, Jesus proclaims that God's hour has struck, that the kingdom of God is about to appear, and that the people must turn back to their God and welcome the glad tidings he brings to them.

QUESTIONS ON MARK 1:14-45

1. What was the signal for Jesus to commence his public ministry, and why (1:14; cf John 3:24)?
2. What did the prophets mean by what Jesus called 'the kingdom of God'? How should we respond to the message of the kingdom of God today?
3. Put yourself in the place of the people who heard Jesus teach in the synagogues of Galilee, as recorded in 1:14-45. Would you have thought of him as a rabbi, a prophet or as ...?
4. What problems are posed by the fact that Jesus says so little about himself? (Note the 'revelations' about Jesus' identity from heaven and from demons.)
5. How does Mark tell us the kingdom has arrived? How might Jewish and Roman readers have responded to this (cf 1 Corinthians 1:23)?
6. The casting out of demons is somehow connected with the kingdom of God (1:39). What do you think that connection is? In this chapter, do casting out demons and healing the sick have the same role?
7. Why does Jesus silence the demons and the sick (1:25,34, 43-44)? Why does he appear reticent to heal the leper (1:40-43; cf 1:35-38)?
8. How do Mark's references to 'desert' places (1:35,45) give us insight into Jesus' ongoing temptations (cf 1:12-13)?

10

The Son of Man is revealed 2:1-3:6

Jesus' ministry in the synagogues in and near Capernaum (1:21,39) appears to have provoked the hostility of the Pharisees. Is this why Jesus now ceases to teach in the synagogues but begins to teach in the open, to large crowds of hearers? (And do we see here an anticipation of the ministry of John Wesley who, prevented by the authorities from speaking inside the established church, took his message to the multitudes in the open?)

In the stories that follow we will notice two closely related themes: one is Jesus' conflict with the Pharisees, the other his important statements about himself. Jesus goes out of his way to challenge the Pharisees' beliefs and practices, and to expose their false expectations about the kingdom of God. At the same time it becomes clear that Jesus himself is the kingdom which he is announcing; he embodies it. There is no hint, however, that his small group of disciples understand this.

(1)   Blasphemer! (2:1-12)

After *a few days,* a short but indefinite period after the last incident (1:45), *when Jesus again entered Capernaum,* the local *people heard that he had come home* (ie to Simon's home, cf

44

1:29). As on the first Sabbath evening in Capernaum (1:32-33), the street outside the house is again filled with people. And again, the crowd is chiefly interested in the healing of the diseased and chronically ill.

Jesus, however, *preached* [literally 'spoke'] *the word to them,* the message about the kingdom of God, which he probably gave in the form of parables. In the synagogues Jesus declared the gospel of the kingdom from the Prophets (Luke 4:16-21), but in the open he spoke that message in parables (4:33,34).

Jesus is probably standing in the doorway to speak. A group of men appear at the back of the crowd, and *four of them* are carrying a paralysed man on a stretcher. Unable to bring the man forward to Jesus *because of the crowd* in the street, the four climb up on the roof (probably by means of an outside stairway), make an opening in it and lower the man into the house. The truth of this story is guaranteed by the unimaginable detail.

While Jesus did not seek such healing encounters, he did not refuse any pleas for help from the desperate people of that pre-hospital age. The human context in which Jesus healed, however, was *faith in him:* wherever there was scepticism about him, at Nazareth, for example (6:2-6), Jesus' healing activity was minimal. *When Jesus saw their faith* refers to the faith in him shown by the group of *four* who revealed such enterprise in bringing the man *to him.* This is the first occasion *faith* (Greek *pistis*) in Jesus is reported by Mark, and it is characterised by desperation, determination and dependence (see also 5:34; 10:52; 11:22; cf 4:40).

Jesus' reaction to the men's faith is startling and totally unexpected: he does not say, 'Be healed!' or anything similar (cf 1:41); rather, *he said to the paralytic, 'Son, your sins are forgiven.'*

There is an important, though general, theological connection between sins and illness. Death, and therefore, sickness which is a symptom of death, arises from the sin of our 'parents' Adam and Eve when they first disobeyed God (Genesis 2:16-17). Moreover, there is sometimes a direct physical or psychological connection between sins and sickness (though this is not always, or even often, the case; cf John 9:1-3). In this incident, however, there is no suggestion that the man's paralysis arose directly from sins, either his own or his parents. In fact, the astonishing point being made by Jesus – that the man's sins are forgiven by *God* – will be missed if this connection is insisted on. The man had committed no sin against Jesus, and yet Jesus declared him forgiven.

Jesus' words are prophetic of the time after his death and resurrection, when all those who exercise faith in him are assured that their sins are forgiven, that they are 'saved' (5:34; 10:52; cf 15:30-31).

We now meet a group whom we will encounter many times: the *teachers of the law* (literally 'men of letters' or 'scribes'). They *were sitting there*, presumably in the street, weighing up Jesus' words. They must have been close enough to the door to hear his outrageous words to the paralytic and his friends. Jesus is blatantly provocative towards the teachers in order to make a critical point about his own identity and mission.

Jesus discerned their thoughts (verse 8), which were probably written on their faces and expressed in their body language: *'Why does this fellow* [Greek *houtos*, a term of disparagement] *talk like that? He's blaspheming! Who can forgive sins but God alone?'* From their viewpoint, Jesus was highly offensive, a crude fellow, a blasphemer. It was fundamental to their 'godly' thinking that humans were morally blemished, imperfect in the sight of God and that God alone could declare sins forgiven. If this was the reaction of the religious establishment towards Jesus at the beginning of his ministry it should be noted that it will also be their attitude at the end: ultimately the Sanhedrin condemn Jesus for blasphemy (14:64).

Jesus reponds to the teachers' unasked question with his astonishing question: *'Which is easier: to say to the paralytic, "Your sins are forgiven," or to say, "Get up, take your mat and walk"?'* The implication is that Jesus is equally capable of forgiving *and* healing. Indeed, either or both express the arrival of God's Messianic kingdom as promised by the prophets, for example, Jeremiah 31:31-34: 'The time is coming ... when ... I will forgive their wickedness ...' and Isaiah 29:18: 'In that day the deaf will hear ... the blind will see'. Jesus is saying that the kingdom of God, whose critical nearness he proclaimed, is *manifest* in his words and actions.

But the forgiveness of sins cannot be seen; it is invisible. Because Jesus knows it is not possible to see whether or not the paralytic's sins are forgiven by God, he makes the remarkable statement to him: *'But that you may know that the Son of Man has authority on earth to forgive sins ... get up, take your mat and go home.'* And in living proof that Jesus had the *authority ... to forgive sins,* the paralysed man did exactly as Jesus had commanded: *he got up, took his mat and walked out in full view of them all.*

Son of Man, Jesus' characteristic way of referring to himself, now appears in the narrative. 'Son of man' is prominent in Daniel 7:13-14: the term refers to a human agent who would execute God's saving purposes as God's representative. *The Son of Man* bears God's authority both to forgive and to judge (verse 10; cf John 5:27). This, however, raises an important question: If God alone can forgive and judge, what manner of *man* can act on God's behalf to forgive and to judge? Jesus is preparing the disciples for the truth which he will later reveal to them, that he is not merely a man, but also the Son of God, the one who shares in God's own nature. But because it was a more mysterious term, Jesus could speak of himself as 'Son of Man' without fuelling messianic fires.

The miracle of the paralytic's healing is the undeniable proof that, though a man, Jesus was God's unique and divine representative *on earth – the Son of Man –* having God's full *authority* to do what no other man could do: *forgive sins* and, at the end, pass judgment (John 5:27).

Jesus is not merely the preacher of the kingdom of God but also its mediator and instrument. Although the kingdom is yet to appear, it is already active in Jesus' words and actions. God himself is present in Jesus to forgive and, in demonstration of that, to heal the chronically ill (cf Acts 10:38). Jesus' words and actions are an oblique claim to his deity. Ironically the teachers of the law were correct in asking their question: *'Who can forgive sins but God alone?'* Who indeed.

The reaction of the people in the street outside the house is significant. The healing of the paralytic *amazed everyone and they praised God, saying, 'We have never seen anything like this!'* We the readers share in the amazement of those present, that the kingdom of God had drawn near in Jesus.

(2)   Compromiser! (2:13-17)

It was no light thing for Jesus to be accused of blasphemy. We are not surprised to find him now outside Capernaum, though Mark gives no indication how soon after the dramatic scene at the house of Simon these next incidents occur, nor where exactly. It is likely, however, that *beside the lake* refers to the north-west shore of the Sea of Galilee, in the general region of Capernaum. That part of the shoreline certainly would have afforded areas where Jesus could conveniently teach the *large crowd* which gathered. We may eliminate other segments of the shoreline at this stage of Jesus' ministry: the eastern side of the lake lay outside

Galilee in the tetrarchy of Philip, but Jesus did not take refuge there till later; the south-western part of the lake which was centred on Tiberias, the capital of the tetrarchy and home of its ruler Antipas, was an area which Jesus appears to have avoided. (Commentators sometimes interpret Mark's various references to the lake as darkly foreboding and ominous, but this may be reading into the text a symbolism he did not intend.)

This is the first occasion in Mark's narrative when Jesus teaches a crowd: an indication of his growing fame in the region, but also of the suspicion of the synagogue rulers towards him, forcing him to teach in the open.

Although Mark does not record as much of the actual teachings of Jesus as the other Gospel writers, it is as a teacher, or rabbi, that Jesus chiefly comes before us in this Gospel. He is called 'Rabbi' or 'Rabboni' four times, 'Teacher' on 12 occasions and is said to engage in 'teaching' no less than 16 times. Jesus' teaching at this stage in his ministry was about the rapid approach of the kingdom of God, a message which he taught by means of parables (4:33-34).

Jesus now sets out back to Capernaum, probably travelling along the major road from Egypt to Mesopotamia. Capernaum was the town closest to the border with Philip's tetrarchy and therefore had a customs post. Jesus came to *the tax collector's booth* where the customs official *Levi son of Alphaeus* was sitting receiving toll payments from travellers on behalf of his employer, the tetrarch Herod Antipas.

As with the four fishermen who are now following him, Jesus issues the direct call, *'Follow me,'* whereupon *Levi got up and followed him.* As before (cf 1:17), this is a point of dissimilarity with the rabbis, whose pupils applied to follow and learn from them. But Jesus summoned his disciples to follow and learn from him; his direct call, and their

immediate obedience in leaving their employment, is a sign
of the kingdom whose nearness Jesus proclaimed.

Jesus' calling of a customs official was both deliberate and
provocative, and marks a new departure in his ministry.
Such persons were despised on account of their extortion
of travellers and their demands for bribery. The scribes
regarded them as law-breakers (as they usually were), on a
par with robbers and murderers. Jesus not only called into
his company a man who practised a despised trade and who
was in all probability notorious in that region; he even went
to his *house* and ate dinner with him and *many other tax
collectors and 'sinners'* (= outcasts). J. Jeremias comments,

> Any one engaging in such trades could never be a judge,
> and his inadmissibility as a witness put him on the same
> footing as a gentile slave. In other words he was deprived
> of civil and political rights to which every Israelite had
> claim ... This makes us realize the enormity of Jesus' act
> in calling a publican to be one of his intimate disciples,
> and announcing the Good News to publicans and
> 'sinners' by sitting down to eat with them. (*Jerusalem in
> the Time of Jesus*, SCM, 1969, p 311)

We may suppose that Levi was overwhelmed that one who
was proclaiming the kingdom of God should call him to
follow; the banquet that he gave expressed his love and
gratitude to Jesus.

By calling Levi and attending his banquet, Jesus was
declaring the kingdom of God to be mercifully within reach
of all outcasts. Since the name of Yahweh was invoked in
thanksgiving, eating a meal was a sacred fellowship;
therefore Jews had to be careful not to eat with any whose
lifestyle blasphemed the name of Yahweh (cf Acts 10:28).

So when *the teachers of the law who were Pharisees* heard the
scandalous news that Jesus had eaten at the house of Levi,

they came, saw for themselves and complained, '*Why does he eat with tax collectors and "sinners"?*' Their question foreshadows the teaching of the Mishnah two centuries later which states that '[a Pharisee] may not be the guest of one of the people of the land' (*Demai*, ii.2), the latter being a term for those who were ignorant of the law, clearly including *tax collectors and 'sinners'*.

Mark expresses the teachers' complaint in the form of a question, as with their earlier complaint about Jesus' blasphemy (cf 2:6). Readers too may be asking why indeed Jesus does this. Surely the first psalm declares:

Blessed is the man who
   does not walk in the counsel of the wicked
or stand in the way of sinners
   or sit in the seat of mockers. (Psalm 1:1)

Isn't Jesus compromised by being there giving apparent endorsement to an immoral lifestyle? Why is he eating with these extortioners? Once again these teachers unwittingly ask a deeply perceptive question which is addressed ultimately to us the readers.

Jesus defends his action by quoting a popular proverb: '*It is not the healthy who need a doctor, but the sick.*' As law-breakers, these sinners and tax collectors were *sick*. Jesus says he is among them as a *doctor*, which calls to mind the many references in the Prophets to the messianic age as one of healing, both physical and moral; for example:

In that day the deaf will hear the words of the scroll,
and out of ... darkness
the eyes of the blind will see.
Once more the humble will rejoice in the LORD;

the needy will rejoice in the Holy One of Israel
(Isaiah 29:18-19)

Jesus then expresses his strong sense of mission which, in keeping with his other 'I came to ...' statements, begins with a negative (cf 10:45; Matthew 5:17): *'I have not come to call the righteous, but* I have come to call the *sinners.'* Jesus' 'I have come to ...' statements match others in which he says he has been 'sent' (9:37; 12:6), the divine passive indicating that God is the sender of Jesus. Jesus did not come on his own account; he *came* because he was *sent* by God. Jesus is the apostle of God, the one whom God sent.

The people with whom Jesus was eating were the 'sinners', the very ones whom Jesus had *come to call.* He had come to bring the kingdom of God to them, in his own person. With ironic but profound truth, Jesus' critics called him a 'friend of tax collectors and "sinners"' (Matthew 11:19). The other group, *the righteous,* clearly refers to the Pharisees. Their program of moral triumphalism against 'sinners', like Levi and Jesus who befriended him, blinded them to their own need for forgiveness from Yahweh their God. Jesus, however, declared 'blessed' those who confessed their poverty of spirit, their grief for their sins and who desired true righteousness before God (Matthew 5:3-4,6). 'Sinners' would hear his call; the righteous would not.

In their growing opposition to Jesus in Capernaum, the teachers of the law ask him (and us, the readers): *'Who can forgive sins except God alone?'* and *'Why does he eat with ... "sinners"?'* Mark's answer is that the kingdom of God which Jesus announced is now revealed in his person; Jesus himself is the bringer of that kingdom to 'sinners' like Levi who know they are law-breakers needing God's forgiveness. But the righteous teachers do not see where their questions should lead – to humble confession of sin and joyful acceptance of Jesus' offer of mercy which he extended to all his hearers, themselves included.

(3)   Why no fasting? (2:18-22)

Mark narrates that *John's disciples*, the followers of the Baptist who lived in the region, *and the Pharisees were fasting*, but that Jesus and his disciples (some of whom had come over from John's circle) were not. At that time it was customary for Jews to fast for two days every week – remember the Pharisee in the temple (Luke 18:12) – in addition to the Day of Atonement. The query, 'How is it that your disciples are not fasting?' does not come from the scribes on this occasion, but from *some people* (though the scribes' complaints may have been behind the question). This incident probably occurred in Capernaum where Jesus' disciples, not just the five who had been specifically called, but the wider group from the houses of Simon and Levi, were subject to ongoing scrutiny from the people.

While fasting in the Old Testament expressed mourning (eg 1 Samuel 31:13), in Jesus' time it was seen as hastening the coming of messiah and his kingdom (see Lane, pp109-112). Failure to fast, therefore, would have been viewed as treachery to Yahweh, hindering the coming of messiah and the redemption of Israel.

Jesus' explanation of why he and his disciples do not fast is told in two closely connected parts, both of which are in parable form. The first relates to Jesus' identity; the second to the kingdom of God which Jesus announces.

First, Jesus asks a question in response to the people's question: *'How can the guests of the bridegroom fast while he is with them?'* This is indeed a stunning question: hadn't Yahweh likened himself to a bridegroom and Israel to his bride: 'As a bridegroom rejoices over his bride, so will your God rejoice over you' (Isaiah 62:5)? Jesus is saying there is no need to fast because the messianic age has arrived; it is active and present in his ministry. In Jesus, Yahweh is with his people. This is a wedding banquet; it is no time for fasting, but for feasting. Like the declaration of the paralytic's forgiveness and his presence at the meal in the 'sinner' Levi's house, Jesus' failure to fast was deliberate. His action in not fasting, as he explains by this parable, declares that the messianic age had now come. By this parable, Jesus implies his identity of function with Yahweh the God of Israel: he is the bridegroom of Israel.

Jesus immediately tells two further parables about a new *patch* and new *wine*. Both are related to the presence of Messiah with his people. Like the bridegroom saying, both are in the form of questions. Rabbis typically met question with question.

The bridegroom is present, the time of fulfilment has come. But what will the kingdom be like? The parables teach that the patch and the wine are *new*, that messiah's kingdom cannot be patched on to the *old garment* of Judaism and cannot be poured into its *old wineskins*. Jesus and his message are quite different, not a rehash of the old. The age of messiah will not require his people to observe ceremonial acts like fasting; they are now free in conscience to fast or not to fast.

Jesus will take up the theme of the 'new' in the upper room on the eve of his death, when he speaks of the long-awaited (new) covenant which he was about to establish by his death (14:23-25). In verse 20 of this present passage he speaks enigmatically about that death:

> *But the time will come*
> *when the bridegroom will be taken from them,*
> *on that day they will fast.*

Jesus' words (as set out here) show that '*when* the bridegroom will be taken from them' is in parallel with '*on that day* they [the guests of the bridegroom] will fast'. *That day* will bring death to Jesus and grief to his followers. (The Servant Song of Isaiah 52:13-53:12 may be also in Jesus' mind here. The servant was 'taken away' (53:8); Jesus will be *taken from them.*)

The death of Jesus would indeed be a time of mourning. Ironically it will be the direct result of the failure of the bride, Israel, to welcome her bridegroom. There are some at least who will fast on that day; not the disciples of Jesus, who fall away from him on the night of his arrest, but the grief-stricken women of Galilee who watch his crucifixion 'from a distance' (15:40-41). Nonetheless, the risen Jesus will go before his faithless followers to Galilee and reconstitute them as his flock (16:7). Then they will be the new Israel, his bride. (Both Paul and John later refer to the church of the end-time as the virgin bride of Christ, cf 2 Corinthians 11:2; Revelation 19:7; 21:9.)

(4)   Law-breaker! (2:23-3:6)

The scribes have by now targeted Jesus as a subversive influence. So long as he is based at Capernaum they dog his heels wherever he goes. But Jesus' provocative actions – declaring a man forgiven, eating with 'sinners', failing to fast – have provided him with opportunities to make important statements about himself and his mission. The kingdom of God, which in the previous chapter was centred on *God*, is now seen to be centred on *Jesus*.

Jesus continues to act provocatively, now in relation to the Sabbath. Mark gives two examples which, however, do not appear to have occurred on consecutive Sabbaths. Indeed, it may be that some period of time elapsed between the three previous controversial incidents and the two that follow.

The reference to *ears of corn* establishes the time of year as summer (perhaps June) and therefore a full year after Jesus' visit to Samaria when he observed that the fields were 'ripe for harvest' (John 4:35). From Samaria Jesus had travelled to Galilee in what must have been late summer or early autumn to commence his public ministry (John 4:43,45), which was signalled by the arrest of John the Baptist (1:14; John 3:24).

Before these Sabbath incidents Jesus had probably visited Jerusalem for the Passover, a festival which fell in the spring. Such a visit would have taken at least three weeks – one week to travel there, one week in Jerusalem, one week to return – but Jesus may have spent longer than a week in Jerusalem for the sake of his ministry there (cf John 18:20). Such a visit would have represented a pause in the hostilities of the Capernaum scribes towards Jesus; now, however, matters come to a head.

(i)   *In the cornfields (2:23-28)*

Jesus is possibly guilty of two breaches of the law of the Sabbath in this incident: travelling further than was permissible and plucking heads of grain.

The Mishnah laid down strict limitations on activity from sunrise to sunset on the seventh day. Even going out from your house was not permitted beyond about a kilometre (cf Acts 1:12, where the distance from the Mount of Olives to Jerusalem is called 'a Sabbath day's walk').

To take ears of a neighbour's corn was allowed only so long as hands, not sickles, were used (Deuteronomy 23:25). However, if grain was plucked *on the Sabbath* it was regarded as reaping, one of 39 activities explicitly forbidden on the Sabbath (*Mishnah*, *Shabbath*, vii.2).

Strict observance of the Sabbath was seen as a necessary condition for the appearance of messiah and the redemption of Israel. According to the Talmud, 'If Israel were to keep two Sabbaths according to the rules, they would immediately be redeemed' (*bShab*, 118b). The Pharisees, therefore, would have regarded Jesus as lawless, an obstacle to God's deliverance of his people.

Consistent with custom, their question is put to the teacher, although it was Jesus' *disciples* who were breaking the law. Deliberate Sabbath-breaking would be met by stoning. Perhaps the question, '*Why are they doing what is unlawful on the Sabbath?*' was to ascertain if the action was unintentional: perhaps these ignorant Galileans had not realised what day of the week it was!

In line with rabbinic practice, Jesus responds to the Pharisees' question with a question introducing an appeal to Scripture: '*Have you never read ...?*' (cf 12:10,26). He refers to an incident involving no less a figure than *David*. The *high priest* of the Tabernacle at Nob gave David *consecrated bread* for his men to eat, on the proviso that they were ritually pure at the time; ordinary bread was not available (1 Samuel 21:1-6). Jesus' point is simple: the Pharisees are stricter in their demands than David and the high priest had been in the incident recorded in Scripture.

Jesus is not necessarily in error, as many claim, in saying this event occurred *in the days of Abiathar* even though the priest in 1 Samuel was not Abiathar but his father Ahimelech. Viewed from David's standpoint, those were the times not of Ahimelech but of Abiathar, the friend of David (cf 1 Samuel 22:20).

Jesus concludes the dialogue with a dramatic and profound utterance, which begins: '*The Sabbath was made for man, not man for the Sabbath.*' The original intention of the Creator in creating the world in six days and resting on the seventh was to provide for men and women, the pinnacle of his creation, a day of rest from arduous labour (Genesis 2:2-3; cf Exodus 20:8-11). The Sabbath was not instituted by God to be the burden it had become under the strict rules of the Pharisees, as reflected in the Mishnah's *Shabbath*. And though the New Testament does not confirm the ongoing observance of the seventh day, for Christian believers it remains appropriate to regard one day per week as *made for man*, that is for rest and renewal.

The final part of the saying contains Jesus' second reference to *Son of Man*, God's human agent of the divine plan (see comment on 2:10). That *the Sabbath was made for man* is demonstrated by the Son of Man's freedom to break it; Jesus is not subject to its trivial and legalistic demands.

A deeper meaning is also to be understood by Jesus' words. The Sabbath rest is also a picture of the end-time, the Day of the Lord (Hebrews 4:1-11; cf Matthew 11:28,29; Genesis 5:29). Jesus is Lord of, or over, that Sabbath epoch, the king in God's kingdom.

Lord (Greek *kyrios*) can have two meanings: one is a human master (12:9; 13:35), also roughly equivalent to 'sir' (as in 7:28, where a Gentile woman addresses Jesus); the other use is as the Greek equivalent to Yahweh, the sacred name of God (12:11,29-30,36; 13:20). In the following references, where *Lord* is applied to Jesus, it is clear that he is being referred to not as a human master but as Yahweh, Israel's God:

Prepare the way for the *Lord* (1:3; cf 1:7-8);
Tell them how ... the *Lord* ... had mercy on you (5:19);
David himself calls him *'Lord'*. (12:37)

The description of Jesus as *Lord ... of the Sabbath* belongs to this group of texts and is an implicit affirmation of Jesus' deity. Once again, therefore, we see Jesus deliberately breaking the law of Judaism in order to teach about himself.

The kingdom of God is now revealed to be focused on the Son of Man; it is *Christ-centred* or *Christocentric*.

(ii) In the synagogue (3:1-6)

In this episode Jesus is again in the *synagogue* in Capernaum, though there is no hint that he addresses the congregation. His outrageous actions and words have made him an outcast from the synagogues of the region centred on Capernaum. The big question now is whether he will again break the Sabbath law by healing *a man with a shrivelled hand* who is also present. The authorities knew by this time that Jesus would not withhold healing from the disabled people whom he encountered. *Some of them,* revealed later to have been Pharisees and Herodians (verse 6), *were looking for a reason to accuse* him of blasphemy before the highest court. The scene is set for a showdown.

In the drama that follows, Jesus demonstrates the folly of the existing rules about the Sabbath. He could easily have deferred the healing until the next day since there was no urgency, but he deliberately calls the man to his feet in the middle of the gathering.

Once again we see the rabbinic custom of debating by asking questions. Jesus asks: *'Which is lawful on the Sabbath: to do good'*, that is, *to save* the man's *life*, *'or to do evil?'*, that is, *to kill* Jesus? Jesus knows what is in his opponents' minds; his questions have exposed their hypocrisy. They seek to prevent him doing good at the very moment they are plotting his death; and so *they remained silent.*

Mark's description is so electric that we cannot doubt that Peter's eyewitness recollections underlie it. Jesus *looked around* as in a full circle (Greek *periblepesthai*), something he will do at other critical moments (3:34; 5:32; 10:23; 11:11). Mark also records that Jesus 'looked [hard] at' certain people (10:21,27). Evidently Jesus' manner of looking at people was striking. His look gave expression to his feelings of *anger* and distress *at their stubborn hearts.* The Sabbath was more important to them than the welfare of the disabled man, to say nothing of Jesus' own life.

Jesus' remarkable power was revealed in the instantaneous restoration of the withered hand; but those who had been watching Jesus so closely, the Pharisees and the Herodians, now went out and met to decide how to kill him. They were unlikely collaborators, drawn together to fear Jesus for different reasons.

Galilee had yet to be won for Pharisaism. The noted rabbi Yohanan ben Zakkai, a contemporary of Jesus who had attempted to establish Pharisaism in Galilee, declared in his frustration, 'Galilee, Galilee, you hate the Torah.' Pharisees would have regarded Jesus as a major hindrance to their mission in Galilee.

Herodians, on the other hand, were relatives of Herod Antipas as well as officials who benefited materially from his rule of Galilee. They probably advocated their tetrarch's acquisition of Judea – now a Roman province – as a return to Herod's golden days. A charismatic figure like Jesus might easily become a messianic leader of the volatile and warlike Galileans, and would thus undermine the secure rule of the tetrarch. John the Baptist had done this and had been imprisoned; soon he would pay for it with his life. The tetrarch needed a stable population in Galilee to impress his Roman masters that he was fit to keep ruling, let alone make a case that he was fit also to rule Judea. Jesus must die.

QUESTIONS ON MARK 2:1-3:6

1. In this section why doesn't Jesus teach about God and his kingdom so much as about himself as Son of Man?

2. Why does Jesus deliberately eat with outcasts, fail to observe the twice-weekly fast and break the Sabbath?

3. What point is Jesus making in the twin parables of the new patch and the new wine ?

4. What do you notice about each of sayings of Jesus contained in the following verses:

> 2:10;
> 2:17;
> 2:20;
> 2:27?

11

Jesus calls the Twelve 3:7-4:34

This is the second occasion Jesus withdraws from Capernaum, his adopted home. If the first was necessitated by the clamour for healing (1:37-39), the second is due to the danger Jesus now faces from the conspiracy of the Pharisees and the Herodians (3:6). Jesus is increasingly a field teacher, no longer welcome in the synagogues of the area and at risk in the streets of Capernaum.

(1)   Jesus teaches a great crowd (3:7-12)

Mark wants us to understand this to be a critical new stage in Jesus' ministry. To date, Jesus has spoken in the synagogue in Capernaum (1:21-27), in the synagogues in the immediate region (1:39), to the people in the street outside the house in Capernaum (2:2) and to a large crowd beside the lake (2:13).

The lakeside place to which Jesus and his disciples now go may be the same as that recorded earlier; the crowd that gathers, however, is from all points of the compass – from *Galilee* in the west; *Judea, Jerusalem, Idumea* in the south; *the regions across the Jordan* in the east; and *around Tyre and Sidon* in the north. We are meant to understand that the multitude converging on Jesus is drawn from an area greater than that which came to John the Baptist (cf 1:5). Mark's description implies Jesus' relative greatness over John.

The reason Mark gives for this great assembly (verses 8,10) may not reflect well on the people but is in line with the interest already shown in Jesus (1:32,45; 2:13): it was because *he had healed many. A small boat* had to be ready as *those with diseases were pushing forward to touch* Jesus, forcing him back into the sea.

A sinister detail is added: *the evil spirits ... fell down before him and cried out, 'You are the Son of God.'* This mock worship, from those who from the beginning had recognised Jesus as 'the Holy One of God' come to destroy them (1:24), is full of menace. Jesus is their inveterate enemy, the one who is even now overpowering 'the strong man' and liberating his prisoners (3:27). This conflict between Satan and Christ, beginning in the wilderness and culminating with the crucifixion, is one of Mark's major themes.

Typically, Jesus imposes strict silence on those who know who he is. Obsession with healing was serious enough, bringing ever larger crowds to him; a sudden messianic uprising inspired by the rumour of the appearance of the Son of God in Galilee would have come to the attention of Antipas, bringing Jesus' ministry to an immediate end.

(2)   *Jesus appoints the Twelve (3:13-19)*

In contrast with the great crowd by the lake, we now see Jesus on a mountainside with but 12 men, a further seven having now been added to the core group. These are not merely men who for various reasons were attracted to Jesus: *he called to him those he wanted.* The initiative lay with Jesus.

Significantly, Jesus *appointed twelve*, indicating that here at last is the embryonic new Israel. The choice of this number of men to accompany him was a deliberate and calculated action, an action that made an important statement for all to see. Ten times Mark will refer to 'the Twelve'; it is his distinctive name for the disciples.

Israel had been based on 12 tribes. Now these 12 men are the foundation of the reconstituted people of God with whom Jesus will later make the (new) covenant (14:24). The *kingdom of God* is exercised *over a people* and the *covenant of God* is entered into *with a people,* a people founded on the 12 Galileans chosen by Jesus. Here is the beginning of the community of the end-time, the tiny seed that will become the giant tree (4:30-32).

It is not correct to say, as some do, that the Twelve were called 'disciples' before the resurrection and 'apostles' afterwards. From this time Jesus *designated them apostles* (cf 6:30), a word meaning 'official representatives' or 'sent ones'. As Jesus was sent by God, so these 12 will be sent by Jesus (cf 9:37).

Two reasons are given for calling the Twelve as apostles. First, *that they might be with him* to be instructed by him; henceforth they will normally address him as 'Rabbi' (9:5; 14:45) or 'Teacher' (4:38; 5:35; 9:17,38; 10:35; 13:1; 14:14). Second, *that he might send them out to preach and to have authority to drive out demons.* This looks forward to their mission to the towns of Galilee (6:7-13), a mission which will closely resemble that of Jesus (cf 1:39), namely, to call for repentance in view of the imminent arrival of the kingdom of God, the sign of which is the casting out of demons (cf 6:12-13a). The kingdom of God will mean the overthrow of the kingdom of the Evil One. As with Jesus, the Twelve's healing of the sick is secondary to proclaiming the kingdom, driving out demons and calling for repentance (cf 6:13b).

The apostles' mission to Galilee, however, is not to be an end in itself: it anticipates the greater mission to the nations, with which they will be entrusted after the first Easter. Jesus will now devote months of teaching to prepare them for their mission to Galilee; thereafter he will devote the final year of his life almost exclusively to the Twelve in view of the universal responsibility which will soon be theirs.

The names of the Twelve now follow, the first four indicating some kind of seniority. *Simon* is first, whom Jesus also named *Peter* (Greek *Petros*, 'a rock'; Paul's reference to Peter as *Cephas* in 1 Corinthians 1:12 probably recalls the Aramaic word used by Jesus as Peter's surname.) The *Zebedee* brothers, *James and John*, follow, whom Jesus nicknamed *Boanerges* (Aramaic for 'sons of thunder') on account of their explosive character (cf Luke 9:54). 'Sons of ...' is a typical Semitic expression, encouraging belief in the historicity of the name. The fourth fisherman, *Andrew*, brother of Simon (1:16), comes next.

Little can be said of *Philip, Bartholomew, Thomas* or *Thaddaeus*, as they do not figure by name in Mark's account beyond this point. *Matthew* is called 'the tax collector' in a parallel list (Matthew 10:3), so the customs collector Levi (2:13-14) might have had two names. *James* is the *son of Alphaeus*, which may mean he was brother to Levi (cf 2:14), making three sets of brothers in the Twelve. *Simon* is referred to as *the Zealot*, suggesting a reputation of an extreme, anti-Roman nationalist, a fascinating contrast to the customs official Matthew! Finally comes the name of the disgraced *Judas Iscariot* who *betrayed* Jesus; Mark's introduction of the key word 'betray' is an unambiguous reference to Jesus' death.

(3) More controversy in Capernaum (3:20-35)

Jesus returns once more to his centre of operations, the *house* of Peter at Capernaum (verse 20, RSV; verses 31-32; cf 1:29; 2:1). As happened wherever Jesus now went, *again a crowd gathered*, which in the confined space of the house meant that *he and his disciples were not even able to eat*.

News that Jesus had arrived in Capernaum, and that he was not looking after himself, came to the attention of his family back in Nazareth. Earlier they would have heard of his synagogue ministry in and around Capernaum, his disputes with the Pharisees and his preaching to the great crowds by the lakeside; now suggestions of personal neglect led them to the sad conclusion that Jesus was *out of his mind.*

So they made the day's journey from Nazareth to Capernaum. At this point Mark simply notes the family's concern and their departure from Nazareth; he will record their arrival after the next incident. But the reaction in Nazareth illustrates how controversial a character Jesus was becoming and that radically different opinions were being reached about him.

As Jesus' family in Nazareth had heard about the dramatic events in and around Capernaum so, too, these matters now come to the ears of the leading Pharisees in distant Judea: *the teachers of the law ... came down from Jerusalem.* (Notice that Mark says correctly that they came *down* from Jerusalem to Galilee.) Pharisaism was relatively poorly established in Galilee, so the local Pharisees may have been concerned that Jesus would undo their work in the region. Possibly the local teachers were not equal to Jesus' debating skills. Perhaps these Judean teachers had also come to gather information on the prophet from Galilee, as they had done concerning John the Baptist some time earlier (John 1:19). Mark is hinting that Jerusalem will be a place of opposition and danger for Jesus.

Just as his family say Jesus is 'out of his mind, these learned men from Jerusalem say that he is *possessed by Beelzebub* and that *by the prince of the demons he is driving out demons.* Mark's use of the unusual Semitic-sounding word *Beelzebub* to refer to Satan is good reason to believe that the accusation was made against Jesus in precisely that way. Later in Jerusalem, the teachers of the law would repeatedly refer to Jesus as 'demon-possessed' (John 7:20; 8:48,52; 10:20). This explains the tradition that survives in the Talmud which declares that sorcery was the sin for which Jesus was executed *(Sanhedrin,* 43a). The present accusation that he is *possessed by Beelzebub,* by whose power *he is driving out demons,* is probably the origin of these later traditions.

It is noteworthy that the teachers identify the casting out of demons as Jesus' characteristic activity; this is consistent with Mark's account (1:21-27,32,39; cf 3:11). Significantly, they do not doubt that Jesus successfully performed these actions (therefore the historicity of the actions can hardly be doubted). What is in dispute is the power by which he acted: they say he is Satan-possessed, Satan-empowered.

As is often the case (cf 2:8,19,25; 3:4), Jesus replies to his critics with a question: *'How can Satan drive out Satan?'* He then speaks to the teachers in parables. (A parable can be a one line word-picture: it is not necessarily a full story.) He observes that *if a kingdom* or *a household is divided* it *cannot stand.* Therefore, *if Satan opposes himself ... he cannot stand; his end has come.* Since Jesus is casting Satan out from people, it is illogical for the teachers to say Jesus is Satan-possessed; Satan would be opposing himself.

A second 'house' parable now follows, though it is longer and uses different imagery. It is, in fact, an allegorical representation of Jesus' struggle with Satan. Here is Jesus' own view of his ministry: *'No one can enter a strong man's house* [= Satan's] *and carry off his possessions* [= cast out demons from Satan's prisoners] *unless he first ties up the strong man. Then he can rob his house* [= Jesus' spiritual victory over Satan, in the wilderness and subsequently].

Because Jesus, the stronger man (cf 1:7), has overpowered Satan at the beginning and during his ministry, and because, in particular, he will prevail over Satan by submitting to crucifixion and being raised from the dead, he is 'robbing' Satan of his captives. This parable is, *par excellence,* Jesus' own interpretation of his mission: the kingdom of God is not merely near but may be seen in Jesus' casting out of unclean spirits. Jesus says as much in words recorded outside Mark: 'If I drive out demons by the Spirit of God, then the kingdom of God has come upon you' (Matthew 12:28).

From our side of Easter, the gospel of Christ is, in the language of Revelation, the 'great chain' that binds Satan 'to keep him from deceiving the nations' throughout the period until the second advent (Revelation 20:1-3). Christ bound Satan during his ministry; we now bind Satan with the chain of the gospel, until the Lord's return.

Mark now records Jesus' first *I tell you the truth* statement (literally 'Amen, I say to you'; see 8:12; 9:1,41; 10:15,29; 11:23; 12:43; 13:30; 14:9,18,25,30). Clearly this speaker is greater than any prophet who spoke only *in the name* of Yahweh. Jesus speaks in his own right, as the divinely authorised Son of Man: *'All the sins and blasphemies of men will be forgiven them'*. Jesus came to call sinners (2:17), and as the Son of Man he declared the paralytic's sins forgiven (2:5). Jesus is God's appointed instrument of forgiveness, a forgiveness that is universal in its breadth. One sin, however, is excluded: *'Whoever blasphemes against the Holy Spirit will never be forgiven'*. The present tense verb *blasphemes* indicates not a single act, but a pattern of habitual practice. To resist the ministry of the Holy Spirit convicting the heart and mind about the truth of Jesus is to be *guilty of an eternal sin.* Those who fear that they *might* have committed this sin are to be assured *by their concern* that they have *not.*

This teaching shows that the Holy Spirit was active *during* the ministry of Jesus as well as after it (cf John 16:7-11); Jesus was the bearer of the Holy Spirit from the time of his baptism in the Jordan (1:10,12). However, this severe remark was occasioned because the teachers *were saying, 'He has an evil spirit.'* It was their interpretation that his casting out of demons was due to the power of an evil spirit, not the Holy Spirit. They had called the good that he did 'evil', and affirmed the Evil One, not the Holy Spirit who was doing good through Jesus. They were suppressing every prompting of the Spirit of God.

The family who had set out for Capernaum from Nazareth (verse 21) now arrive: specifically *Jesus' mother* and four *brothers*. Jesus' natural family has come to the house of his adopted family, but they remain *outside*. Jesus is within, probably in an inner courtyard common in the houses of the time, surrounded immediately by the Twelve. This separation between those who were on the outside and those who are within is often noted by Mark (4:10,11; 7:17; 9:28; 10:10).

A message is sent to Jesus: *'Your mother and brothers are outside looking for you.'* They had come because they believed that he was out of his mind (3:21). Though Mary had expressed joyful faith at the time of Jesus' conception (Luke 1:46-55), his brothers did not at this time believe in him (John 7:5). After the resurrection, however, both Mary and Jesus' brothers would be part of the community of believers in Jerusalem (Acts 1:14).

Characteristically, Jesus begins speaking with a question: *'Who are my mother and brothers?'* Mark then records for the second time (cf 3:5) Jesus' unforgettable way of looking *at those seated in a circle around him,* probably in this case referring to the Twelve. After this moment of silence, Jesus answers his own question with a weighty utterance. He points to the Twelve who have followed him, doubtless including the outcast Levi (see 2:13-14) and says, *'Here are my mother and my brothers!'* Then, thinking of others beyond the Twelve who are present, he adds, *'Whoever does God's will is my brother and sister and mother.'*

To follow Jesus and to learn from his teaching, as the Twelve and others with him were doing, is to do God's will and to be part of Jesus' true family. These learners are the community of the kingdom of God, a community which is a family, and a family, moreover, which is *Jesus'* family. This is Jesus' answer to the members of his natural family who said he was mad.

(4)   Parables of the kingdom of God (4:1-34)

This is the third time Jesus teaches a crowd by the lakeside (2:13; 3:7-8). It was probably the same place on each occasion, and not too far from Capernaum. The content of his teaching on the two earlier sessions is not given, but it is reasonable to suppose that what is recorded here was typical of those other times.

This time the crowd *was so large* that it was necessary for Jesus to get *into a boat* and to teach them as he *sat in it out on the lake*. He had to speak in the open: the synagogues were no longer available for the controversial teacher. In the synagogues he had taught from the Prophets that all was now fulfilled and that the kingdom of God was at hand; in the open he teaches about the kingdom of God *by parables*. In the synagogue he was a scholar with scroll in hand; in the open he is a popular prophet teaching his message in terms the crowds can understand. Jesus announces the nearness of the kingdom of God and summons Israel to repent.

(i)   The parable of the sower (4:3-9)

The first parable, about the sower, is Jesus' simple but profound story explaining his ministry, what its end will be and why there are such wide-ranging responses to his message. The *seed* that *fell along the path* is immediately eaten by the *birds;* the seed which *fell on rocky places* sprouts *quickly* in the *shallow soil* but is soon *scorched* and *withered;* the seed *among thorns* is *choked,* so that it does *not bear grain*. But *other seed fell on good soil.* It *came up, grew* and ultimately produced a *crop.* The harvesting of the crop portrays the end of history, the seed of which Jesus the Sower was at that very time sowing in the world.

But how would Jesus' hearers receive his seed-word? He begins and ends his parable with the urgent commands: *'Listen!* and *'He who has ears to hear, let him hear'* (the same Greek word *akouein* is used both times). His challenge to 'listen ... hear' is thrown into relief by his hearer's failure to do so.

There was, as we have seen in Mark's account to date, great variety in human reponse to the seed which the Jesus the Sower had cast. There were the Galilean and Judean scribes who were closed-minded and rejected Jesus' message outright. There were the over-ready, clamouring sick who had no will to continue with Jesus for any distance. There were the impulsive messiah-expecting multitudes who followed Jesus without understanding his message, and would finally desert him. And there were the Twelve who had glimmerings of understanding about his message, who would follow him to the end. Jesus' message is: 'If you want to be part of the great crop of the end-time, listen to the Sower and hear what he is teaching; be good soil, not bad.'

But this parable was not understood by Jesus' hearers. Later, *when he was alone* with *the Twelve and the others* who formed his close circle, they *asked him about the parables.* In his reply Jesus distinguishes between the crowd and those whom he had chosen to be with him.

To those whom he had chosen – the Twelve and the others close to him – *the secret of the kingdom has been given.* Although the disciples reveal considerable spiritual obtuseness right through the Gospel (4:40; 8:14-21,33; 9:5-6,32; 10:13,24-26,32), they remain Jesus' disciples, learning from him: he privately explains to them the meaning of parables and other teaching which they do not

71

understand. After the first Easter they will be given the Spirit who completely transforms their understanding. These are the means – educational and spiritual – by which the Twelve were *given* the secret of the kingdom; the passive verb indicating that God was the giver of their understanding.

But to those on the outside, that is, the crowds, Jesus said *everything ... in parables*. He then gives the purpose for teaching the crowds in parables, *so that,*

> 'they may be ever seeing, but never perceiving,
> and ever hearing, but never understanding;
> otherwise they might turn and be forgiven!'

For the multitude, those not called and chosen by Jesus (cf 3:13-14; 7:16,17; 9:30-31), the parables are seen but not perceived, heard but not understood. They hear and understand the parables intellectually. Jesus, indeed, taught in such simple terms for that reason (verse 33). But the hearers do not identify themselves in them, for example, as the various kinds of bad soil; nor do they identify Jesus as the Sower sent by God to them; and they do not see their need, before God, to listen and hear his words. It will be no different with the other parables Jesus will speak: *'Don't you understand this parable? How will you understand any parable?'* In the end, Jesus and his word, despite its eloquent simplicity, have no impact on them. That is why there was so little recollection of Jesus among the Jews who did not respond to his message, and the reason that such recollection as there was is negative.

In this context Jesus' quotation of Isaiah 6:9-10 is significant. It refers to a specific moment in Israel's past when Yahweh visited his people in retribution. God had commissioned Isaiah to speak so as to harden the people's hearts against God who would bring his terrible judgment against them (Isaiah 6:9-13). It appears that Jesus sees his ministry to Israel, in part at least, in terms of Isaiah's prophetic vocation, as a visitation of judgment. Nonetheless, this was not Jesus' active purpose but an inevitable passive consequence of his ministry; otherwise he would not have urged his audience 'listen ... hear'.

Yet, to be realistic, Jesus foresaw a new and reconstituted Israel based on the Twelve – to whom the secret of the kingdom was given – replacing the old. But as the multitudes failed to understand the parables, the apostles also will fail to understand Jesus. At a later stage in his ministry, when he leaves ministering to crowds and concentrates on the Twelve, Jesus complains that they too 'have eyes but fail to see, and ears but fail to hear' (8:18). Nonetheless, it is to the Twelve that Jesus now speaks.

Jesus explains this parable in terms which will also apply after Easter to the preaching of the gospel (verses 14-20). *The farmer* (literally 'the sower', meaning Jesus) *sows the word*, the word of the kingdom of God when God will reap his end-time harvest. But there are various obstacles to the word taking root and giving grain at the harvest: *Satan* who *takes away the word; persecution ... because of the word*, which causes people to *fall away;* and *worries, wealth* and *desires* which *choke the word* and make it *unfruitful*.

Jesus' warning to us, the readers of the Gospel, is the same as to those who originally heard him speak that day from the boat; we must also 'listen ... hear'. We ignore the forces which endanger the word in our lives, of which Jesus warned us, at our peril. For the time being, the risen Sower continues to sow his word in the world through his servants, but the end-time will surely come. Will we be part of the harvest?

(ii)   The parable of the lamp (4:21-23)

Jesus' second parable is as simple as the first, though domestic not rural in its imagery. It speaks of a darkening room into which an oil *lamp* is brought. Because its purpose is to illuminate, Jesus says: 'Surely a lamp is not brought in to be put *under* a bowl or a bed but *on* a stand.' God's end-time will be like a bright light in the darkness, revealing behaviour which people had thought was hidden from view: *'For whatever is hidden is meant to be disclosed, and whatever is concealed is meant to be brought out into the open.'*

As a modern analogy, imagine a power failure plunging a department store into darkness. Then, just as suddenly, the lights come on again, catching many in the act of stealing. The Day of the kingdom of God will be like that — sudden, unannounced, revealing everything. But the kingdom was, and is, present in Jesus, not only at the end. The light came in his historic person (cf John 1:4-9) and is present wherever the gospel is preached, illuminating the attitudes and behaviour of his hearers. This parable is a call to repent: *'If anyone has ears to hear,'* teaches Jesus, *'let him hear.'*

(iii)   The parable of the measure (4:24-25)

The exhortation to *hear* leads into the subsidiary parable of the *measure*. Offering your ears to Jesus to hear fully what he says is likened to bringing a measure to the grain seller. According to the size of the measure or receptacle people use, the grain will be measured back to them – *and even more.* Present a small measure and you will be given correspondingly little; in other words, Jesus is saying to his hearers, 'Be big eared! Listen and hear what I am saying to you!'

Christians may be described as people who give all they know of themselves to all they know of God. God spoke in and through Jesus and he continues to speak through Jesus' words. Before we can give all that we know of ourselves to all we know of God, we must first listen and hear what the Sower has to say to us.

(iv)   The parable of the growing seed (4:26-29)

Jesus' third parable is like the first except that it is introduced by *'This is what the kingdom of God is like.'* Jesus says, *'A man scatters seed on the ground'* but this man pays no attention to the soil into which the seed falls. The focus is on *the seed,* which *night and day ... sprouts and grows* regardless, whether the man *sleeps or gets up.* The man does not know how the seed germinates, grows and then finally matures; it happens all by itself. Only when *the grain is ripe* at the time of *harvest* does he reappear to put *the sickle to it.*

Jesus is teaching two things from this parable. First, he tells us not to be deceived by the apparent sameness of daily life. God has not gone away, nor is he asleep. At the right time the sudden harvest of the end-time will occur. The sleepiness and ordinariness of daily life will dramatically change: reapers and labourers will appear in a whirl of frantic activity. The message is: 'Be prepared for the harvest.'

Second, we are to think of Jesus as the farmer who both sows and reaps. He has sown the seed, which will grow on its own without him reappearing in the fields until the time of the harvest. Indeed, so far as appearances are concerned, he might as well not be there. The seed he has sown will grow, without his physical presence, into the mighty universal crop of the church.

Near the beginning of his ministry, Jesus depicts himself as a sower; just before his death he will speak of himself as a reaper: '*The Son of Man ... will send his angels and gather his elect from the four winds, from the ends of earth to the ends of the heavens*' (13:26-27).

This parable is an allegory of the first and second advents of Jesus – the first was to sow, the second will be to reap – with 'life as usual' in the time between. But do not be deceived: the Sower is watching his crop; he knows exactly its stages of growth, and he will know when to put in the sickle. Despite his physical absence from the crop, the Son of Man will know when the time is right for the harvest. By his imagery of sower and reaper, Jesus teaches that he overarches the process of salvation; he is its beginning and its end.

(v)   The parable of the mustard seed (4:30-32)

Jesus' fourth parable relates the growth of a tiny *mustard seed* into *the largest of all garden plants*. The point of this parable is the contrast between the smallness of the seed and greatness of the tree into which it grows, *with such big branches that the birds of the air can perch in its shade.*

The end-point of the parable reminds us of the theme of the giant tree with nesting birds which occurs in the Old Testament (Ezekiel 17:23; Daniel 4:11-12,14,20-21). The most comprehensive picture occurs in Ezekiel 31: the birds of the air which nest in the tall tree represent 'all the great nations' (31:6,12); the tree, however, stands for the pride of Assyria (31:3), which Yahweh will give to the ruler of the nations to cut down (31:10-12).

God will have his giant tree in which the birds take shelter. Here is a picture of the multitude of God's people of the end-time which will be composed not just of the people of Israel but also of people from the nations. Given the extreme Jewish nationalism of the period and the hatred the

Jews felt towards the nations (= the Gentiles), this was radical teaching.

If the giant tree with the birds portrays the glorious end, what is signified by the tiny seed? Again Jesus is referring to himself from Daniel 7, as the 'one like a son of man' (7:13) who, together with the 'saints of the Most High' (7:18), form the people of God in embryo. In other words, the tiny seed is Jesus and the Twelve; so ordinary, powerless and unexceptional at that time, but from which the giant sheltering tree will grow.

Jesus' parable was, and remains, profoundly encouraging. The tiny seed will grow into the giant tree, providing shelter for the birds of the air. Jesus and the Twelve were indeed tiny, and in our time, too, the people of God often appear confused and of diminishing significance in the world. Yet there will be a great end-time people of God, composed of Jews and Gentiles.

So Jesus concludes his teaching from the boat. Mark notes that *with many similar parables Jesus spoke the word* – the message of the kingdom of God – *to them*; he has given us only a sample. In fact, *he did not say anything to them without using a parable.* Parables told by other rabbis of the period were rather complex and obscure, told for the benefit of fellow rabbis, not for the simple people. Jesus' parables, however, were given for the people, *as much as they could understand.* Their failure to comprehend his message was not due to any failure on his part in explaining his message in the simplest terms; rather it lay in their own spiritual and moral obtuseness.

This was true also of the Twelve: *when he was alone with his own disciples, he explained everything.* They and the people at large were blind and deaf to his parables (cf 4:11-12), as later Jesus would complain to them about their blindness and deafness to the miracles he had performed (8:18). When at last they recognise him to be the Christ (8:29) it is in nationalistic terms, so Jesus must reinterpret their concept of the messiahship (8:31). From that point he will also teach them that he is God's Son (8:38; 12:6; 13:32). Yet it will not be one of the Twelve, nor indeed a Jew, but the Gentile commander of the crucifixion squad who finally identifies Jesus as the Son of God (15:39).

This is the last occasion Jesus teaches in the open on the western side of the lake. The area had by now become full of menace for him, due to the conspiracy of the Pharisees and the Herodians (cf 3:6). Indeed, he and the disciples do not even bring the boat in to the shore but set out immediately for the other side of the lake (4:35), to the Decapolis, outside the tetrarchy of Herod Antipas.

Jesus' initial period with the Twelve is now complete. They have been called to his side to learn from him; they have heard the accusations of the teachers of the law and Jesus' replies to them. They have seen his brothers and mother seeking to take him back to Nazareth; they have heard him declare that they, the Twelve, are doing the will of God. They have heard him speak to the crowds in parables and been mystified about their meaning; they have heard him speak to them alone, explaining the parables.

But now the Twelve must accompany Jesus and be confronted by dreadful and terrifying forces.

QUESTIONS ON MARK 3:7-4:34

1.   Why did the evil (literally 'unclean') spirits fall down before Jesus (3:11; cf 1:24,34; 5:6)?
2.   Why did Jesus choose the twelve apostles? How did he prepare them, and for what purpose (3:13-14; cf 6:7,12)?
3.   How did various groups explain Jesus' activities (3:21-22,30)
4.   Why is attributing Jesus' power to an evil spirit 'an eternal sin' (3:28-30; cf 3:22)?
5.   How should hearers respond to the parable of:
                 the sower (4:3-9);
                 the lamp (4:21-23);
                 the measure (4:24-25);
                 the growing seed (4:26-29);
                 the mustard seed (4:30-32)?

12

The Lord is revealed to the Twelve 4:35-6:6a

A series of episodes now follows which reveals Jesus' control over evil and chaotic forces: storm, unclean spirits, chronic illness and death. Jesus' initial proclamation of the rapid approach of the kingdom of God, in the synagogues centred on Capernaum (chapter 1), might have suggested that his ministry was *theocentric*, God-centred. However, the sequence of controversies in Capernaum, with Jesus' important pronouncements about himself, shows that he saw his ministry as *Christocentric*, centred in himself. In the next four incidents Jesus reveals both by word and action that the kingdom of God is indeed focused on himself: the kingdom of God is exercised through Jesus.

It is sometimes suggested that these stories might not have occurred in the sequence as narrated but were put side by side because they are similar in character; but such a view is unwarranted. Given the conspiracy against Jesus by the Pharisees and Herodians (3:6), his decision to depart immediately to the eastern side of the lake beyond the reach of Herod Antipas is understandable. Both the storm and the 'Legion' incident occur in the course of these movements.

Then, after an unspecified period of time in the Decapolis, Jesus and the Twelve re-cross the lake to a westside town where Jairus was the synagogue ruler, where two further incidents occur. Possibly this town was to the south of Capernaum, and it is from here that Jesus and the Twelve go directly up to Nazareth. In other words, Jesus' journey is geographically coherent and quite consistent with the political realities of the region.

(1)   The storm at sea (4:35-41)

The story contains many details which are best explained as coming from an eyewitness, most probably Peter. The precise time note *(when evening came)*, the immediate departure (taking Jesus *just as he was*) to the eastern side, the gratuitous reference to *other boats*, the mention of the *cushion* on which Jesus was asleep *in the stern*, the disciples' rather rude question: *'Teacher, don't you care if we drown?'* and the unexpected nature of his reply: *'Why are you so afraid? Do you still have no faith?'* all suggest the recollections of someone who was present at the time.

This is the first occasion Jesus is addressed as *'Teacher'* (= *'Rabbi';* cf 9:5; 11:21; 14:45), though it will be commonplace from now on (5:35; 9:17,38; 10:17,20,35; 12:14,19,32; 13:1; 14:14).

Sudden wind squalls on the Sea of Galilee are not uncommon. Mountains surround the sea, except to the south where the Jordan continues its journey south towards the Dead Sea. Strong winds from the Mediterranean entering from the south-west still create violent storms on the lake today.

The power of Jesus evident in this passage is similar to that in two other incidents, one earlier, the other later. In the earlier incident Jesus rebuked and silenced the unclean spirit in the synagogue in Capernaum (1:25); here Jesus rebukes and silences a storm. In the later incident, the command of Jesus results in 'Legion', the uncontrollable man, 'sitting there, dressed and in his right mind' (5:15); here Jesus' words to the storm are followed by complete *calm*. In all three incidents Jesus reveals his control over evil and destructive forces.

Jesus' questions to the Twelve, *'Why are you so afraid? Do you still have no faith?'* imply criticism that they do not yet understand who he is. He has drawn them apart from the crowds to devote himself to teaching them; he has explained to them the mystery of the kingdom of God. By now they should have had a better idea about him. However, the blindness of the Twelve to Jesus' true identity as the Son of God remains throughout his ministry until the first Easter and Pentecost; only then will they understand (cf Romans 1:3-4).

The disciples' question, *'Who is this? Even the wind and the waves obey him!'* invites the answer that only Yahweh the God of Israel commands the obedience of wind and waves (cf Psalm 106:9). Again, Mark's way of recording this question reveals his skill as a writer. As with the scribes' question, 'Who can forgive sins except God alone?' (2:7), he reflects the question of the moment while at the same time putting it in such a way that the reader also asks it. For us the readers, the question is the more powerful in being unanswered. As with the question, 'Who can forgive sins?' this question, too, can only be answered: God, or one who is uniquely authorised by God. Only such a person can forgive sins and control wind and waves.

Nonetheless, although Mark provokes his readers to reflect on the supernatural identity of Jesus, he does not obscure the historical perception of the disciples and others that Jesus was a human teacher (= rabbi). Nor does Mark put into the mouths of the disciples exalted faith confessions about Jesus which we find, for example, in the letters of Paul and which predate this Gospel (eg Philippians 2:5-11; Colossians 1:15-20). Mark never loses touch with Jesus' historical situation. Thus, despite the apparent simplicity of his words and innocence of style, the author displays considerable ability as a historian, recording what happened while at the same time forcing us to ask questions of an ultimate kind about Jesus.

(2)   Legion, the uncontrollable man (5:1-20)

After the storm the boat came to rest on the eastern shore of the Sea of Galilee. This is the first recorded occasion Jesus visits a Gentile region, namely, *the Decapolis.* 'Decapolis' literally means 'Ten Cities', and refers to a league of independent cities which were established in the period after Alexander's conquest of Palestine three centuries earlier. Each city had a region surrounding it, with dependent towns and villages. These ten cities formed an alliance for mutual protection. The greater region of the Decapolis formed a rough triangle: from Damascus in the north to Scythopolis (modern Bet Shean) in the west – the only city on the west of the Jordan – to Philadelphia (modern Amman) in the south.

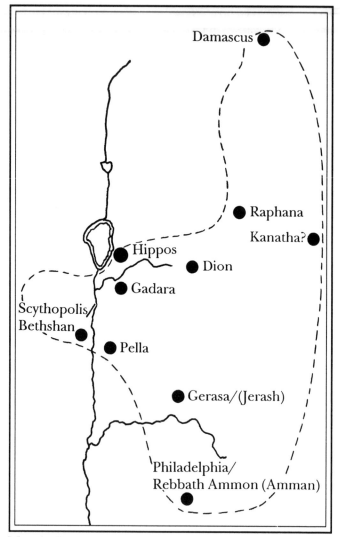

Map 3 *The Decapolis*

The region of the Gerasenes is probably close to modern Kersa, where within a short distance there is a steep slope and also caves which have been used as tombs. (Any reference to 'Gadara' or 'the Gadarenes' is probably incorrect: see Lane, p181, n6).

Even as Jesus is getting *out of the boat*, he is confronted by *a man with an unclean spirit* who *came from the tombs*. (Had he watched the boat approaching?) Local people, distressed at his madness and perhaps concerned for their own welfare, had *often* attempted to overpower the man by chaining him *hand and foot*. But with superhuman strength *he tore the chains apart and broke the irons on his feet*. Eerily *he lived among the tombs* in the hills, and *night and day* his cries could be heard as *he cut himself with stones*. The account is so vivid, immediate and unimaginable as to be true, presenting again a strong case that the story rests on the recollection of someone who was there (Peter, once more?).

A moment's reflection prompts us to feel the suffering of all those involved in this tragic scene. The local townspeople were anxious for their welfare, as witnessed by their many unsuccessful attempts to capture this frightening man. We can readily imagine the sense of helplessness of the man's immediate family too, forced to live with the tragedy of their deranged relative. The unclean spirit gives his name as *Legion,* revealing something of the greatness of the man's own inner pain and sense of dislocation.

As the man advanced, he fell on his knees before Jesus, not in the menacing mock worship of an earlier occasion (see 3:11) but in a sincere, if confused, manner. And consistent with his approach elsewhere with the demon-possessed (though not with the otherwise sick), Jesus takes the initiative: *'Come out of this man, you evil spirit!'* he commands.

This is the second of only two confrontations between Jesus and *an evil spirit* (literally an 'unclean spirit'; see

1:23,26,27; 3:11,30; 6:7; 7:25; 9:25) *where the unclean spirit speaks*. The words of both unclean spirits – one in the synagogue in Capernaum, this one on the eastern shore of the Sea of Galilee – are strikingly similar, as the following comparison shows:

> Gerasa – 5:7 : Capernaum – 1:24
>
> What do you want with *me* : What do you want with *us*, Jesus: Jesus of Nazareth?
> Son of the Most High God? : I know who you are – the Holy One of God.
> Swear to God that you won't torture *me*? : Have you come to destroy *us*?

Both statements echo an Aramaic way of speaking which the NIV translators smooth out – literally the words are 'what to us and to you?' – but note that at Gerasa *one* unclean spirit speaks, whereas at Capernaum there was more than one. On both occasions the unclean spirits express the great, unbridgeable gap between them and Jesus. They are *unclean* spirits; he is the Son of the Most High God/ the Holy One of God, the bearer of the *Holy* Spirit. Both sets of unclean spirits recognise that Jesus has come to torture/destroy them, and that he has the power to do so. Both also use Jesus' name in their attempts to overpower him.

Jesus addresses the spirit, asking, '*What is your name?*' Initially Jesus called him '*you evil* [=unclean] *spirit*', but now he demands to know his name. The unclean spirit obediently replies, '*My name is Legion ... for we are many.*' A Roman 'legion' had about 6000 soldiers, and the Latin word *legio* had been adopted into Aramaic (another echo of the actual words which were spoken); the one spirit who speaks at Gerasa speaks for *many*. Thus, on both occasions when the words of the unclean spirits are recorded, it is clear that each man was host to a *community* of unclean spirits.

The one who spoke for the unclean spirits *begged Jesus again and again not to send them out of the area.* This is a curious request: Why would unclean spirits need to remain in a specific area? Was it that the host had consulted the dead on account of the many tombs in that area, and for that reason the unclean spirits did not want to leave? If they were to be cast out from their present host, where might they hope to find another as suitable?

Accordingly, the unclean spirits begged Jesus to send them among *a large herd of pigs* which *was feeding on the nearby hillside,* doubtless expecting these pigs to remain near the area where they were feeding. The unclean spirits cannot bear to be free-ranging, without a host (cf Matthew 12:43-45). The presence of pigs in the Gentile Decapolis region is an authentic detail: swine were unclean to the Jews.

Jesus *gave them permission* and the unclean spirits *came out* of the man *and went into the pigs, about two thousand in number,* which, however, against expectation *rushed down the steep bank into the lake and were drowned.*

Mark concludes his story with starkly contrasting human responses. The owners of the pigs, and others from the neighbouring region who had been told what had happened, converged on Jesus and the man who had been demon-possessed. *They were afraid,* sensing the presence of the supernatural, when they saw the previously deranged man *sitting there, dressed and in his right mind.* Yet despite the astonishing change in the man they *began to plead with Jesus to leave their region.* We might have expected a request for Jesus to come and bring his powers to bear on others similarly afflicted in the area. But, they asked him to go away, a sad commentary on their distorted sense of priorities which preferred property to people.

Mark lets us not only see the dramatically changed man, but also hear him beg *to go with* Jesus as one of his group. Did he not owe him his life? But now, Jesus tells him to *'Go home to your family and tell them how much the Lord has done for you, and how he has had mercy on you.'* Jesus silences Jews whom he has healed or those from whom he has cast out unclean spirits; but this Gentile is to testify to his loved ones that Yahweh, the God of Israel, has shown him mercy, through the ministry of Jesus. Jesus is in fact making another oblique claim to be the Lord of Israel. Obedient to this command, the man *began to tell in the Decapolis how much Jesus had done for him.* In future times Jesus would return to the Decapolis and find considerable interest in his ministry (cf 7:31-37). Was this due, to some degree at least, to the testimony of the man previously possessed by a legion of unclean spirits?

What does Mark want us to learn from this passage? We should understand that Jesus is the Son of the Most High God who has come like a victorious warrior against the community of the unclean spirits and their ruler, Satan. The casting out of unclean spirits is evidence of the coming kingdom of God which Jesus had come to proclaim. We are reminded once more that Jesus takes the initiative against the unclean spirits, as opposed to his more passive approach to healing.

Further, Mark wants us to see that, in Jesus, Yahweh the God of Israel is present in both mercy and power to deliver those who are oppressed by evil forces. At the word of Jesus the unclean spirits are expelled, just as at the word of Jesus the storm was stilled (cf verses 35-41). The picture of the man clothed and in his right mind now restored to his family, in contrast with the deranged man who had lived among the tombs, is silent but eloquent testimony to this. In Peter's words:

God anointed Jesus of Nazareth with the Holy Spirit and power ... he went around doing good and healing *all who were under the power of the devil*, because God was with him. (Acts 10:38)

(3)   *The chronically ill woman (5:21-34)*

After a passage of time – Mark does not say how long – Jesus re-crosses the lake, probably arriving at a village in the Gennesaret region a few kilometres to the south of Capernaum. On the arrival of the boat he is met by a large crowd and by *Jairus ... one of the synagogue rulers* of the village, who wants to take him immediately to the bedside of his daughter who is 'at the point of death' (verse 23, RSV).

But hidden among the *large crowd* who go with Jesus to Jairus' house is a chronically ill woman. *For 12 years* she *had been subject to bleeding*. It was as if her monthly menstrual periods were permanent. This would have involved great suffering for her physically, conjugally, personally and socially. Physically, because of vaginal bleeding; conjugally, because she could engage in no normal sexual relationship (it is possible that her husband had divorced her); personally, because she could bear no children; and socially, because the menstrual period made her ritually unclean.

Her recourse to *many doctors* had only made things worse. Under their treatment *she suffered a great deal*, to say nothing of the cost, for she *had spent all she had*. But, despite the expense, *instead of getting better she grew worse*. So the woman's approach to Jesus is a mixture of fear – *she came up behind him* – as well as desperate hope and superstition: 'If I just touch his clothes, I will be healed'.

Something happened, as both the woman and Jesus knew, the moment she touched his clothing: *Immediately ... she felt in her body that she was freed from her suffering. At once Jesus realised that power had gone out of him*. But Mark does not say how either the woman or Jesus knew that she had been healed.

Jesus' pastoral care of this poor woman is instructive. He could have allowed her to go on her way healed and done no more. But that would have left her with the superstitious belief that his clothing had some kind of magical power. His concern about the desperate and superstitious lengths to which the chronically ill and their families would go is well placed. When he next visited that region the sick from the surrounding villages would be brought on their mats and lined up in the marketplaces, begging to touch the hem of his garment as he passed by (6:53-56).

Jesus' enquiry to the crowd *'Who touched my clothes?'* is met with incredulity by the disciples who say, *'You see the people crowding against you, and yet you ask, "Who touched me?"'* Typically they do not understand the spiritual issues at stake (cf 4:38-41; 6:37; 7:17-19; 8:14-21; 8:33; 9:6,10,17-29,33-34; 10:13-16,32,35-45; 13:1-2; 14:37).

But while *Jesus kept looking around ... the woman ... came and fell at his feet and, trembling with fear, told him the whole truth.* He addresses her in kindness — *'Daughter'* — though wishing her to understand that touching his garments has not healed her. He, not his clothing, has brought the restoration of her health. He says, therefore, *'Your faith* — your conviction about me — *has healed you.'*

Once more, as in other stories in this cycle, we see Jesus addressing a situation of human distress; in this case, a chronic illness with accompanying personal and social stigma. And again, his word, simple and unrepeated, is sufficient: *'Go in* [literally 'into'] *peace,'* he says, *'and be freed* [literally 'be healed'] *from your suffering.'* The pain of the past twelve years is replaced by the peace of the future.

The word *heal* (Greek *sozein*), which is so important in this passage (28,34), is important in Mark's Gospel overall (cf 3:2,5; 6:56). In the story about Bartimaeus (10:46-52) identical words are used as here: 'Your faith [your conviction about me] *has healed* you' — the Greek perfect tense signifying that permanent healing has resulted from the single action of faith being directed towards Jesus.

But *sozein* also carries the broader meaning 'to save'. Thus the passers-by at the scene of the crucifixion said to Jesus: 'Come down from the cross and *save* yourself!' (15:30; cf 8:35; 10:26; 13:13,20; 15:31). Mark wants the readers of the post-Easter period to apply the broader word 'saved' to themselves so that, as faith in Jesus had healed these sick people then, faith in Jesus will bring the salvation of God — complete restoration — to all people, the readers included.

As with the two previous incidents in this sequence, the narrative is marked by considerable detail. The crowd which physically pressed in on Jesus; the woman's furtive manner within the crowd — consistent with the nature of her sufferings; the medical information about her bleeding; the ironic remarks about her suffering through the doctors' 'care' and the extent and ineffectiveness of her expenses; the awareness of both the woman and Jesus that something had happened when she touched his garment; Jesus' persistence in identifying the hidden supplicant — all combine to support the idea of an eyewitness report (probably Peter's) on which Mark has based his narrative.

(4)   Jairus' dead daughter (5:35-43).

Throughout this prolonged episode, Jairus – whose daughter was *in extremis* — has been waiting patiently. But while Jesus was still speaking to the woman some men came from the house of Jairus with the grim news, *'Your daughter is dead,'* adding insensitively, *'Why bother the teacher any more?'* (We note in passing that the title 'teacher' is now widely applied to Jesus, not just by the disciples, cf 4:38 — doubtless

91

this is an accurate report of the popular perception at the time.)

Again we hear Jesus setting *faith* in him against *fear* inspired by the destructive forces of nature. To his disciples terrified by the storm at sea he had asked: 'Why are you so *afraid*? Do you still have no *faith*?' To the woman afflicted with chronic illness he said: 'Daughter, your *faith* has healed you. Go in *peace* ...'. Now, to Jairus faced with the death of his young daughter, he says: *'Don't be afraid; just believe.'* (Notice, too, Jesus' gentleness with Jairus in contrast with the insensitivity of the messengers.)

The sequence of events which follows again illustrates Jesus' passive attitude to healing. In regard to the casting out of unclean spirits Jesus adopts 'a search and destroy' policy, whereas with the clamorous and multitudinous needs for healing he does not take the initiative but responds to requests as they arise. He wants to be known as the proclaimer of the kingdom of God and the caster-out of demons but not as a healer (cf 1:38-39). The previous incident and another that will follow (6:53-56) show how easily healing could degenerate into magic in the common mind.

Thus, he *did not let anyone follow him* to the house of the synagogue ruler except the inner circle of *Peter, James and John*. This is the first occasion their independence from the twelve is noted (but see 9:2 and 14:33). In the years to come, Peter and John will be the only members of the original twelve to have any prominence in early Christianity: Peter becoming the source of the tradition about Jesus which gave rise to the Gospel of Mark, and John being the source of the tradition from which came the Gospel of John, the letters of John and the Revelation.

When they came to Jairus' home, *Jesus saw a commotion, with people* [i.e. relatives and professional mourners] *crying and wailing loudly.* When he told them, *'The child is not dead but asleep,'* they laughed at him. Thereupon *he put them all out* (literally 'cast out' – the same word as of demons; cf the leper, 1:43, and the traders in the temple, 11:15). Jesus did not want this miracle to be witnessed by the crowds or the mourners – that would have stimulated even more interest in healing. He took only the *father and mother* of the child and the three disciples and went in to the dead child. Then, Jesus, taking her hand, spoke to her in Aramaic: *'Talitha koum!'* (which means, 'Little girl, I say to you, get up!'). His words understood literally are 'Little lamb' – the gentleness Jesus showed to Jairus he now shows to his daughter.

As with the earlier stories in which Jesus confronted the destructive forces of storm, unclean spirits and chronic illness, the word of Jesus is immediately powerful and, in this case, as Jesus confronts death, leads to the restoration of the child to her parents. *Immediately the girl stood up and walked around* (for she was no child who needed to be carried but *twelve years old*), at which those present *were completely astonished.* But consistent with his desire not to be known as a healer, Jesus *gave strict orders not to let anyone know about this.* At the same time he *told them to give her something to eat.*

The vivid description in this episode reflects the underlying memory of an eyewitness (once more, Peter's?). The arrival of the men from the house with the tragic news while Jesus was still talking to the woman; the commotion inside the house; the father and mother with Jesus and the three disciples in the room with the child; the words *talitha koum* which Jesus spoke in his vernacular Aramaic; the age of the child and her walking around – all are very impressive, authentic details which assure us that we are reading an accurate account of what occurred.

On the other hand, this story is also told from the perspective of fully fledged Christian belief that deceased believers are not dead but 'asleep' and will be awakened at the resurrection (cf 1 Corinthians 15:18). Jesus' statement that the girl was 'not dead but asleep' is in line with later understanding and in all probability was the genesis of it. Mark's words that the girl 'stood up' (literally 'rose up'; cf 1 Thessalonians 4:14) is also resurrection language.

It is part of Mark's ability as a gospel writer that, on the one hand, he narrates events in such detail so that we feel confident of their accuracy, and, on the other hand and at the same time, he infuses his stories with subtle reminders of the wider truths of the Christian gospel – in this case that Jesus will wake sleepers from the dead, who shall rise up alive again.

The miracles of Jesus described in this sequence are not freakish or against nature, as were the signs of the Messianic age expected by the Pharisees (cf Luke 17:20-21). Rather, Jesus' miracles restored to nature the goodness which God had originally bestowed on it (cf Genesis 1:31). Here in Jesus' miraculous actions is a picture of the better future God has in mind for his creation, the salvation which God will finally bring. As the proclaimer and bearer of the kingdom of God, Jesus shows us unambiguously what God is like.

(5)   Tragic epilogue: Unbelief at Nazareth (6:1-6)

Jesus, *accompanied by his disciples*, now returns *to his hometown*. After the remarkable events (perhaps in the Gennesaret region) in which the chronically ill woman and the deceased child of Jairus were healed, we might have expected that Jesus would return to Nazareth as a local hero. That he did not return in triumph, however, may have been due in part to the relative isolation of mountainous Nazareth from the northern lakeside towns and villages. Perhaps the people of this southern village had heard little of the ministry of Jesus in Capernaum and Gennesaret. By now his way into the northern synagogues had been barred, forcing him to teach in the open, but his ready access to the Nazareth synagogue supports the idea that his reputation had not yet reached his local region. Perhaps, too, there was some resentment that Jesus had left his own town to make his mark elsewhere: 'Here he is back home with twelve men, none of whom are from Nazareth. Aren't our local men good enough?'

When the Sabbath came Jesus was permitted to *teach in the synagogue.* Doubtless he took a scroll containing the Prophets and gave the translation from Hebrew into vernacular Aramaic, commenting that the prophetic scripture was now being fulfilled and that the kingdom of God was upon them. It is also likely that he cast out evil spirits and healed the sick in this context of teaching in the synagogue in Nazareth (cf 1:21-25; 3:1).

Those present *were amazed* – signalling Jesus' supernatural character – *at the wisdom ... given him* – as heard in his teaching – and at his *miracles.* Inconsistently, however, the people do not associate God with the teaching and miracles of Jesus. Indeed *they took offence* at Jesus for presuming to do what he had done: 'Isn't he just a local carpenter? Isn't he just Mary's son, and don't his brothers and sisters live in this town?'

Jesus was *amazed at their lack of faith*, that is, at their complete failure to see the hand of God on him (cf 9:19). Their prejudice had blinded them to the things of God; they were without spiritual understanding. As such, the people of Nazareth are bracketed with the unbelieving disciples at the time of the storm on the lake (4:40) and seen in unfavourable contrast with the haemorrhaging woman and distraught Jairus, both of whom showed faith in Jesus in the midst of anxiety (5:34,36).

Mark's words, that Jesus *could not do any miracles there*, are difficult. Do they mean that Jesus' power was limited by the people's unbelieving response? Or do they mean that Jesus chose not to exercise his power among people who displayed no confidence in him? The former option is simply unacceptable, since everywhere else Jesus' word is all powerful. The second option is preferred.

Jesus' own words spoken in another setting may be applicable here: 'Do not give dogs what is sacred; do not throw your pearls to pigs' (Matthew 7:6). Jesus would not force people to respond positively to him. Prejudice against him – as in Nazareth – blinds people to his glory. To them he remains just the carpenter, just the brother of some men and women of Nazareth.

Nonetheless, this passage is valuable in supplying historical information about Jesus. He was by trade a *carpenter* (Greek *tekton* – one who works any 'hard' building material, eg stone, metal, timber); he might have built houses, ploughs or household furniture. He was the oldest of five sons, whose names were drawn from the Old Testament (*Jesus* = Joshua, *James* = Jacob, and *Joseph*) and from the Maccabean heroes (*Judas and Simon*). The names or number of his sisters are not supplied, consistent with that male-dominated society. Mark's failure to mention Joseph, the father, probably means he was by then deceased.

Jesus' proverb about the dishonoured prophet is also helpful in establishing something of the social networks of a village like Nazareth. Jesus mentions, in diminishing concentric circles, his *hometown* (Greek *patris* – the local district), his *relatives* (Greek *suggenes* – the extended family) and his *own house* (Greek *oikia* – the immediate family). At every level of Nazareth society, the people failed to honour him.

QUESTIONS ON MARK 4:35-6:6

1. Against what dread forces does Jesus contend in
    4:35-6:6?
2. What picture of Jesus emerges in each of the five
    episodes?
3. Who is Jesus in relationship to the kingdom of God?
4. What can be said about faith and 'unfaith' in this
    sequence (cf 4:40; 5:34,36; 6:6)?
5. Which details in these stories suggest authentic history?

13

Two feasts, two kings 6:6b-56

This part of Mark's Gospel is particularly important. The mission of the Twelve brings to a climax the process which began when Jesus called these men to follow him. Duly trained by the Teacher, they too must now proclaim the kingdom of God, but by themselves. This anticipates the time when Jesus would be permanently absent from them.

In turn, the mission of the Twelve is climaxed by the convergence of the Galileans on Jesus in the wilderness, where he teaches them and feeds them. This 'wilderness feeding', in which he is assisted by the Twelve, represents the end of Jesus' public ministry in Galilee. One year later, after a period of ministry to the west, east and north of Galilee, Jesus will go to Jerusalem, where he will be put to death.

In between the mission of the Twelve and the wilderness feeding, Mark places a flashback scene: the birthday banquet of Herod Antipas, when the prisoner John the Baptist is beheaded. Mark contrasts the godless feast of King Herod Antipas, at which John is killed, with the desert feast of the Shepherd-Messiah of Israel, at which the people are fed in their minds by Jesus' teaching and in their bodies by simple peasant fare which he generously provides.

(1) The mission of the Twelve (6:6b-13)

Undeterred by his rejection at Nazareth, Jesus *went around* (Greek *kuklo* = in a circle or circuit) teaching *from village to village.* Earlier, soon after his arrival in Capernaum, Jesus had gone on a teaching tour of the synagogues in that region, that is surrounding the northerly part of the Sea of Galilee (1:38-39). But as we have seen, Jesus was no longer welcome in the northern synagogues, and was being forced to take his message into the open by the lakeside (2:13). Back now in Nazareth, and beginning from there, Jesus visits villages of the high country between the southern part of the Sea of Galilee and the Mediterranean. Perhaps the Pharisees were not so active here in Jesus' home territory; he was still free to bring his good news of the kingdom of God to these southerly synagogue congregations.

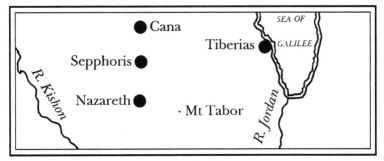

Map 4 *Nazareth and southern Galilee*

Many questions arise in regard to the so-called mission of the Twelve: Where was Jesus during the mission? From which village were the disciples dispatched? To which part of Galilee did they go? How long did the mission last?

Since Jesus was then in the region of Nazareth, it is possible that he sent the Twelve forth from Nazareth and remained there himself during the course of the mission. We are told that the five thousand Galilean men who later converge on Jesus, as a result of the mission of the Twelve, came from '*all* the towns' (6:33,44), so we can conclude that the total area the disciples covered must have been considerable. According to Josephus there were 204 cities and villages in Galilee (*Life*, 235), so if the six pairs of disciples visited each town for a week the mission would have lasted about nine months. Of course, we do not know exactly how many towns the disciples visited nor how long they stayed, but a mission of such duration is conceivable.

The location of the mission in relation to Jesus' ministry overall is easier to establish. It is followed immediately by the feeding of the multitude (6:30-44), which took place at the Passover season (John 6:4) exactly one year before the crucifixion (14:1,12,16). Thus, we are able to say that the mission of the Twelve occurred in the months immediately before the feeding, and that the mission and the feeding brought Jesus' Galilean ministry to its close, one year before his death.

Mark's account of the mission falls into three parts: Jesus' calling and sending of the Twelve (verse 7), his instructions to them (verses 8-11) and a summary of what they accomplished (verses 12-13).

First, Mark narrates Jesus' calling and sending of the Twelve. To a remarkable extent, the words used here exactly echo those found in Jesus' initial assembling of the Twelve (cf 3:13-19): *calling* (Greek *proskalein*); *sent* (Greek *apostellein*); *authority* (Greek *exousia*) over *evil spirits* (demons in 3:15); *preached* (Greek *keryssein*); and *drove out* (Greek *ekballein*). Moreover, in both passages the twelve men are called *apostles* (3:14; 6:30).

Going back even earlier to the beginning of Jesus' ministry in Galilee, it is clear that this mission is the 'fishing for men' to which the Lord originally called his disciples

(1:17). The five thousand men who gather in the wilderness in response to the mission are part of the great haul of 'fish' gathered in by the Twelve.

That Jesus sent the Twelve *two by two* may deliberately reflect the legal requirements of the Old Testament in regard to court proceedings. At least two witnesses were needed to testify when someone had been killed (Numbers 35:30; Deuteronomy 17:6); Jesus' dispatch of *two* disciples per village added weight to the message of his apostles.

Second, Jesus gave instructions to the Twelve. They were to rely on God. They were to *take nothing* with them — *no bread, no bag, no money*. They were to *stay* as guests in one *house* within each *town*, not to beg from door to door. The *staff* and *sandals* called to mind the Hebrew fugitives who were to be ready with their sandals on their feet and staff in their hands (Exodus 12:11); like Egypt before the exodus, Israel was now a doomed land. That Israel was now analogous to Egypt — a place from which to escape — is further confirmed by Jesus' command to the Twelve to *'shake the dust from your feet'* if any place would not welcome them or listen to the call to repent. Such action would be a *testimony* to the inhabitants, a vivid demonstration that they were now living in a 'Gentile' town, subject to the coming judgment of God (cf Acts 13:51; 18:6).

Third, Mark summarises what happened to the Twelve. As directed by Jesus, they *went out* and, like Jesus and doubtless based on his message that the kingdom of God was at hand (1:14-15), they *preached that people should repent*. Further in line with Jesus' instruction and example, they *drove out many demons*. The casting out of demons in the gospel bears close relationship to the announcement of the kingdom of God; clearly the kingdom of God overturns the domination of Satan. Mark adds that the Twelve, though they were told to cast out demons, also *healed* many sick people, having *anointed* them with oil. Once more we note that, as with Jesus, healing the sick was secondary and responsive, whereas proclaiming the kingdom/casting out demons/calling for repentance was primary (1:21-27;38-45). Mark also shows us that casting out demons and healing the sick represented *two* separate forms of suffering and two separate actions from Jesus, not *one* problem resolved by the one ministry of exorcism, as some suggest today.

This mission to the towns of Galilee is central to the purposes of Jesus in the Gospel of Mark. It is the logical progression from Jesus' initial call to the four fishermen, to Levi and then to the Twelve as a whole. The mission also anticipates the greater mission of the Twelve, no longer to the towns of Galilee, but to the nations of the world (Mark 13:10; 14:9; cf Matthew 28:19-20).

The modern 'signs and wonders' movement assumes that the mission of the Twelve to Galilee and to the nations is still in force today in a *direct* way: if these men cast out demons and healed the sick, then surely it is the will and intention of the risen Christ that Christian people continue to exercise such ministries right through history until the Lord returns. But it must be understood that the Twelve enjoyed a special place in God's purposes. Just as Jesus and no one else represented God, so these men and no others represented Jesus. They were called and given authority in a ministry which was an extension of the ministry of Jesus, and limited to the generation in which the Son of God came.

This is not to minimise the power of God to answer prayer in subsequent generations, including our own. But it does mean that the effortless casting out of demons and healings by the Twelve, and later by the apostle Paul, are not duplicated beyond their own age. The miracles of the signs and wonders movement — usually ambiguous in character, difficult to verify, dependent on the right atmosphere being created and generally explicable on psychosomatic grounds

— are not the same as the apostles' miracles. They may indeed be God's answer to faithful prayer, but the miracles of Jesus and the Twelve were declaratory in character and did not usually arise from intercession.

(2) News reaches Herod Antipas (6:14-16)

The deeds of the Twelve came to the notice of many Galileans and then to the tetrarch Herod Antipas who was based at the lakeside city of Tiberias. It is interesting that it was *Jesus' name* and not the names of the Twelve which *had become well known.*

Some Galileans were saying that *John the Baptist* had been *raised from the dead;* they attributed the *miraculous powers* of the Twelve to his supernatural resurrection. Others were saying that the prophet *Elijah* had returned, as indeed many expected (cf John 1:21). But others were saying that it was the work of *a prophet, like one of the prophets of long ago.*

It is clear from all these reactions that in popular perception Jesus was a prophet. The Twelve probably saw Jesus both as a prophet heralding the kingdom of God and as a rabbi or teacher. Though struck by his miracles (4:41), apparently it did not dawn on them until the final six months of his public ministry that Jesus was in fact the Christ (8:29). Then Jesus set about the dual task of reinterpreting their nationalistic concept of the Christ (8:31) and establishing with them that he was the Son of God (8:38; 12:6; 13:32; 14:36). But those who stood outside the number of the Twelve continued to see him as a prophet, even after his crucifixion (Luke 24:19). Thus we can conceive of Jesus as having two 'faces': the public face of a prophet or rabbi which the people saw; and one which was known only to those whom he had chosen — the face of the Son of God (cf Matthew 11:25-27; Mark 4:11).

But when Herod heard these reports and reactions he could only guiltily conclude, *'John, the man I beheaded, has been raised from the dead!'*

(3) The feast of Herod the King (6:17-29)

Mark recorded earlier that John had been arrested but gave no explanation (1:14). The arrest of John was simply the signal for Jesus to commence his public ministry in Galilee. No sooner was Herod Antipas rid of one troublesome prophet than he was confronted with another — one, moreover, who appeared to be active in many places!

In flashback, Mark now tells us that Herod Antipas had specifically ordered the arrest of John. This detail is confirmed by Josephus, who adds to the picture by stating that John was imprisoned in the fortress Machaerus in Perea (*Jewish Antiquities*, xviii.119). That Antipas had John arrested means that John must have been prophesying in Perea, within Antipas' jurisdiction. John's Gospel makes clear that John had indeed been baptising on the 'further', or Perean, side of the Jordan (John 10:40), so again we note the accuracy of Mark's account.

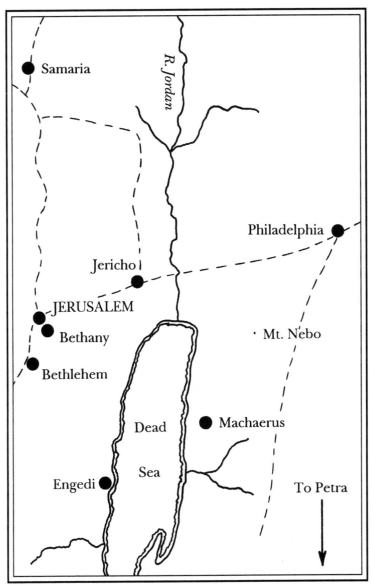

Map 5 *Perea, including Machaerus and Petra*

Josephus and Mark, however, give divergent accounts of John's arrest. According to Josephus, Herod Antipas arrested John for *political* reasons. John's eloquent prophesying had attracted great crowds, something which led the tetrarch to believe that the people might rise up behind John as a popular leader. It was to avoid any such uprising that Antipas had John arrested and killed.

Mark, on the other hand, gives *theological* reasons for John's arrest. John had raised his voice in protest that in his second marriage Herod Antipas had married his brother's wife. '*It is not lawful for you to have your brother's wife,*' he said (see Leviticus 18:16; 20:21). Josephus confirms this detail by noting,

> Herodias, taking it into her head to flout the ways of our fathers, married Herod [Antipas] her husband's brother...; to do this she parted from a living husband. (*Jewish Antiquities*, xviii.136)

Mark's theological reason is not necessarily at odds with Josephus' political explanation. It is quite possible that Antipas perceived political danger in the popular prophet's public denunciation of his marriage to his brother's wife.

But which brother did Antipas sin against? Here Mark and Josephus do appear to be in conflict. According to Mark, *Herodias* had been the wife of Antipas' brother, *Philip*. Josephus, however, states that Herodias' former husband was a certain *Herod*, a son of Herod the Great and Mariamne II (*Jewish Antiquities,* xviii.136). Some scholars believe Mark has confused Philip with Herod, but Mark and Josephus may be referring to the same man, whose full name was 'Herod Philip'. The family tree of Herod the Great is very complicated: he had nine wives and numerous children, many of who were called 'Herod' (eg Herod Antipas, Herod

Agrippa, etc). It is not possible to say for certain that Mark has made an error.

To marry Herodias, it was necessary for Antipas to divorce his then wife, the daughter of the king of Nabatea whose kingdom bordered Perea and whose capital was located at Petra. Antipas' father, Herod the Great, had an ongoing border conflict with the Nabateans, so Antipas had married the Nabatean princess for political reasons, namely to secure the eastern and southern border to Perea. But when Antipas was staying with his brother Herod (Philip), he became infatuated with Herodias and they secretly agreed that he would divorce the Nabatean woman and that she would leave Herod (Philip) and marry Antipas. To that point in time Antipas had successfully ruled Galilee-Perea for more than thirty years; Herodias was to be his downfall.

Mark briefly contrasts the different attitudes to John taken by Antipas and his consort. For her part, *Herodias nursed a grudge against John and wanted to kill him*. On the other hand, *Herod feared John and protected him* from Herodias, *knowing him to be a righteous and holy man*. The tetrarch would go to John's prison cell, and though *greatly puzzled* by what he heard, *he liked to listen to him*.

However, Herodias' opportunity came on the evening of the tetrarch's birthday, when *Herod gave a banquet for his high officials and military commanders and the leading men of Galilee.* The former two groups were senior administrators and military leaders, the latter the wealthiest landowners in the tetrarchy. These men had come from Galilee proper to the frontier fortress-palace of Machaerus in Perea. Perhaps Antipas was in this remote corner of the region to oversee the strengthening of his frontiers with the Nabataeans who by now would have been infuriated because of the indignity inflicted on their king's daughter.

During the festivities, by what must have been part of her plan, *the daughter of Herodias came in and danced*. Mark comments that *she pleased Herod* and those who reclined with him at the feast. There can be no doubt that the dancing was lascivious and took place in a context of heavy drinking (see Josephus, *Jewish War*, ii.29).

So, predictably, surrounded by his courtiers, Herod foolishly promised the girl, *'Ask me for anything that you want and I'll give it to you,'* rashly adding, *'up to half my kingdom'* (cf Esther 7:2).

The girl withdrew and asked her mother, *'What shall I ask for?'* The designs of Herodias were falling into place; she could now be rid of this prophet. She replied, *'The head of John the Baptist.'*

At once the daughter of Herodias hurried back to the king. *'I want,'* she said, *'you to give me right now the head of John the Baptist on a platter.'*

The tragedy comes quickly to its carefully planned end. Herod Antipas, outmanoeuvred by his wife, *was greatly distressed.* He obviously believed John to be a man of God, yet he dared not lose face by revoking the *oaths* he had uttered in the presence of his courtiers. He would not *refuse her,* and he *immediately* gave the order to kill John. The *executioner* went to the prison, *beheaded John* and *brought back his head on a platter* and *presented it to the girl.* The daughter in turn finally gave the head of John the Baptist to her mother, Herodias.

When they heard of this, *John's disciples,* who were apparently close at hand (visiting and caring for the imprisoned prophet?), came to the fortress-palace and *took his body and laid it in a tomb.* Thus, the great prophet was probably buried in the bleak high country of Machaerus which overlooks the Dead Sea. (The tradition that John was buried in Samaria seems not to have an historical basis.)

But the death of John continued to haunt Herod Antipas (the man Jesus called 'that fox' — Luke 13:32). The ministry of Jesus and of the Twelve raised in his mind the question:

'Is this John the Baptist, the man I beheaded ... raised from the dead?' (see 6:16). And four years later, Aretas' Nabatean army poured into Perea, decimated Antipas' troops and captured his military equipment. His loss of face among people within his own tetrarchy, to say nothing of his Roman masters whose borders he was responsible to protect, must have been considerable. The Jewish people immediately concluded that the humiliation of Antipas was God's vengeance for the death of John (*Jewish Antiquities*, xviii.117).

It was Herodias, however, who had instigated both the divorce of the daughter of the king of Nabatea and the murder of John the Baptist, and she was also responsible for Antipas' final downfall. When in AD 37 Caligula appointed her brother Agrippa as *king* of Philip's tetrarchy, she incited Antipas to seek the upgrading of his title from tetrarch to king of Galilee. Hadn't Antipas been named king of the whole of Herod's realm in the old man's earliest will? Hadn't he ruled Galilee-Perea effectively for more than forty years? Surely the emperor could do no less for Antipas than he had done for her villainous brother Agrippa in a smaller tetrarchy? Doubtless her reasoning ran along these lines.

But reasonable Caligula was not; he was, in fact, quite mad. Antipas and Herodias made the long voyage to Rome where they made their representations to Caligula. But instead of promotion, Antipas and Herodias were dismissed from office by the capricious Caligula. They did not return to Galilee but were banished to Spain where they died. Ironically, Caligula gave their territory to Herodias' brother, Agrippa, who reigned there as king in place of Antipas!

(4) To the wilderness (6:30-33)

In these few verses Mark skilfully narrates how those who
were gathered in the wilderness feeding – the Twelve with
Jesus and the five thousand Galilean men – came to be there.

Their mission completed, the six pairs of apostles
converged from various places around Galilee. They
gathered around Jesus and reported to him all they had done –
cast out evil spirits and healed the sick – *and taught* – the
imminence of the kingdom of God and the call to repent –
during their weeks and months away from him.

But they were not alone. Each pair of disciples was
followed by people *from all the towns* they had visited. As a
result, *so many people were coming and going* during their
reunion that Jesus and the Twelve *did not even have the chance
to eat* together. Therefore, Jesus said that they should come
with him by themselves *to a quiet place and get some rest*.

Both groups then move *to a solitary place* (Greek *eremos* –
a 'desert' place; see verses 31,32,35). Jesus and the Twelve
travelled *in a boat*. But the Galileans *saw them leaving* and
together *ran on foot* and got to their destination *ahead of them*.
A *large crowd* was waiting on the shore when the boat arrived.

What was the rendezvous where Jesus arranged to meet
the Twelve? Neither Mark nor the other Gospel writers say
precisely where it was. But we do know that the crowds
originally converged on Jesus and the Twelve at Bethsaida
at the northern tip of the Sea of Galilee (Luke 9:10). Thus,
it must have been from Bethsaida that they set out in the
boat. On its return trip the boat headed for Bethsaida (6:45),
though it actually arrived at Capernaum about six
kilometres to the west (John 6:24; cf John 6:17). In all
probability, therefore, the 'solitary place' was on the eastern
side of the Sea of Galilee within running distance of
Bethsaida, that is, a few kilometres south of that city. There
are also high hills in that region, one of which is probably

to be identified with the mountain where Jesus went to pray (6:46; John 6:15).

This short passage is important *historically* and *theologically*. Historically, it is clear that these envoys of Jesus created a considerable impact in the towns and villages of Galilee as they proclaimed the kingdom of God and cast out demons. We have noted already that their activities came to the notice of many Galileans, including the tetrarch Herod Antipas (6:14-16). The assembling of so many Galilean men *from all the towns* (of Galilee) who, having reached Bethsaida, *ran on foot* to get to Jesus' destination *ahead of him,* speaks of some considerable agitation on their part. It is reasonable to assume that they came with a heightened expectation of the appearance of the kingdom of God, the coming of which the apostles had proclaimed. Consistent with this, John tells us that at the conclusion of the feeding, those present attempted to make Jesus their king (John 6:14-15). This incident, therefore, is filled with political significance, especially in view of the paranoid tetrarch across the waters in Tiberias, who had already shown his enmity by removing John the Baptist for fear of a public uprising against him.

Theologically Mark makes many references to *a quiet ... solitary ... remote place* (6:31,32,35). Though the NIV translates the phrase in three different ways, it is one in the original Greek: *eremos topos.* This is probably to be understood as 'a desert place', a place with particular theological significance in the Old Testament (see comment on 1:12). It should also be noted that like the baptising of John and the temptations of Jesus, the feeding occurred on the eastern or *desert* side of the Jordan/Sea of Galilee. As we shall notice in commenting on the major incident which follows, there are elements both of blessing but also of temptation present in this desert setting too.

(5) The feast of Jesus the Messiah (6:34-46)

The drama that follows is acted out in eight short scenes.

(i) Arrival in the wilderness (6:34)

Immediately Jesus *landed,* awaiting him on the shore was the *large crowd* which had gathered from wider Galilee. This will be the final occasion Jesus teaches a great crowd in the north of Palestine (cf 2:13; 3:7; 4:1).

Mark tells us that, in Jesus' perception of the people, they were *like sheep without a shepherd.* Perhaps Jesus said something to that effect to the disciples in the boat as he looked out on the crowd waiting for him. His words call to mind Moses' prayer:

May the LORD ... appoint a man over this community to go out and come in before them, one who will lead them out and bring them in, so the LORD'S people will not be *like sheep without a shepherd.* (Numbers 27:15-17)

The passage continues: 'So the LORD said to Moses, "Take Joshua son of Nun, a man in whom is the spirit, and lay your hand on him"' (Numbers 27:18). In the original Semitic languages, Jesus' name was *Joshua.* By quoting from this passage in Numbers, Jesus apparently saw himself as a new Joshua, a shepherd-leader of God's people who have been called out from the resistant towns of Israel to the wilderness in a new exodus.

Related to this idea is the oracle of the prophet Ezekiel, where the Lord says:

I will save my flock ... I will place over them one *shepherd,* my servant David, and he will tend them ... I will make my covenant of peace with them ... so that they may live in the *desert* ... in safety. (Ezekiel 34:22-23)

These were people for whom Jesus felt *compassion* on account of their lack of understanding. Because he was their shepherd, or leader, Jesus *began teaching them many things.* We are not told by Mark exactly what Jesus taught them: perhaps he attempted to correct the heightened apocalyptic and nationalistic hopes inflamed by the apostles during their mission to Galilee, on account of which these men had gathered.

(ii) The hunger of the crowd (6:35-37)

By now it was *late in the day.* The disciples came to Jesus and asked him to *send the people away ... to the surrounding countryside and villages* to *buy themselves something to eat.* The northern and eastern side of the lake, today without towns, must have had a number of settlements then.

Jesus' rejoinder,'*You give them something to eat,*' foreshadows two future ministries of the disciples, one immediate, the other more distant. In the immediate future the disciples will indeed give out the food provided by Jesus to the crowd. He will be the provider, but they are to have an important role as dispensers of the Messiah's food to his people. They have begun to fulfil this role already, metaphorically, in their mission to Galilee. But Jesus also has in mind the time when he will no longer be with them physically. Then, too, they will give the Messiah's bread — the word of God — to the people (see Isaiah 55:10-11).

But in line with the spiritual dullness they show throughout his ministry, the Twelve fail completely to grasp Jesus' meaning (cf 4:40; 8:14-21,33; 9:5-6,32; 10:13,24-26,32,35). *'That would take eight months of a man's wages!'* they exclaim. *'Are we to go and spend that much on bread and give them something to eat?'* Clearly a very substantial sum of money was needed to give even a small amount of food to five thousand men. (In the original Greek we are told that the sum of money needed was 200 denarii. We know from the parable of the labourers in the vineyard that the wage

113

for a day's work was one denarius — Matthew 20:2. Hence, one man's wages for 200 days' work would have been needed to feed this multitude.)

(iii) The discovery of five loaves and two fish (6:38)

Jesus then asks the Twelve to *go and see* how many loaves of bread they can find among the crowd. They return and tell him that there are *five loaves* and, they add, *two fish.* John's version of the story (see John 6:9) reveals that the loaves were made from 'barley' — as for poor folk — and that the fish were not freshly caught but 'dried' (Galilee was a centre not only for catching but also for drying fish).

(iv) The seating of the crowd (6:39-40)

Jesus now takes his role as the Messianic provider of this meal for the hungry multitudes in the wilderness. But first the great assembly must recline in orderly *groups on the green grass* – green because, as John notes (John 6:4), this event took place at the time of Passover, that is, in the spring. The word for *groups* (Greek *prasiai*) was used of flower beds, so the vivid recollection of an eyewitness is implied, remembering people seated on green grass, appearing like garden beds. Once more we may be in contact with the reminiscences of Peter.

Jesus directs the Twelve to organise the men into groups of *hundreds and fifties.* In the Old Testament, Moses had organised the Israelites into groups of thousands, hundreds, fifties and tens for the sake of settling minor disputes (Exodus 18:17-26). These same groupings appear in the literature of the desert community of Qumran, depicting the end-time warriors of the people of God in the last battle. Each company of a thousand, a hundred, fifty or ten was to have its own chief and its own standard with words appropriate for the holy war about to take place (*War Rule*, iv.1-5).

It may be that despite the thoroughly unmilitary style of Jesus' ministry, his careful avoidance of Messianic titles and the markedly non-violent character of his teaching, the Galileans placed a warlike interpretation on their meeting with Jesus in the desert. Jesus might have meant only to group the men in an orderly manner by a pattern suggested by Exodus 18:17-26. But the men themselves appear to have seen the grouping in Messianic and martial terms, as the enigmatic conclusion of the episode will indicate.

(v) The thanksgiving (6:41)

The people being seated, Jesus now gives thanks for the food set before him. Four actions are described: first, Jesus took the loaves and the fishes in his hands; second, he lifted his eyes to heaven and *gave thanks* to God for the food; third, he *broke the loaves f*or the people; and fourth, he *gave* the food to the Twelve, for them to distribute to the people.

Since Jesus does exactly the same four actions with the bread at the Last Supper (14:22), many Christians have believed that this meal in the wilderness was a kind of Last Supper, that Jesus was somehow symbolising his death through his actions. But there are two problems with this view. One is that the wine cup, so important in the Last Supper, does not figure at all in the wilderness feeding. The other problem is that these same actions are taken by the apostle Paul on a ship during a storm (Acts 27:35). It is clear from that incident that Paul offers a typical Jewish thanksgiving for food about to be eaten. In the wilderness story Jesus is simply doing the same: offering God thanks for food about to be eaten, as all Jews were bound to do. It is, therefore, not clear that any Last Supper or eucharistic overtones should be found in this incident.

(vi) The feeding (6:42)

Mark then states briefly that *they all ate and were satisfied.*
He is emphasising the reality of the miracle: from such a
small supply of food, not just a few people, but *all* ate; they
did not eat a token amount, they were *satisfied.*

It is not altogether clear from Mark's account, however,
if the people knew that a great miracle had occurred. Some
indeed argue that those present were unaware of the
miracle. John, however, leaves us in no doubt that the men
'saw the miraculous sign that Jesus did' (John 6:14). And
regardless of Mark's silence, the men must have known that
initially there had not been enough food available for them
to have eaten their fill. Moreover, as we shall see, the
mysterious conclusion of the incident is consistent with the
crowd's awareness that a miracle had taken place.

(vii) The oversupply of food (6:43-44)

Scholars have sometimes treated the careful collection of
surplus food in the story as symbolic, for example, of
reverence for any unused bread in the sacrament of the
Eucharist. However, such an interpretation is uncalled for,
as the following passage from the Babylonian Talmud
shows:

> Abaye [a Jewish teacher] said:
> Formerly I thought that the sweeping away of crumbs
> took place for the sake of neatness, but [it is] because
> [letting crumbs lie on the ground] leads to poverty. Once
> the spirit of poverty pursued a man; but [the spirit of
> poverty] was not able to do anything against him, because
> he was very careful with the crumbs. One day the evil
> spirit thought: now he has certainly fallen into my hand
> [because the crumbs cannot be swept away]. After he had

eaten he took a shovel, dug off the grass and threw it into a river. Then he heard the evil spirit exclaim: alas he has chased me out of his house. (*Hullin,* 105, b)

Just as Jesus' thanksgiving was according to Jewish custom, so was the disciples' gathering up of the uneaten food. Uncollected surplus food invited poverty.

The baskets used by the Twelve were the ordinary small wicker-baskets used by Jewish men for carrying personal bits and pieces. Gentiles sometimes mockingly called Jews *cophinoi* — the Greek word for these dillybags which they characteristically carried.

The greatness of the miracle is indicated by the size of the crowd of five thousand fed by Jesus from such a tiny amount of food. Both Mark and John specifically state there were *five thousand men* (cf John 6:10). Matthew adds that there were also women and children present (Matthew 14:21).

(viii) Conclusion (6:45-46)

The story began with unexplained references to many people from all the towns of Galilee converging at Bethsaida and then running together to get to the 'desert place' before Jesus arrived by boat. What had precipitated this frenetic gathering? Had the Twelve spoken to the Galileans of the nearness of the kingdom of God in terms which inflamed their nationalistic hopes? Did Jesus' instructions to carry a staff and wear sandals suggest to them that a new exodus was imminent? Did his words that the dust was to be shaken from the disciples' feet in the unresponsive villages imply that the fiery apocalyptic end would soon be upon them? The answer to all these questions is probably yes.

The conclusion of the incident is as mysterious as its beginning. Jesus takes three dramatic actions. First, he *immediately made* [literally 'forced'] *his disciples get into the boat and go on ahead of him to Bethsaida.* Second, he *dismissed the crowd* and took his leave of them. The words used (Greek *apoluein* and *apotassein*) suggest a formal and final farewell. Third, Jesus *went up on a mountainside to pray.*

Evidently something occurred which made Jesus conclude the incident in such a peremptory manner. What was it that provoked such a speedy end to the gathering in the 'desert'? Mark, for reasons known only to himself, does not say what took place. It is John who tells us that 'After the people saw the miraculous sign ... they began to say, "Surely this is *the Prophet* who is to come into the world."'

Based on what they read in Deuteronomy 18:15-18, Jews had been looking for God to send them a prophet like Moses. When John the Baptist came, some supposed that he was that great, long-awaited, Moses-like prophet (John 1:21). Herod Antipas had had John arrested precisely because he feared the multitudes would rise up against him under John's leadership. Josephus tells us: 'Herod became alarmed [about John]. Eloquence that had so great an effect on mankind might lead to some form of sedition' (*Jewish Antiquities,* xviii.118).

The Galileans, inflamed by the preaching of the apostles in the towns of Galilee, moved by Jesus' grouping of them into what they saw to be holy war configurations, and now inspired by this great miracle which reminded them of Moses in the wilderness, hailed Jesus as the long-awaited prophet. John continues: 'Jesus, knowing that they intended to come and make him *king* by force, withdrew again to a mountain by himself' (John 6:15).

So this is the mysterious missing piece of the jigsaw — not found in Mark but found in John — which caused Jesus to disengage so abruptly from the crowd, to send the disciples packing and to retreat to the solitude of the mountain to pray: the attempt by the Galileans to force the kingship of Israel on him. This meant nothing less than the beginning of a Galilean revolution, a Messianic uprising in which the kingship of Israel was being forced upon Jesus.

And it was an attempt in which the disciples probably took a leading part. They pointed to Jesus in purely external ways, they allowed him to be cast in the role of a new Moses or a new Joshua, a military Messiah who would deliver the people from the Gentiles. Had Jesus been with the Twelve for so long that they still could not comprehend him in other than triumphalist and nationalistic terms?

The disciples' presentation of Jesus in apocalyptic terms not only failed to help the Galileans see who Jesus really was and what he had in truth come to do. Equally unfortunately they typecast Jesus in a role that false prophets and false Messiahs would be quick to exploit over the next three decades. During that time certain prophetic figures were followed to the Jordan, into the wilderness or around the walls of Jerusalem in the mistaken belief that God would bring salvation and liberation through them. Indeed, ten years later, one such figure was Theudas who, according to Josephus,

> persuaded the majority of the masses to take up their possesssions and follow him to the Jordan River. He stated that he was a prophet and that at his command the river would be parted and would provide them with an easy passage. (*Jewish Antiquities*, xx.97-98)

As it happened, the Romans heard of this and killed Theudas before he could attempt his Joshua-like attempt to part the waters of the Jordan.

Jesus once made a statement which can serve as his reaction to the attitude of the Galileans, who followed the lead of his own disciples: 'From the days of John the Baptist until now, the kingdom of heaven has suffered violence and men of violence take it by force' (Matthew 11:12, RSV). In other words, for the past three years, since John came on the scene and was followed by Jesus, 'men of violence' — Jews of nationalistic zeal — had attempted to *force* the kingdom of God into existence by violent means. The attempt to force Jesus to become 'king' or Messiah during the wilderness feeding is a good example of the 'violent' mindset to which Jesus was so much opposed.

From Jesus' standpoint, the feeding of the five thousand bore important similarities with his initial time of temptation (1:12-13). Both events occurred in the 'desert'; both were periods of acute moral and spiritual pressure for him to deviate from the path God had set him to walk. Satan tempted Jesus to conquer and bring justice through power and violence, but Jesus' prayer to his Father here on the mountain in the 'desert' strengthened his resolve to press on in obedience to the divine will. The former temptation in the desert set Jesus firmly on his non-violent and obedient path; the latter confirmed him in it.

Jesus also suffered temptation in the 'desert' regions of Galilee, when he was confronted with the many desperately ill and disabled people who pressed in on him for healing (1:35,45). How difficult it must have been not to allow compassion for the sick to replace the casting out of demons/the announcement of the kingdom/the call to repent (1:41-45). And he will be tempted again on two further occasions — at Caesarea Philippi and in Gethsemane (8:33; 14:32-36) — when he will be under pressure to take the political option rather than the way of the cross.

Today there is still the 'temptation' for us to cast Jesus into the role of political saviour or healer. The temptation is all the more powerful on account of the corrupt and unjust regimes under which the poor live and because of the endless misery caused by disease. But these evil circumstances were no less real in Jesus' time. In response, he did not withhold healing, yet it was not central to his mission.

The feeding of the five thousand marks the end of Jesus' open ministry in Galilee. The news of his very public, even seditious, action could not have failed to come to the attention of the tetrarch in Tiberias, visible across the water. For the next six months Jesus will move outside Antipas' province, to the west, the north and the east. When he is briefly in Galilee, he will travel swiftly and spend time indoors. Then, in exactly one year — at the time of the next Passover — Jesus will once more take the bread, bless God for it, break it and give it to his disciples. That feeding, however, will mark the end of his ministry on earth.

But what did Jesus, as portrayed by Mark, think was the significance of this feeding? For his part, Mark is surely wishing us to contrast the drunken banquet of the ruler Antipas, at which the prophet John was cruelly beheaded, with the gracious feast in the 'desert' provided by the true leader of God's people, Jesus.

Jesus did not wish to be seen as a Messiah in terms of contemporary Jewish hopes. He saw himself as the Shepherd of Israel who would compassionately feed the hungry people with the truth of God — if only they would heed him. By acting as host and presiding at this austere meal, by which he fed the people with plain food of bread and fish, Jesus foreshadowed the Messianic meal in the kingdom of God, to which the people of God were to be looking forward (14:25).

While the Twelve have their part to play in the feeding as those who bring his provision to the people, it is Jesus who is the focus of all the activity. It is he who teaches the people, sends the Twelve to find such food as there is, organises the multitude into groups, gives thanks to God for the food and breaks it for the people. He is the Good Shepherd of Israel who gives all things to his disciples to give in turn to the people. How blind they are not to see this!

But now a dramatic event takes place which will enable them at last to see who Jesus really is.

(6) Jesus walks on the sea (6:47-52)

When they set out, the disciples intended to sail north-west across to Capernaum (John 6:17), but to compensate for the flow of the Jordan as it entered the northern part of the Sea of Galilee they probably pointed the boat in the direction of Bethsaida to the north.

It is now *evening*. Jesus is *alone on land*, on the mountain; the disciples are in *the boat ... in the middle of the lake*. Separated from him, their position is very difficult. The story, as it unfolds, is told first from Jesus' point of view, then from theirs.

From the mountain, Jesus *saw* [by lightning flash or moonlight?] *the disciples straining on the oars, because the wind was against them*. They had not progressed towards Bethsaida, but were in the middle of the lake. At about 3 o'clock the next morning (about the time of *the fourth watch* kept by Roman sentries during the night), Jesus *went out to them, walking on the lake*.

Many people seek to explain away what Mark wants us to understand was a miracle. One such humanistic explanation is that Jesus was walking on some kind of shallow sandbank. But Mark tells us that because *their hearts were hardened* the disciples had neither understood about the miracle of the loaves the previous day, nor about Jesus' miracle in walking upon the sea in the early hours of this day. God-given miracles occurred on both occasions, but to those with hearts hardened against God they appeared only as wonders or marvels and nothing more. The true identity of Jesus as the Son of God remained hidden from the disciples.

At this point, the axis of the narrative shifts dramatically. The story is now told from the viewpoint of the men in the boat. Desperately tired from many hours of hard rowing against the strong wind, the disciples saw Jesus coming towards them. The account reflects two stages in their perception of him. When they first saw him, they concluded that *he was about to pass by them*, probably assuming he was in another boat standing up. Their first reaction, therefore, was anxiety that he would not be reunited with them at this time of great difficulty. But then, as Jesus drew nearer, they could see that there was no boat and that he was *walking on* the surface of *the lake*. Anxiety was replaced by terror: they thought he was a *ghost* (Greek *phantasma*).

Jesus' words to the Twelve are of great importance. Their mission to the towns of Galilee, followed by the feeding in the wilderness, had only served to show up their lack of understanding about his identity and mission. They were locked into existing ways of thinking about the one who was to come, that he was some kind of prophet or human Messiah. But this event and Jesus' words to them reveal him to be the Son of God.

The key words uttered by Jesus are, *'It is I,'* which could mean, 'It's not a ghost, but me, Jesus.' On the other hand, the words are literally, 'I am' (Greek *ego eimi*); in which case they are the same as the words of Yahweh by which he revealed himself to Moses at the scene of the burning bush (Exodus 3:14). We do not have to choose between these alternatives: both were probably meant by Jesus. That the latter option was indeed intended, however — namely that Jesus identified himself with Yahweh the God of Israel now come among them — is strengthened by two considerations.

First, Jesus' words understood as such make good sense when seen against the behaviour of Jewish boatsmen in storms. According to the Talmud, seafarers kept a paddle engraved with the words, 'I am that I am, Yah, the Lord of hosts...' Whenever their safety was threatened by high seas, the sailors would beat the waters with this paddle. But Jesus did not beat the waters with a piece of wood: he walked upon the sea and declared himself to be 'I am'. And when Jesus *climbed into the boat ... the wind died down* at once. His words appear to have been carefully chosen.

Second, Jesus' other words, *'Take courage! ... don't be afraid,'* are often used alongside the divine 'I am' in the Old Testament; for example: 'I am the LORD, your God, who ... says to you, Do not fear ...' (Isaiah 41:13; cf 43:1-5; 44:2-6; 51:12; Psalm 115:9-11; 118:5-7). Jesus' words clearly call to mind Yahweh's characteristic way of addressing Israel.

By this event and by his words, it is clear that Jesus intends to deepen the understanding of the Twelve about his identity. He is no mere prophet or Messianic king cast in their nationalistic mould. Nonetheless, just as their hardened hearts prevented them recognising Jesus as the Son of God when the loaves were multiplied, so, too, they do not see who he is even in this most spectacular demonstration of his divine power.

(7) The sick seek healing (6:53-56)

Their desperate night-time lake crossing is now completed; the disciples anchor the boat at the town of Gennesaret, which gave its name to the small, fertile plain nestling between the hills to the north-west side of the Sea of Galilee. Jesus would have passed through the plain of Gennesaret whenever he travelled between Nazareth and Capernaum.

What follows reminds us of the events of the previous day at Bethsaida (cf 6:33). Once again the appearance of Jesus in public creates tremendous interest. Great crowds are again drawn magnetically to him. Immediately *they got out of the boat, people recognised Jesus*. And this recognition sparked off great activity. As at Bethsaida, the people *ran throughout that whole region* (of Gennesaret). They collected *the sick* and carried them *on mats to wherever they heard he was* — developments which were anticipated by the story of the paralysed man carried by his four friends (or relatives) to Jesus at the house in Capernaum (cf 2:1-3).

Wherever [Jesus] went in that thickly populated area, whatever the size of the settlements — whether *villages* (medium-size towns), *towns* (places with the largest populations) or *countryside* (tiny hamlets) — the sick were brought by those desperate to help them and placed in the *marketplaces* (Greek *agora*) or town squares. Like the superstitious woman from this same region who had met Jesus earlier (cf 5:27), the sick begged Jesus *to let them touch even the edge of his cloak* as he passed by.

Notice that Mark comments that *all who touched him were healed,* as if to emphasise that it was not the garment but *Jesus* who was the source of healing. It is doubtful that Mark approves of these actions of the sick. First, while faith in Jesus is commended and lack of faith censured (6:5-6), Mark, following the declared attitude of Jesus on the subject, does not at all favour superstition. Though the woman with the issue of blood was treated with great pastoral care by Jesus when she said, 'If I just touch his clothes, I will be healed,' Jesus ensured that she did not go away with a superstitious belief that his garment had healed her (5:25-34): 'Your faith has healed you,' he said. But these people were as superstitious as the woman had been at first. Also, there is no mention of Jesus teaching the people or of the people responding to his words. Their interest was not directed towards the kingdom of God, but only on the relief of their sickness.

Jesus' attitude to healing here is consistent with that shown elsewhere in the gospel. He does not initiate healing of the sick; rather, he responds with compassion to needs as they confront him. His was a passive rather than an active policy towards healing. He came to proclaim the kingdom of God, not to be a healer (see comment on 1:38).

QUESTIONS ON MARK 6:6b-56

1. How was the mission of the Twelve different to Jesus' mission (6:7,12; cf 1:14-15,39)?

2. Why do you think the five thousand men from the towns of Galilee converged on Jesus in the 'desert' (6:31-33)?

3. Consider the contrasts between Herod's banquet and Jesus' wilderness feeding.

4. Can you explain why the feeding ended so quickly (6:45-46)?

5. In view of earlier references to 'desert' associated with 'temptation' (1:12,35,45), what temptation might Jesus have faced at this time?

6. What is the significance of Jesus' words during the storm, especially in view of what had happened in the desert (6:50)?

14

Uncleanness
7:1-23

The reference to 'the house' (7:17; cf 1:29; 2:1; 3:20,31; 9:33) suggests that Jesus is once again in the house of Peter in Capernaum, the centre of his activities. Capernaum is on the way from Gennesaret to the border of Tyre. The previous incidents were located in the Gennesaret region immediately to the south of Capernaum; soon, Jesus will travel north then west, into the city-state of Tyre (7:24).

Now Mark narrates a dispute over ritual uncleanness between Jesus and the teachers of the law. Their earlier disputes — over *blasphemy* (2:7), *fasting* (2:18) and the *Sabbath* (2:24; 3:2) — had apparently forced Jesus out of the synagogues to become a popular preacher to the crowds. That this dispute is not thematically grouped with the earlier ones suggests that it did in fact occur at this point in time.

The exchange is over the matter of uncleanness: Jesus' disciples had failed to separate themselves ritually from the Gentiles. As such it may be bracketed with Jesus' offensive table fellowship with 'sinners' in the house of Levi the customs collector (see comment on 2:13-17).

(1) Eating with unwashed hands (7:1-4)

The local *Pharisees* were apparently so intimidated by Jesus that they had called in the assistance of the high-powered *teachers of the law ... from Jerusalem*. On a previous occasion these teachers from Jerusalem had declared Jesus to be empowered by Beelzebub, the prince of demons (3:22). Mark does not say why the teachers came to Capernaum at this time. Perhaps it was because of the impact on the region of the mission of the Twelve which had culminated in the great assembly of Galileans on the eastern shores of the Sea of Galilee. The Galilean Pharisees probably felt considerable disquiet at these developments: Were they concerned about losing popular support to Jesus?

Mark says that the Jerusalem and Galilean teachers *gathered around* Jesus. This suggests he had a kind of magnetic appeal, even to those who opposed him. The 'gathering' of people (Greek *synagein*) to Jesus is something Mark often notices (2:2; 4:1; 5:21; 6:30). The teachers found fault not, in the first instance, with Jesus but with *his disciples* (see also 2:18). *Some* (not all) of them had sinned by coming inside the house and *eating food with hands that were ... unwashed*. (Perhaps Levi, the outcast customs collector, was among those who had erred in this regard.) Mark explains that *the Pharisees and all the Jews [did] not eat unless they [gave] their hands a ceremonial washing*. Every Jewish house had large stone jars placed near the entrance (John 2:6) for people to wash and purify themselves from the defilement of contact with goods which may have been handled by Gentiles. Thus, as Mark explains, whenever Jews *[came] from the marketplace they [did] not eat unless they [washed]*. They also washed *cups, pitchers and kettles* in the same way and for the same reason.

This washing — by means of water in cupped hands, as water was scarce — was not so much for hygiene as for the washing away of moral and spiritual defilement. For Jews, the problem was the kind of things which Gentiles customarily did: they ate food sacrificed to the gods; they were known to be sexually promiscuous, adultery and sodomy were commonplace, and they aborted their unborn, thereby defiling themselves by contact with the dead. God's people, his holy ones, must be protected from any possibility of such defilement.

While it was true that the Old Testament called for various washings from defilement, significantly they were only prescribed for the priests (Exodus 30:19; 40:12). It seems that, in their desire to make the laity of Israel conform with the holiness of the priests, the Pharisees went beyond the demands of the Scriptures and, as this incident bears witness, put pressure on the people to observe these rules.

Mark further comments that this practice was according to *the tradition of the elders*. The Scriptures had been added to for several generations by *the elders* (= the teachers of the law), who amplified the teachings of the Torah for the needs of the moment. It had been calculated that there were 613 commandments which could be found in the Old Testament, and the teachers had multiplied that number many times. As Mark notes, *they observe many other traditions*.

(2) Their question (7:5)

As with other exchanges between Jesus and the Pharisees, the opening words are put as a question. The Galilean Pharisees and the Jerusalem teachers ask him: *'Why don't your disciples live according to the tradition of the elders instead of eating their food with 'unclean' hands'?*

We should have some sympathy for these teachers of the law. Theirs was the task of purifying and sanctifying a semi-literate people who, in Galilee in particular, were exposed to Gentile influence. Along comes this awkward prophet with a growing peasant following, who blasphemes the name of God, fraternises with unholy people, breaks the Sabbath, and whose disciples neither fast nor wash themselves from defilement before eating. The entire Pharisaic program in Galilee was under challenge from this man and his followers.

(3) Jesus' answer (7:6-13)

Jesus replies by quoting Isaiah who, he tells the Pharisees, had *'prophesied about you hypocrites'*. The word 'hypocrite' originated with the Greeks who used it of actors in a play. Since Jews disapproved of plays and, therefore, did not have their own word for 'hypocrite', it is probable that Jesus had some familiarity with the Greek language. His reason for calling his questioners *hypocrites* is made clear in the example he will soon give.

'Isaiah was right,' says Jesus, quoting the prophet. *'These people,* these actors, *honour me* outwardly *with their lips, but their hearts,* their real concerns, *are far from me.'* Again, Jesus' specific example, soon to be given, will explain what he means. He adds, *'They worship me in vain* because *their teachings are but rules taught by men.'*

Because the Pharisees and teachers of the law went beyond what the Scriptures required, they were not teachers of the word of God, but inventors of the rules of men. Therefore, their worship of God was in vain. God's commands, sanctioned in Scripture, were being ignored. Instead, these people were holding to man-made teachings devised in recent days by the teachers of the law. As Jesus says to them, *'You have let go of the commands of God and are holding on to the traditions of men.'*

Jesus' words stand as a great affirmation of the authority of Scripture alone, for the beliefs and behaviour of God's people. Article Six of the Thirty-nine Articles of Religion puts it well:

> Holy Scripture containeth all things necessary to salvation: so that whatsoever is not read therein, nor may be proved thereby, is not to be required of any man, that it should be believed as an article of the Faith, or be thought requisite or necessary to salvation.

The principle of *sola scriptura,* as Luther called it, goes back to Jesus himself in this dispute with the Pharisees and teachers of the law over the means to the holiness of God's people.

In the last few years the 'new quest for the historical Jesus', as it is called, has arisen. In principle, this is a good development, a healthy reaction to the scepticism that has marked the study of the Gospels for most of the twentieth century. Nonetheless, many 'new quest' scholars, in their efforts to locate Jesus within the framework of first-century Judaism, are denying his uniqueness as the Son of God. Some regard Jesus as a rabbi who was one of the Pharisees. Yet Jesus' present dispute with the Pharisees reveals that he differed sharply from them in their most distinctive beliefs, namely the authority of their oral tradition and the achievement of purity by ritual washing. So, despite the claims that are now being made, it is clear that Jesus was not a Pharisee. Rather, he was in headlong conflict with the Pharisees in matters of fundamental importance.

Jesus now cites the case of negligence in keeping the law which was the basis of his appeal to the prophet Isaiah. 'It is the will of God that parents are to be honoured,' he says. *'For Moses said, "Honour your father and mother," [Exodus 20:12] and, "Anyone who curses his father or mother must be put to death"'* [Deuteronomy 5:16]. 'But,' says Jesus, using the precepts of the very teachers of the law who attack him, 'you are siphoning off the money people set aside to care for their parents and diverting it to the coffers of the temple. You call it 'a gift devoted to God', and say it's permissible because the person has said a religious formula over it, 'Corban', which he then can't retract. Thus, *you no longer let him do anything for his father or mother.'*

Disobedience of the word of God in the Scriptures had led to a serious social consequence – the neglect of people's parents. So Jesus accuses the Pharisees, *'You nullify the word of God by your tradition that you have handed down.'* Purification, the matter in dispute, was only one area where the word of God was being nullified by man-made tradition. Jesus further accuses: *'You do many things like that.'*

The people of God in every age must resist the imposition of new rules and practices which are not consistent with the word of God and which have the effect of nullifying it. Christians today need to engage in what the Reformers called the 'continuous reformation' of the Church by the word of God, purging out all those things which are contrary to scriptural teaching.

(4) Jesus' parable to the teachers and the crowd (7:14-15)

Jesus now summons the crowd to him and makes a great pronouncement on the matter of purity. Concern for purity before God was critical for God's people. He begins with the striking words, *'Listen to me, everyone, and understand this.'* Jesus is about to make an earth-shattering declaration on a critical subject and he wants everyone to hear and understand. His single-sentence 'parable' (as Mark calls it in verse 17) contains the seed of teaching about the origin of 'uncleanness' which later profoundly influenced the writers of the New Testament as they developed a Christian view of Man. The parable is in two parts.

'*Nothing,*' Jesus declares in the first part, '*outside a man can make him 'unclean' by going into him.*' Food which is eaten, even if it has been sacrificed to pagan gods, cannot defile the eater before God. Hence, the ritual washing of hands is irrelevant to purity.

Jesus' parable provokes us to ask, '*What, then, does make a person "unclean"?*' The second part addresses that question, but enigmatically, without providing a clear answer. '*It is,*' says Jesus, '*what comes out of a man that makes him unclean.*'

Jesus explains nothing more to those present — the Galilean Pharisees, the Jerusalem teachers, the crowd. As with the earlier parables which the public found baffling, Jesus will explain the meaning only to his disciples (cf 4:11).

(5) Jesus explains the parable to the disciples (7:17-23)

Now inside *the house* (of Peter in Capernaum?), the *disciples* (by which we infer the Twelve) ask Jesus about the parable. This private explanation, as distinct from public teaching, should be noted (cf 3:31-35; 4:10; 9:28; 10:10,23). Once again Jesus draws attention to their spiritual obtuseness; despite his exhortation to 'understand' the parable (verse 14), he must ask them, '*Are you so dull?*'

Jesus draws a critical distinction between the *stomach*, the receptacle of food, and the *heart,* which today we would call the 'mind'. He comments that food *enters* a man's *stomach,* then goes *out of his body* as human waste into the lavatory (Greek *aphedron* — English translations delicately mask Jesus' plain speaking on this subject!).

The *heart* (= mind), however, is not defiled by food nor, by implication, can it be spiritually purified by washing. This was an incredible thing for Jesus to say at that time, and it reminds us how futile it is to attempt to put him neatly into a first-century Jewish pigeonhole. He was no Pharisee!

Moreover, Jesus had moved into uncharted territory, far beyond the dispute over ritual washing of hands before eating. By his words, as Mark says, *Jesus declared all foods 'clean'*. Since, as Jesus taught, food did not defile anyone before God, people were free to eat whatever they chose — the restrictions under the old covenant were annulled. And the repercussions did not stop there. Not only were God's people free to eat *what* they chose, Jesus' declaration meant they were free to eat *with whom* they chose, even with Gentiles. In one sentence Jesus smashed forever the great ritual barrier that had prevented Jews and Gentiles sitting down together at table.

But may the heart (= mind) ever be defiled? Indeed, yes, as Jesus now proceeds to teach. It is not food that goes *in*, but behaviour that comes *out of a man*, that is, out of his heart or mind, which makes him 'unclean'. Jesus then refers to *actions* which break the commandments of God: *sexual immorality, theft, murder, adultery,... deceit,... slander*. And, equally important, he includes the underlying *attitudes* of the heart which, as he teaches in the Sermon on the Mount, also constitute a breaking of the commandments: *evil thoughts,... greed, malice,... lewdness, envy,... arrogance and folly*. Evil actions are like a defiling stream that flows out of the heart's evil attitudes; such things *make a man 'unclean'*.

This whole passage is of great importance to the New Testament. On one hand, Jesus sets to one side the notion of unclean foods, which belongs to the old covenant and to the oral tradition of the teachers of the law. In recent generations the Pharisees had attempted to create a holy priesthood out of the laity of Israel, but they had, in fact, brought the people under the bondage of religious legalism. By his words, Jesus liberates his people both from the Levitical food laws and the strictures of the Pharisees. Table fellowship with the Gentiles was now possible. God's people, under the new covenant of Jesus, would be free to be a multi-racial people. So important is this teaching that when Peter later forgets it, having heard this from Jesus and learned it from the vision of the clean and unclean animals (Acts 10:9-16), he has to suffer the fiery admonition of the apostle Paul (see Galatians 2:11-21).

Nonetheless, Jesus strongly upholds the moral law of God, as found in particular in the Ten Commandments. Parents are to be honoured and, as appropriate, provided for by their children; Jesus rejects pious oaths relieving children of such obligations. Jesus not only upholds the law of God regarding sexual immorality, theft, murder, false witness and the like; he also imparts his great insight that committing such evils originates in the wellspring of the human mind. Human 'uncleanness' does not come from negligence in ritual matters, but from the wickedness of the human mind as expressed in the breaking of the laws of God.

This passage also illustrates the public and private character of the ministry of Jesus. Overall, the incident takes place in two parts. The first is in *public,* as Jesus debates with the teachers of the law and addresses the crowd (verses 1-15). The second part is in *private,* as Jesus explains his parable to the Twelve (verses 17-23). In public Jesus speaks parables which the hearers, including his own disciples, do not comprehend. In private, however, Jesus explains the meaning of his parables to the Twelve. In this two-sided ministry, Jesus reveals his two profiles or faces.

Jesus' public profile was seen by the crowds, by his critics and also by the Twelve. His public face was that of a prophet who announced the nearness of the kingdom of God, an unorthodox rabbi who rejected the established canons of scriptural interpretation. This is the face which is sketched by Josephus and, less favourably, by later Jewish writers. And it is the public face which Jesus showed to the Jewish people of his own time that modern 'new quest' scholars tend to portray to us today.

But Jesus revealed another face to the Twelve, a face which at first they did not understand: the 'filial' face, the face of the Son of God. When Jesus prayed to God in their presence he said: 'Father ... you have hidden these things from the wise and learned, and revealed them to little children' (Matthew 11:25). What are 'these things' which Jesus in public *hides* from 'the wise and learned' (= the teachers of the law) and in private *reveals* to 'little children' (= the Twelve)? It is God himself, God as the *Father* of Jesus his *Son,* whom Jesus hides from the public and reveals to the Twelve (see Matthew 11:27).

As part of this hiding and revealing process, Jesus teaches in public by means of parables about the kingdom of God and, in this incident, about 'uncleanness'. But it is only to the Twelve in private that Jesus explains the meaning of the parables and, in this case, the true source of 'uncleanness'. The public teaching of Jesus was only grasped superficially, if at all, by the Jewish people of his time. The private teaching of Jesus, as it eventually came to be understood by the Twelve, especially after the first Easter and the first Pentecost, survives in the writings of the New Testament.

QUESTIONS ON MARK 7:1-23

1. How do you respond to the suggestion of some scholars that Jesus should be regarded as one of the Pharisees (7:3-4,8)?

2. What did the Pharisees do to the word of God, and why (7:8-9)? What does this lead to (7:13)?

3. Is Jesus against the commandments in any sense (7:10,21-23)?

4. If the body cannot be made 'unclean' by what touches it, or what goes into it, is it possible for the heart (= mind) to be made 'unclean' (7:20-23)?

5. What are the momentous consequences of Mark's passing comment in verse 19: 'In saying this, Jesus declared all foods "clean"'?

15

Jesus in Gentile regions 7:24-8:26

From this point, Jesus does not again appear in public in Galilee. Clearly his life was in danger, and two recent events would have further displeased his enemies, the Pharisees and the Herodians who, a year earlier, had formed their unlikely alliance seeking his death (see 3:6).

One event was the Galileans' attempt to appoint him king after the feeding of the five thousand (6:30-45; cf John 6:14-15), an action which must have angered Herod Antipas and his supporters, the Herodians. Antipas had already killed one prophet, John the Baptist; he would not hesitate to kill another popular leader.

The other event was the dispute over 'uncleanness' with the local Pharisees and their allies, the Jerusalem teachers of the law (7:1-23). These religious leaders must have regarded Jesus as a major threat to their influence in Galilee.

So for the next six months, Jesus and the Twelve will travel in the Gentile lands to the west, east and north of Galilee, out of reach of Herod Antipas. During this period of 'wandering', as it is sometimes called, we are shown the first glimmerings of understanding of Jesus' true identity and mission — not, however, by Jews, but by Gentiles. Mark's account of the healings of a deaf-mute (7:31-37) and a blind man illustrate the confession and insight of these people in

Gentile regions (8:22-26). Ironically, however, the *unbelief* of the Twelve also reaches new heights at this time (8:17-21). Those who were not God's people 'see' in Jesus and 'say' about him what the Jews, including the Twelve, do not yet 'see' or 'say'.

(1) In Phoenicea: The Gentile woman's insight (7:24-30)

Jesus left Capernaum *and went to the vicinity of Tyre.* This is not to say that he went to the *city* of Tyre on the Mediterranean coast, but that he crossed the border (Greek *horia*) from Galilee into the political *region* of Tyre, which consisted of a number of dependent villages around Tyre, the capital. Here Mark reveals his awareness of the boundaries of the Gentile city-states to the west, north and east of Galilee.

In all probability Jesus would have avoided travelling north-west from Capernaum through the brigand-infested mountainous region of Galilee. It is likely that he travelled instead up the valley of the north Jordan River, and then crossed westwards into the region of Tyre. And here, for the first time, Jesus meets a representative of the Gentile world.

He entered a house there, but *he did not want anyone to know it,* because the long arm of the tetrarch of Galilee might still reach into a small neighbouring city-state like Tyre (cf Acts 12:20). Yet such was Jesus' fame that *he could not keep his presence secret.* People from Tyre had gone to Galilee early in his ministry, attracted by all that they *heard* he was doing (3:8). Now Mark focuses on one person who comes into this house seeking help from Jesus, *a woman whose little daughter was possessed by an evil* [= unclean] *spirit.*

This Gentile woman was from *Syrian* [or coastal] *Phoenicea,* and she is further described as *a Greek.* Large numbers of Greeks had settled in Palestine after Alexander's conquests 300 years earlier. Through the

140

easterly migration from Greece the Greek language became widely known. It is not clear whether this woman was of Syrian or of mixed Greek-Syrian parentage but, either way, it is clear that she spoke Greek. This is evidence that Jesus also spoke Greek as well as Aramaic, something which is not unlikely since bilingualism was common among Jews at that time. Pontius Pilate probably addressed his question to Jesus and received his answer in Greek (15:2-5).

Desperate to find help for her daughter, the woman is very determined in both *action – as soon as she heard about him [she] came and fell at his feet –* and *word – she begged Jesus to drive the demon out of her daughter.*

Jesus replies in a brief parable: *'First let the children eat all they want,... for it is not right to take the children's bread and toss it to their dogs.'*

But who are the *children*, who are the *dogs* and what is the *bread*? The 'children' are the children of Israel, the 'dogs' are the Gentiles and the 'bread' is the kingdom of God which Jesus is bringing, the sign of which is the casting out of demons. The bread of God's kingdom is to be given first to the children of Israel, he says.

But, as the woman understands it, that does not mean that there will be nothing at all for the Gentile dogs. Showing further determination (as well as an understanding of the habits of dogs!), she seizes on Jesus' gracious word *first*. In an instant she grasps that 'first' means *priority* for the children, not exclusion to the dogs. She understands that Jesus holds out great hope to a Gentile woman like her.

Quick as a flash, and showing insight foreign to the Twelve, she grabs the hand of hope held out to her, meeting Jesus' parable with her own. 'Yes, Lord,' she replies, *'but even the dogs under the table eat the children's crumbs.'* The woman shows humility as well as insight: she is prepared to acknowledge that she is a Gentile — a dog —with no prior claim on the blessings of the kingdom.

141

The woman has thus completed Jesus' parable, as he virtually acknowledges: *'For such a reply, you may go; the demon has left your daughter.'* Although Jesus had spoken to her in a parable, as he typically did in public, this Gentile woman understood who he was. Her grasp of the situation and her determined faith in Jesus is in stark contrast with the dullness of the Twelve (cf 7:18) and the opposition of the Pharisees and other religious leaders. Because of this, she is bracketed by Mark with the paralytic and his friends, the bleeding woman, Jairus and Bartimaeus as a person of faith (cf 2:5; 5:34,36; 10:52).

Jesus knew that, although the girl was not there with him, she was already free of the unclean spirit. Indeed, when the mother *went home*, she *found her child lying on the bed, and the demon gone.*

Mark has brought us to an important milestone. This is the first Gentile to turn to Jesus. In the years to come, after Jesus was no longer physically present on earth, churches would be established in Phoenicea, including Tyre (Acts 15:3; 21:3-4; 27:3). This woman who fell at the feet of Jesus and showed such powerful understanding of his ministry anticipated the response to the gospel of her fellow countrymen. Perhaps she was present when Paul visited the churches of Phoenicea fifteen years later. In Mark's Gospel this Greek woman anticipates the Roman centurion who confesses at the crucifixion (15:39). Both symbolise the great future response to Jesus by Gentile people.

(2) In the Decapolis: The people's confession (7:31-37)

Mark now gives his most detailed statement of Jesus' travels so far, though his account has often been criticised, even ridiculed. To travel from *Tyre through Sidon, down to the Sea of Galilee and into the region of the Decapolis* may be likened, say, to travelling from Sydney to Brisbane via

Melbourne. Thus, this highly improbable route is cited as conclusive evidence that Mark lacked accurate historical knowledge about Jesus' ministry.

But such scepticism is unwarranted. It does not take into account the danger Jesus faced from Herod Antipas after the attempt to make him king at the feeding of the five thousand (6:44-46; John 6:14-16). And Jesus' dispute with the Pharisees in Capernaum over 'uncleanness' may well have provoked further plotting with the Herodians to remove him (cf 3:6). The route taken is, in fact, a circuit which skirts the borders of Galilee. Jesus had to avoid being in public within or near Antipas' region.

From inside the borders of Tyre, Jesus and the Twelve travelled north into (the territory of?) Sidon, crossing eastwards over the upper reaches of the Jordan (past Caesarea Philippi?), turning south through the midst of the borders (Greek *horia*) of the Decapolis, before moving west to arrive ultimately at the eastern side of the Sea of Galilee. This roundabout trek through the Gentile countries bordering on Galilee must have taken many weeks.

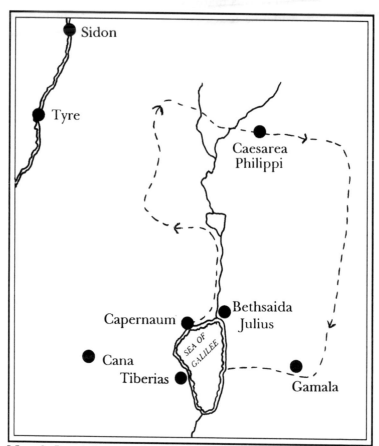

Map 6 *Jesus' journey through Gentile territory*

Mark probably selected the healing story that follows for two reasons. First, the healing of deafness may point symbolically to the growing *hearing* of the word of God at this time in Gentile regions, in contrast to the deafness of the Jews, including the Twelve (4:12; cf 8:18). Jesus opens the ears of a deaf man, pointing to the beginning of people's understanding of Jesus and his message.

Second, this miracle indicates that Jesus engaged in ministry during this lengthy period. Naturally, we are curious to know what else he did in this time. The gathering of the four thousand in the Decapolis in the passage following (8:1-10) probably represents the climax of an extensive ministry in these Gentile regions, just as the feeding of the five thousand represented the climax of his ministry to the Galileans.

While somewhere within the region of the ten city-states known as the Decapolis (literally 'ten cities'; see comment on 5:1-20), *some people brought to [Jesus] a man who was deaf and could hardly talk.* (Possibly he had partial hearing, otherwise he would not have known how to speak at all.) *They begged [Jesus] to place his hand on the the man,* doubtless with a view to his healing. These people of the Decapolis region might have heard of Jesus as a result of the remarkable restoration of the man who had been known as 'Legion' (see comment on 5:20). Jesus' use of his hands in healing may also have been well known by this time (see 1:31,41; 3:5; 5:23,41; 6:5; 7:33; 9:27; 10:16).

Jesus' actions towards the man illustrate his pastoral care. *He took him aside, away from the crowd,* to engage the (partial) deaf-mute in an undistracted way. He then physically identified the defective organs by putting *his fingers into the man's ears* and touching *the man's tongue* with spittle. Even Jesus' prayer is dramatised for the man: *he looked up to heaven and with a deep sigh said to him,... 'Be opened!'* — the passive verb indicating that his deaf ears would be opened *by God.* Why, in a Gentile region, does Jesus address the man in the Aramaic *'Ephphatha'* (cf 5:41; 15:34)? Probably because this man and the people who brought him were Jews, living among the Gentiles in the Decapolis.

As was his usual practice, Jesus commands those present *not to tell anyone* about the healing. The problem that he had faced from the beginning — of being overrun by the sick in that pre-hospital society — was now compounded by the need for secrecy in the face of the life-threatening menace posed by the Pharisees and the Herodians. *But the more [Jesus] did so*, implying that there were other miracles of healing at that time, *the more they kept talking about it* (literally 'proclaiming' it).

Mark's comment that the *people were overwhelmed with amazement* indicates the powerful impact this healing made. Such a miracle was listed in Isaiah's prophecy of the coming Messianic age: 'Then will the eyes of the blind be opened and the ears of the deaf unstopped' (Isaiah 35:5). Therefore, when those present say, *'He has done everything well. He even makes the deaf hear and the mute speak,'* it is clear that they recognise that in Jesus, *God* has 'come to save' his people (Isaiah 35:4), that the long-awaited kingdom of God's Messiah is now present in Jesus' ministry.

Once again we note insight into Jesus far greater than any shown by the general run of Jewish onlookers, or even by the Twelve. These people may have been Jews, but they were not Jews from Jerusalem, nor even from Galilee. They were Jews living among the Gentiles, who had identified Jesus as the fulfilment of the prophetic hope.

(3) In the Decapolis: The feeding of the people (8:1-10)

This episode by the eastern shore of the Sea of Galilee marks the end of the long circuit which began inside the borders of Tyre and which swept in an arc through Gentile territories to the north and east of the tetrarchy of Galilee (7:31). It is important for three reasons.

First, it reveals once more the response Jesus made to people in need, in this case people who were hungry. Jesus did not directly initiate social action or political reforms to change the structures of society; his mission was to proclaim the kingdom/cast out demons/call for repentance. Nonetheless, as we have repeatedly seen, whenever Jesus was confronted with hunger or illness, he relieved whatever needs people had. Jesus himself was in real life the compassionate Good Samaritan of whom he spoke in his famous story (Luke 10:25-37). He said that his people were to be likewise Good Samaritans, so the compassion of Christ which we see here should inspire us to be in the forefront of those who serve their neighbours.

Second, this feeding occurs as the culmination of Jesus' ministry in Gentile regions. Just as Jesus concluded his ministry to the people of Galilee by feeding those present (the five thousand), demonstrating his Messianic care of them, so Jesus now provides for the mixed Gentile and Jewish people of the Gentile regions (the four thousand). This incident foreshadows the future extension of the Messianic rule of Jesus to the Gentiles.

Third, this incident reveals once more to the Twelve Jesus' control over nature. A few months earlier, also on the eastern side of the Sea of Galilee, Jesus miraculously fed a large crowd. But then the Twelve did not understand either the fact or the significance of the miracle (see 6:52). From the time of his calling of the Twelve they have not grasped who Jesus is or why he has come among them.

But the feeding of the four thousand enjoys a special place in their eventual illumination about Jesus. As we shall see (8:17-21), following this incident Jesus will bitingly rebuke them for their spiritual blindness, challenging them to think first about the feeding of the five thousand, then about the feeding of the four thousand. Soon afterwards, Peter, spokesman of the Twelve, will declare Jesus to be the Christ, a confession which is a major turning point — both spiritually and geographically — in the Gospel of Mark (8:27-30).

But did the event actually occur? Some scholars doubt its historicity on two grounds. First, the feeding of the four thousand closely resembles the feeding of the five thousand at a number of points. For example, both feedings occur in a *remote place* or 'desert' (Greek *eremos, eremia* — 6:35; 8:4); both express the *compassion* of Jesus (6:34; 8:2); both report Jesus' question, *'How many loaves do you have?'* (6:38; 8:5); and in both, those present *ate and were satisfied* (6:42; 8:8). Is this merely a recycled version of the earlier feeding?

Similarity of detail and description, however, do not logically demand a negative verdict on the factuality of the story. Given Mark's fairly limited choice of words to describe miracles, it is likely he would describe two similar events in roughly the same way.

In any case, there are as many differences of detail as there are similarities. Here the crowd has been with Jesus *three days,* as opposed to one in the previous incident (6:35; 8:2). Other numbers are also different: of people present (6:44; 8:9), of the loaves and fishes available (6:38; 8:5 — the number of fish is unspecified in the second incident) and of the baskets of unused food collected (6:43; 8:8). Moreover, the type of basket (Greek *kophinos*) used in the first incident had distinctly Jewish associations and was small (cf Juvenal, *Satires* iii.p14; vi.p542), whereas the baskets (Greek *spuris*) used in the second are large and are associated with Gentiles (Paul was lowered down the walls of Damascus in a *spuris* — Acts 9:25). A straightforward reading of the text leads to the conclusion that there were two separate feedings.

Second, scholars seize on the disciples' question, *'Where in this remote place* [Greek *eremia* — 'desert'] *can anyone get enough bread to feed them?'* How could the Twelve ask this question in view of Jesus' earlier feeding in similar circumstances? This second story must be unhistorical.

But this is to miss the very point Mark is making. Due to
their spiritual blindness, the Twelve 'had not understood
about the loaves' (6:52). Because of their lack of insight, the
feeding of the five thousand remained ambiguous to them:
Had it really happened? Perhaps they had been mistaken
about it. By contrast, the people of the Gentile Decapolis
have just made what amounted to a Messianic confession of
Jesus (7:37). But the question which the Twelve ask implies
lack of faith with overtones of resentment. 'Well,' they are
saying to Jesus, 'what do you propose to do now?' They
imply that the present situation is hopeless. But Jesus will
feed the four thousand, then, when he returns with the
Twelve by boat from the other side, he will admonish them
for their spiritual blindness and deafness (8:17-21). Their
question here shows that their unbelief is reaching new
heights; however, the light of understanding will soon begin
to dawn upon them.

(4) The Pharisees seek a sign (8:11-13)

Jesus and the Twelve have crossed to the western side of
the Sea of Galilee at Dalmanutha (8:10). The incident that
now takes place, though brief, is very important. It is yet
another episode in the continuing dispute between Jesus
and the Pharisees.

Earlier, the Pharisees had accused Jesus (and his disciples)
of blasphemy (2:7), of eating with 'sinners' (2:16), of failing
to fast (2:18) and of breaking the Sabbath (2:23-3:4).
Reinforced by the teachers of the law from Jerusalem, they
also charged him with being the instrument of the devil
(3:22) and with ritual defilement (7:1-5). Now they question
him about something which goes to the heart of his message,
namely the imminent appearance of the kingdom of God.
In the light of Jesus' ministry in Galilee and the mission of
the Twelve, they perhaps sensed that something dramatic

was about to happen, hence their question at this time about *a sign*.

The appearance of the kingdom of God was viewed by Jews as a mighty and divine intervention which would be heralded by unmistakable signs. A few years before Jesus' ministry, an unknown Jewish author had written that cosmic signs would precede or accompany the kingdom of God:

> Then [God's] kingdom shall appear throughout all creation ... the horns of the sun shall be broken and ... be turned to darkness ... the moon will not give her light ... the circle of the stars shall be disturbed. *(Assumption of Moses,* 10)

And some years after Jesus, as the siege of Jerusalem drew to its tragic climax in AD 70, the people believed they saw bizarre visions in the heavens and heard supernatural voices. The great door of the temple, which needed twenty men to shut it and which was securely bolted in place, suddenly swung open of its own accord. A weird prophet named Jeshua son of Ananias appeared in the streets of the city uttering oracles of doom against Jerusalem, despite having been flogged to the point of death by the Roman authorities (Josephus, *Jewish War*, vi.288-309). Jesus and the Twelve were heralding the kingdom of God, but where were the signs — signs from or in the heavens — such as these?

In deep distress, Jesus *sighed deeply* and replied by an oath, *'I tell you the truth, no sign will be given ...'* So far as Jesus was concerned, the casting out of demons, which accompanied his announcement of the imminence of the kingdom of God, revealed the nature of the kingdom. This was the sign. He said, 'If I drive out demons by the finger of God, then the kingdom of God has come to you' (Luke 11:20). But there would be no freakish signs such as the Jews sought.

Though the casting out of demons was Jesus' sign of the kingdom of God, the Pharisees held that Jesus did this as an instrument of the devil, not by the finger of God (see 3:22). This view would become the standard Jewish interpretation of Jesus in the centuries to come; according to the Talmud, Jesus was executed for 'sorcery', as a magician (*Sanhedrin*, 43a). In any case, this was not the kind of sign the Jews sought.

Jesus' words *'I tell you the truth'* (literally 'Amen, I say to you') are his solemn and authoritative way of speaking when matters of great importance are in dispute (cf 3:28; 9:1,41; 10:15,29; 11:23; 12:43; 13:30; 14:9,18,25,30). The original words underlying *'no sign will be given to it* [this generation]', which follow, are a literal translation of the Aramaic words Jesus used. The awkward grammar of this phrase breaks the flow of Mark's Greek and lets us hear echoes of Jesus' emphatic rejection of the Pharisees' request.

In his crucifixion, Jesus was destined not to wield power but to be subject to power, the power of the Gentiles. A Messiah who was crucified (by Gentiles!) and who performed no sign could expect only repudiation from the Jewish people of his time, as the apostle Paul later grimly testified (1 Corinthians 1:22-24). Popular Jewish Messianic hopes were utterly different from God's wisdom.

The warning for us implicit in this is that we should be careful about our expectations of what God will do, in particular, how he will wield power for us in answer to our prayers. God's power to save was seen in the crucifixion of Jesus, and is experienced by believers in circumstances of weakness (2 Corinthians 12:9). Naturally, we look for a quick resolution of our illness or distress, and it is right that we pray for that. But equally, God may answer our prayers and show his power in our lives by giving us Christ-like qualities of patient endurance and graciousness.

This incident, as with the earlier confrontations between Jesus and the Pharisees, occurred near the north-western shores of the Sea of Galilee. The geographical consistency of these disputes suggests that the Pharisees may have been concentrated in that region; they are not in evidence in the high country around Nazareth. There Jesus was free to teach in the synagogue, unlike the synagogues centred on Capernaum.

(5) Warning and rebuke in the sea crossing (8:14-22)

The story of the eastward boat crossing from Dalmanutha to Bethsaida has a number of links with three earlier incidents. Jesus' references to the numbers of people fed and the baskets of uneaten food (verses 19-20) take us back to the feeding of the five thousand and the feeding of the four thousand; and the lack of bread on board the boat (verse 14) may have been due to the dispute with the Pharisees at Dalmanutha and the need for Jesus to re-embark hurriedly for Bethsaida, out of Herod's reach. Jesus' warning about the Pharisees arises directly from this dispute, while his warning about Herod may have been suggested by the close proximity of Dalmanutha (8:10) to Herod's capital, Tiberias, a few kilometres to the south.

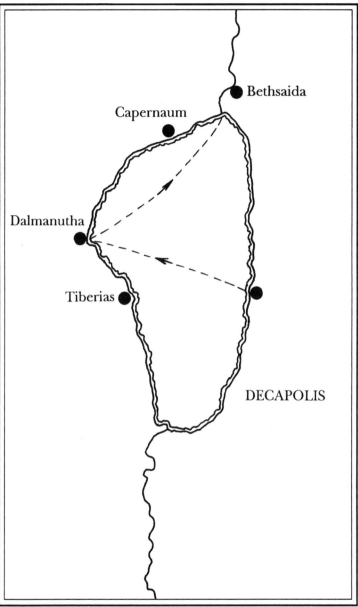

Map 7 *The Sea of Galilee*

This incident also contributes dramatically to the developing climax of Mark's narrative. It is a critical time for these twelve men. On two previous journeys across the lake, Jesus had revealed himself as Lord of the storm and sea (4:35-41; 6:45-52). On both occasions, however, the Twelve failed to understand his true identity (4:40-41; 6:49-52). On this journey, Jesus reveals himself in a different way. The period of the disciples' wilful deafness and blindness is past; it is time for plain speaking, for warning and rebuke.

At some point during the voyage (probably when they became hungry!) the disciples discovered that they had only *one loaf* of bread with them. Jesus uses this simple discovery first to warn, then to rebuke the Twelve.

First, Jesus warns them about *yeast*, which has great influence in breadmaking in inverse proportion to its size. He says, *'Be careful* — even a small quantity of *the yeast of the Pharisees and that of Herod* spells grave danger.'

What does Jesus mean by this parable? The Pharisees' question about 'a sign from [or in] heaven' (8:11) revealed a hankering after spectacular and freakish proof that the kingdom of God was in fact about to appear. The followers of Jesus, however, had to forget about that kind of sign-seeking. Otherwise, like yeast, it would affect and finally dominate their thinking. Here is a warning for people today who become preoccupied with signs and wonders, or whose fascination with fanciful interpretations of Revelation leads them to see political events as sure signs of Armageddon.

The meaning of *the yeast ... of Herod* is more problematic. Jesus knew that Herod sought his life (Luke 13:31), just as he had earlier succeeded in killing John the Baptist (Mark 6:14-29). He said that Herod was like a fox (Luke 13:32) — a coward, yet cunning and dangerous. Jesus is possibly referring to Herod as a schemer and activist who sought to extend his influence by military power and political manipulation. He may be cautioning the Twelve against any notion that the kingdom of God would appear by the methods associated with the tetrarch of Galilee.

But the point of the parable is lost on the Twelve. They say to one another, *'It is because we have no bread,'* doubtless puzzled by Jesus' references to yeast.

It is difficult to think that in reply Jesus does not speak with some heat. *'Why are you talking about having no bread?'* he asks, exasperated by their vacuity. And this question is followed by others in rapid succession, beginning with words which call to mind the prophets' rebukes to Israel (cf Jeremiah 5:21; Ezekiel 12:2): *'Do you still not see or understand? ... Do you have eyes but fail to see, and ears but fail to hear?'*

The Twelve, who are the new Israel in embryo, are as blind and deaf to Jesus as old Israel was to Yahweh. According to Isaiah, the Messianic age would be marked by the deaf hearing and the blind seeing (Isaiah 35:5). Jesus has unstopped the ears of a deaf man (7:31-35) and he is about to give sight to a blind man (8:22-26). The Messianic age has indeed come but the Twelve, unlike the Gentiles (cf 7:26-30,37), still neither hear nor see. Their unbelief is at its height.

Jesus appeals specifically to the disciples' memory of the two great feeding miracles. *'Don't you remember?'* he asks. *'When I broke the five loaves for the five thousand, how many basketsful [Greek* kophinous] *of pieces did you pick up?'* They reply, *'Twelve.'* He asks further, *'And ... the seven loaves for the four thousand, how many basketsful [Greek* spuridon] *did you pick up?'* They answer, *'Seven.'*

There was clearly no problem with the disciples' memory for numbers! Their problem was comprehending the one who miraculously provided the bread, and with such spectacular oversupply. They have eyes but have not seen, ears but have not heard. Did they not understand that he who had stilled the storm, walked on the sea and fed those multitudes is the Lord who would not allow them to go hungry now? *'Do you still not understand?'* Jesus asks.

We, the readers, sense the quickening pace of the story. A climax has been reached. But we are also challenged. From the first sentence of Mark's book, we have been told who this man is (see 1:1). We have watched the Twelve groping hopelessly to identify Jesus, and all the while Mark has made his identity known to us. But do we know who he is? Or have we 'eyes but fail to see, and ears but fail to hear'? Jesus is asking us the question he asks the Twelve: *'Do you still not understand?'*

(6) The healing of the blind man at Bethsaida (8:22-26)

After the brief stop on the Galilean side of the lake, Jesus and the Twelve return by boat to the safety of the eastern side at *Bethsaida,* away from the grasp of the Pharisees and Herod Antipas.

The city of Bethsaida lay just inside the territory of Philip the Tetrarch. It was re-founded by Philip about 3 BC and, although renamed by him 'Julias' in honour of Julia the daughter of Augustus, it is referred to by Mark under its older name. Bethsaida was a twin city to the smaller Capernaum, which lay just inside Antipas' region. Both cities were located on the northern shores of the Sea of Galilee, to the east and west, respectively, of the Jordan River as it entered the lake.

The village to which Jesus came was not Bethsaida proper, but one of fourteen smaller settlements nearby which depended on the city (see Josephus, *Jewish Antiquities,* xx.159). Mark's accuracy on this point should be noted: he does not refer to Bethsaida as a city (Greek *polis*) but to one of its satellite villages (Greek *kome*).

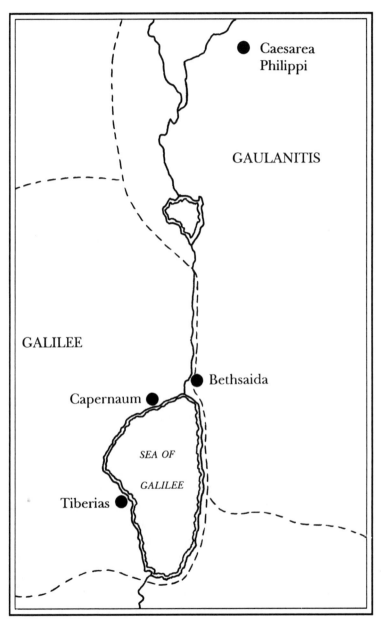

Map 8 *Bethsaida and Capernaum*

Since the feeding of the five thousand occurred just a few kilometres to the south of Bethsaida, it is no surprise that *some people* recognised Jesus and *brought a blind man* to him so that he might *touch him.* Doubtless they wanted Jesus to heal him.

As we have often noticed, Jesus does not take the initiative to heal, but responds to requests from friends and relatives of the sick or disabled. Consistent with this, Jesus *took the blind man by the hand and led him outside the village* away from everyone else. Then, when the healing was completed, he directed him not to go back *into the village* but to go straight *home.*

What were Jesus' reasons for this privacy? First, it seems that he wanted to avoid being venerated as a healer, especially in a society where disease and disability were endemic. But it may also be that Jesus desired a personal relationship with the man. It should be noted that he used his *hands* in ministering to him. He took the blind man *by the hand* and he twice applied his hands to the eyes of the blind man. Many other men's hands are instruments of crime and violence (eg 9:31,43; 14:41,46-47), but Jesus' hands were sensitive instruments of healing. Jesus' hands outwardly express and communicate to others his inner compassion for them (see 1:31,41; 3:5; 5:23,41; 6:5; 7:33; 9:27; 10:16).

But why did Jesus *spit on the man's eyes?* We are not told why, but it may be significant that the only other recorded occasions of Jesus' use of spittle are the healing of a blind man (John 9:6) and the healing of a deaf-mute (Mark 7:33), that is, where organs of perception are impaired but where the sense of feeling remained. Perhaps Jesus' spittle on eyes that could not see and on a tongue that could not speak served to identify the organs in need of healing in a dramatic way; the person healed would have been in no doubt that it was Jesus who had healed him.

It must not be thought, however, that healing by the use of hands or spittle was in some way magical. Jesus healed from a distance on a number of occasions, with no physical contact (eg 7:29-30). He healed by his powerful word. Jesus' hands and spittle merely served to demonstrate his compassionate identification with the sick or disabled.

This miracle is unusual in that it occurs in two stages. For reasons Mark does not give, it was necessary for Jesus to lay his hands twice upon the man's eyes. At first, when the man *looked up*, he said that he saw: *'I see people ... like trees walking around'*. Perhaps his vision was partially restored but blurred. Still, we sense the man's great excitement, and his vivid words give a sense of authenticity to the story. His reference to people and trees suggests that he had not been blind from birth but was beginning to see things of which he still had mental images. But when *Jesus put his hands on the man's eyes* a second time, *his eyes were opened, his sight was restored, and he saw everything clearly.*

This miracle of healing the blind man matches the earlier miracle of giving hearing and speech to a deaf-mute (7:32-37). Both miracles are described in similar ways, and they relate to sight and hearing on a spiritual as well as a physical level. Both occur in Gentile lands, symbolising the appreciation of non-Jews to Jesus in contrast with the spiritually mute and blind disciples, who represent the unyielding response to Jesus of the Jewish people as a whole. Both perform a particularly important role in the overall structure of the gospel. In writing his story, Mark chooses and locates the healing of the deaf and the blind with great care.

Mark writes his narrative with Isaiah's great Messianic prophecy in mind: 'Then will the *eyes* of the blind be opened and the *ears* of the deaf unstopped' (Isaiah 35:5). In narrating these two miracles of sight and hearing, Mark demonstrates that Jesus is the Messiah and that the

Messianic age has come. But up till this point, the Twelve are portrayed by Mark as not yet comprehending this great reality.

But at Caesarea Philippi — the next episode after this healing of the blind man near Bethsaida — Peter, speaking for the Twelve, will at last recognise Jesus to be the Christ and confess him to be so. These 'blind' and 'mute' men will finally see and give utterance to the truth about Jesus which they have not understood before.

QUESTIONS ON MARK 7:24-8:26

1. Why does Jesus commend the Greek woman (7:26-29)?
    How does this incident relate to his words to his
    Jewish disciples (7:18)?
2. What is this significance of a deaf-mute and a blind
    man being healed in Gentile territories (7:31-35; 8:22-26),
    while the Twelve are spiritually tongue-tied and blind
    (8:17-18)?
3. What manner of signs were the Pharisees seeking
    (8:11)? Were the disciples any different (8:17-21)?
4. What was the 'yeast' of the Pharisees and Herod (8:15)?
    What 'yeasts' are dangerous to us?
5. How should the feedings of the five thousand and
    the four thousand have given the disciples a better
    understanding (8:16-21)? In what way is Mark also
    directing Jesus' questions to readers today?

16

The Christ
8:27-9:1

We come now to the first of two great moments of recognition in the Gospel of Mark. The first, by the Twelve — that Jesus is the Christ — occurs approximately in the middle of the story; the second, by the Roman centurion — that Jesus is the Son of God — occurs near the end (15:39).

Although Jesus began by announcing that the hour of *God's kingdom* had struck (1:15), all the subsequent focus has been on *himself*. Mark has allowed us to watch the Twelve struggling with this baffling development. They appear to be obtuse, spiritually blind, deaf and dumb. Mark does not want to suggest that the Twelve are heroic, super-spiritual figures, but ordinary mortals with whom we can all readily identify. He challenges the readers to see that everybody — the Twelve included — needs God's help to grasp Jesus' identity.

Jesus has called the Twelve, trained them and sent them on a mission to Galilee. They have left everything to follow him, believing him to be a prophet or herald of the kingdom of God. They saw themselves as being caught up (as 'fishers of men') in God's final intervention in history. But while the Twelve believed that Jesus was the prophet of God's soon-to-arrive kingdom, could they also believe he was the bringer of that kingdom, its instrument or agent? Would they ever understand that he himself was the long-awaited one, the Messiah in God's Messianic kingdom?

The Twelve are now prepared to take a great step forward, to make that confession. At last they recognise Jesus to be King in God's kingdom, and not merely its prophet or herald. Nonetheless, great though this step is, it is nothing compared to the quantum leap which still lies ahead of them, and which they do not take even as the Gospel draws to its close.

(1) Messiah (8:27-9:1)

Jesus and the Twelve continue their journey 40 kilometres from Bethsaida up to the northern extremity of Philip's tetrarchy. Passing alongside the upper reaches of the Jordan River, they travelled towards *Caesarea Philippi*, which was built beneath snow-capped Mount Hermon which towered almost 3000 metres above sea level.

Fifty years after Jesus visited this region the historian Josephus wrote:

> At this spot a mountain rears its summit to an immense height aloft; at the base of the cliff is an opening into an overgrown cavern; within this plunging down to an immeasurable depth, is a yawning chasm, enclosing a volume of still water, the bottom of which no sounding line has been found long enough to reach. Outside and from beneath the cavern well up the springs from which, as some think, the Jordan takes its rise. *(Jewish War,* i.405-406)

The grotto mentioned by Josephus was named *Paneas* (or Baneas) after the Greek god Pan, who was said to love mountains, caves and lonely places. The region had been Hellenised 300 years earlier, after the conquests of

Alexander the Great. It was a Gentile region with few Jewish settlers. Herod had built a temple here of white marble for his patron, the Emperor Augustus. And in 3 BC, Herod's son, Philip, had built a great city as his residence and capital on the site of Paneas, naming it *Caesarea* in honour of Caesar Augustus. It was known, however, as Caesarea *Philippi,* after its founder, to distinguish it from Caesarea, Herod's port on the coast of Palestine. Bethsaida, from which Jesus had come, and Caesarea Philippi which Jesus now approached, were the major cities in Philip's tetrarchy. As with Bethsaida, Mark's accuracy can be seen in his reference to the *villages around* Caesarea Philippi. Like Bethsaida, this major city had a cluster of dependent villages adjacent to it.

Mark does not relate why Jesus came to this remote region, though it is probable that he had passed by some weeks earlier when travelling between the territories of Sidon and the Decapolis (see 7:31). Was his real destination the high mountain on which the transfiguration would occur (9:2)? Though not mentioned by name, there can be no doubt that the towering Mount Hermon is in mind there.

On the way — an important and evocative phrase that Mark will use often from now (cf 9:33,34; 10:17,32,46,52) — Jesus asks the disciples a question that will lead to the greatest climax in Mark's story to date: *'Who do people say I am?'*

Of course Jesus' real interest is to know who *the Twelve* think he is. Do they think he is who the people in general think he is? At first they reply, *'Some say John the Baptist; others say Elijah; and still others, one of the prophets.'* For some time, the people at large, and in all probability the Twelve also, have concluded that Jesus was a prophet come to announce God's great intervention (cf 6:15).

But what do the Twelve themselves think, having seen and heard so much from this man for so many months? Peter's reply on their behalf shows that at last the light of recognition has dawned on them. Here is the first soaring

climax of the gospel story: *'You are the Christ,'* Peter answers.
'You are not merely a prophetic signpost pointing to the
imminent coming of God's kingdom; you yourself are its
King! The future is fulfilled in you, focused in you; you bring
God's future into the present. In you, God's *then* has become
his *now*. Prophet and Christ are not two persons, but one.'
('Christ' is Mark's Greek for the Aramaic word Peter would
have used, namely *Messias;* see John 1:41.)

Moreover, it is symbolic of things to come that the
Messiah of Israel is recognised in a Romanised city, *Caesarea*
Philippi, with its great temple to Emperor Augustus. Here
is the anticipation that the Gentiles' belief that the Roman
Caesar is master of all will be supplanted by the belief that
Jesus the Messiah of the Jews is in reality master of all. It is
no coincidence that both great confessions of Jesus in Mark
— that he is the Christ and that he is the Son of God (15:39)
— occur in what can be called a Roman context. The former
comes from the lips of a Jew near the Roman city of *Caesarea*
Philippi; the latter comes from a Gentile, a Roman *centurion*
outside the walls of Jerusalem. In general, Jews in Galilee
and Judea will not grant Jesus this recognition. It will be
given to him primarily by Gentiles on Gentile soil.

How did Jesus react to this momentous confession? It is
certain that he regarded himself as the Lord's anointed, his
Christ or Messiah. His manner of ascent to Jerusalem on
horseback will deliberately fulfil Messianic oracles from the
Old Testament (see comment on 11:1-11). There can be no
doubt that Jesus knew he was the Messiah of God.
Nonetheless, he warned the Twelve *not to tell anyone about
him* because of the nationalistic expectations associated with
that title.

About a hundred years earlier an anonymous writer
stated what the Jews were expecting from their Messiah:

Behold, O Lord, and raise up for them their king, the son
of David ...
And gird him with strength, that he might shatter
unrighteous rulers,
And that he may purge Jerusalem from nations that
trample her down to destruction ...
He shall have the heathen nations to serve him under his
yoke. (*Psalms of Solomon*, 17)

According to this, the Jews were looking for a Messiah
who would shatter 'unrighteous rulers', 'purge Jerusalem
from [the] nations' and bring the nations under 'his yoke'.
The mere mention of the word 'Messiah' among Jews at that
time would have ignited a nationalistic bushfire.

So, although the Twelve have taken a giant stride in
recognising Jesus as Messiah, they must unlearn every
nationalistic hope they have cherished about the coming
one. And Jesus must yet show them that the new Israel, of
which they were the embryo, will also be quite different
from their expectations.

(2) Messiah will be killed (8:31-34)

Now that the great point of recognition has been reached,
the Twelve must abandon their beliefs about a warrior
Messiah and accept what Jesus teaches them. Thus, *he ...
began to teach them that the Son of Man must suffer many things.*
Once more he speaks of himself as the *Son of Man* (see
comment on 2:10,28). That the Son of Man *must* suffer
(Greek *dei*: 'it is bound') means that God had ordained his
suffering in Scripture, something that is discerned in
particular in two passages from the Old Testament: Daniel
7:15-28 and Isaiah 52:13-53:12.

Daniel 7:15-28 speaks of suffering, but there it is not the
Son of Man who suffers, but his persecuted people, 'the

saints of the Most High' (Daniel 7:21-22,25). The twelve disciples of Jesus are the seed of the saints of the Most High. So close is their relationship with Jesus, that he can depict their suffering as his and his exaltation as theirs. It is the suffering of persecution which he first, and they subsequently, will endure from the beast-like, ungodly human empires (cf Revelation 13). For Jesus, it will mean death at the hands of the rulers — Roman and Jewish — who stand to lose once his Messiahship is recognised. For his people, it will mean the leaving of family and possessions for Jesus and the gospel (10:29; cf 9:41) and punishment because of their witness (13:9-10).

Isaiah 52:13-53:12 also speaks of suffering — a suffering servant. He is not, however, a servant who suffers *with* his people but *for* his people. In this Scripture, Jesus sees himself as the righteous sufferer who offers himself to God on behalf of an unworthy people, in the first instance, the Twelve, but including 'many' others, even the Gentiles (cf Isaiah 52:15).

Both passages are important. Isaiah 53 teaches that Jesus bears the sins of an ungodly people; Daniel 7 teaches that a close union exists between Jesus and his people as together they suffer at the hands of the persecutors. Thus, Jesus completely reverses the nationalistic triumphalism of the Jews of his time. There will be triumph and vindication; however, it is not won through the exercise of power over the enemy, but through the patient suffering of the Son of Man with his people and the Servant of the Lord for his people.

Jesus amplifies the meaning of his suffering by predicting that he will be *rejected [Greek* apodokimazein = *to discard after testing, declare unworthy; cf 12:10] by the elders* [= the wealthy aristocrats], *chief priests* [= the high priest and top echelon of temple ministers] *and teachers of the law* [= leading Pharisaic scholars]. The meeting place of these persons was the Sanhedrin. Jesus is foreshadowing that he will be *killed* in Jerusalem through the rejection of this ruling body of the Jewish people. They are the wicked tenants who kill the heir to the vineyard in the parable Jesus will give in the temple when he arrives in Jerusalem (12:1-12).

Although Jesus also says *'and after three days [the Son of Man] will rise again'*, it is clear that the Twelve are unaware of his meaning (see 9:10). Their horizons were filled with hope when they recognised him to be Messiah. But his words about suffering, rejection and death, his identification as the Son of Man and his resurrection after three days are somehow not heard.

Nonetheless, Jesus *spoke plainly about this* (his suffering, rejection, death and resurrection); more literally, 'he spoke the word plainly'. Earlier, in Galilee, Jesus spoke the word of the kingdom of God in *parables* (4:2,34). Now, at Caesarea Philippi, he speaks the word *plainly* or openly. The word of the kingdom of God is now revealed as the word of the death and resurrection of the Messiah. Here is the central truth of the Gospel of Mark, indeed the message of the New Testament itself (cf 1 Corinthians 15:3-5).

It is a message, however, that Peter finds deeply offensive. As a Jew, he was looking for a Messiah bloodstained in victory, not defeat. Some time after Jesus, a Messianic prophecy appeared. Paraphrasing Genesis 49:10, it gives us a good idea of what Jews like Peter hoped for in their Messiah:

> How beautiful is the king, the Messiah, who will arise from those who are of the house of Judah! He girds up his loins and goes forth and orders the battle array against his enemies and slays the kings along with their overlords, and no king or overlord can stand before him; he reddens the mountains with the blood of their slain,

his clothing is dipped in blood like a winepress. (*Palestinian Targum,* Genesis 49:10)

Jesus, the Messiah, would be bloodstained, but in his own blood, not that of the enemies of Israel. Far from being victorious, this Messiah would stand defeated. Scandalised, *Peter took [Jesus] aside and began to rebuke him* for this teaching. In his mind a crucified Messiah spelt the death of hope for the people of God. Peter is but the first of many Jews who will take offence at the idea of a *crucified* Messiah; according to Paul, the preaching of 'Christ crucified' was a 'stumbling block to Jews' (1 Corinthians 1:23).

But Peter has it wrong. Mark captures the scene brilliantly: *Jesus turned and looked at the disciples.* As spokesman for the Twelve, Peter above all must understand. They must jettison their views of the Messiah and accept what Jesus says. For the disciples' sake, *he rebuked Peter.*

Peter's nationalistic view of the Messiah — that glory and vindication would come through power not through suffering — expresses the mind of *men,* not of *God.* It is nothing less than Satan's own view. Here once more, in the persona of Peter, Satan is tempting Jesus (cf 1:13,35; 6:45; 14:36), this time to accept the role of a triumphant king of the Jews. But Jesus says, *'Get behind me, Satan!'* , rejecting the temptation to bypass the cross.

(3) Messiah's followers will be crucified (8:34-37)

Jesus' words about the Messiah were unexpected. But now he speaks about the Messiah's *people* in terms equally unexpected. Earlier he had issued a radical call to the disciples to leave all and follow him, to become 'fishers of men' for the kingdom of God, the appearance of which, he said, was immediate (1:14-20). Now he tells them in stark terms what following him will mean.

When Jesus spoke about the kingdom of God, it transpired that he spoke chiefly about himself, not about God. Astounded by his miracles, the Twelve asked, 'Who is this?' (4:41) Finally, it dawned on them that he was God's Messiah (8:29). Naturally they would think that, as the chief lieutenants of the Messiah, they would wield enormous influence and power (10:35-37). As they follow him and turn to march to Jerusalem, they probably think that the power of God will immediately envelop Jesus on arrival in the City of David and that the kingdom of God will then appear (cf Luke 19:11).

But, as Jesus now tells the Twelve, 'If anyone would come after me, he must deny himself and take up his cross and follow me.' Following Jesus the Messiah will not mean power, but crucifixion. Jesus reveals that the kingdom of God consists of a crucified King *and* a crucified people. To be a follower of Jesus means openly identifying with him as the rejected leader, sharing his rejection and, if necessary, his death. To follow Jesus the Messiah means not being ashamed of him or of his words (8:38). Secret discipleship is a contradiction in terms. To affirm him means to deny your very self, to be willing to die.

As we read on, we will find that the disciples fail, Peter in particular. They deny Jesus and desert him. It is, however, no light thing to deny Jesus as Messiah, as he declares in this powerful paradox: '*Whoever wants to save his life* [from martyrdom] *will lose it* [in the kingdom of God], *but whoever loses his life for me and for the gospel* [in martyrdom] *will save it* [for the kingdom of God].'

Note the close connection between Jesus and the gospel (cf 10:29). Before the first Easter, disciples were literally followers of Jesus. In the post-Easter dispensation, however, we express our loyalty to Jesus as loyalty to the *gospel*, which we are to proclaim in the whole world, to every nation (13:10; 14:9). This is discipleship — following Jesus — for us.

170

As the first disciples, pre-Easter, were willing to lose their lives for Jesus, we, post-Easter, should be willing to lose our lives for the gospel.

Jesus reinforces this teaching with a parable about the value of one human life. As the saying goes, 'life is cheap' — but not with God. From his viewpoint, just one human life outweighs the accumulated wealth of the whole world. *'What good is it,'* asks Jesus, *'for a man to gain the whole world, yet forfeit his soul?'* (When I think about it, I agree with Jesus that my soul [= life] is of immense value. His estimate of my personal worth and my own are in agreement!) Any follower of Jesus must carefully weigh up the consequences of 'saving' his or her life, that is of denying his or her allegiance to Jesus and the gospel. For to do this would mean losing one's life — something of immeasurable value — in the kingdom of God.

(4) Messiah's followers will be glorified (8:38-9:1)

While Jesus has not denied that he is the Christ, it is interesting that he prefers to call himself *Son of Man* (cf 14:61-62; John 1:49-51). From one point of view the term 'Son of Man' was unexceptional, being a common way of referring to a person's self; some scholars claim that all Jesus meant to say was 'I'. Yet the contexts of the only two earlier occasions of its use in Mark — when Jesus pronounced the forgiveness of sins (2:10) and claimed he was Lord of the Sabbath (2:28) — surely invest 'Son of Man' with supernatural status. It is better, therefore, to regard 'Son of Man' as Jesus' careful choice of a term which conveyed the mystery of his person without focusing on himself as a political Messiah.

From now on, however, Jesus uses the term in a more striking way, namely with reference to the human figure in Daniel 7:1-14. In Daniel's vision, evil, beast-like empires each

171

fall in sequence after short-lived glory, giving way finally to a kingdom that will be universal and everlasting. This is God's kingdom, which God ('the Ancient of Days') gives to a man to rule ('one like a son of man'), as opposed to a beast. Jesus here claims that *he* is that Son of Man, the one to whom God gives his kingdom which will be exercised over all people for all time.

According to Jesus there will be two great 'moments' for the Son of Man, which he speaks about in reverse chronological order. First, he speaks about the coming of the Son of Man as judge: *'If anyone is ashamed of me and my words ... the Son of Man will be ashamed of him when he comes in his Father's glory with the holy angels.'* During his last week in Jeruasalem, Jesus will say more about this final coming of the Son of Man (13:26-27; 14:62). He also speaks about the immediate future, introducing his words with the solemn *'I tell you the truth'* (literally 'Amen, I say to you'; see comment on 3:28). Jesus, the trustworthy witness to God, declares, *'Some who are standing here will not taste death before they see the kingdom of God come with power.'*

Although these two moments are separated from our viewpoint, from God's perspective they are connected. The kingdom of God 'come with power' begins with the crucifixion and resurrection of the Son of Man and ends with his triumphant return as judge. These two moments, considered as one, also fulfil the vision of Daniel 7 in which the Son of Man received from the Ancient of Days

> authority, glory and sovereign *power;* all peoples, nations and men of every language worshipped him. [The Son of Man's] dominion is ... everlasting ... his *kingdom* is one that will never be destroyed. (Daniel 7:13-14)

When will these moments happen? One will occur within the lifetime of those who are standing here listening to Jesus near Caesarea Philippi, in fact, at Jerusalem within the year. Paradoxically, 'the kingdom of God come with *power*' will be fulfilled when God's King is, so it will seem, *powerless*. Of all people, those responsible for his crucifixion express the truth of God: *He saved others, but he can't save himself [literally 'he is not* powerful *to save himself']! Let this Christ, this* King *[Greek* basileus] *of Israel, come down now from the cross, that we may see and believe* (15:31-32).

Mark's repetition of the keywords *king* and *power* here in the mouths of the chief priests and teachers of the law explains the meaning of Jesus' words at Caesarea Philippi. Astonishingly, the kingdom of God will begin to come with power when the king is crucified in powerlessness. Despite the appearance of powerlessness, however, the power of God will be at work in him saving others by the destruction of the demonic world (1:24; cf 3:11,27; 5:7). In the words of Paul, the message of 'Christ crucified', though regarded as a 'stumbling block to Jews and foolishness to Gentiles', is the 'power of God' (1 Corinthians 1:23-25).

At every level Jesus' teaching must have taken the disciples entirely by surprise. They expected a triumphalist Messianic kingdom, but Jesus taught that the kingdom of God would be characterised by suffering — his and theirs. According to them, triumph would be political and, to that extent, timebound; according to him, the triumph would be heavenly, unlimited and everlasting, above and beyond anything they imagined.

At Caesarea Philippi Jesus dramatically re-defined the Messiah and God's Messianic kingdom in three ways. First, contrary to current Jewish hopes, the kingdom of God is not nationalistic and triumphalist, but is characterised by suffering, the suffering of the Messiah for and with his people.

Second, in parallel with the suffering that is imminent, there is an unimaginable kingdom that Jesus, the heavenly

173

Son of Man, will assume. His kingdom will continue throughout the time of suffering, after which he will reappear. Then the Son of Man will express either shame or pride in his people in the presence of God, depending on their fidelity to him during the period of suffering.

Third, the Son of Man is not merely a human agent or attorney of God: God is *his Father* (verse 38). From this point in the gospel, Jesus draws attention to the unique filial relationship he enjoys with God. In Jerusalem, he will call God 'the Father' (13:32) and 'Abba, Father' (14:36), and he will speak of himself as 'a son, whom [God] loved', (12:6) and 'the Son' (13:32). Jesus is not alone in regarding himself as the Son of God. At the mount of transfiguration he is declared to be 'my Son, whom I love' by the voice of God (9:7), and at Golgotha 'the Son of God' by a Roman centurion (15:39).

Caesarea Philippi is the hinge around which Mark's gospel turns. Up to this point Mark has let us see Jesus proclaiming the kingdom of God while at the same time focusing on his own identity. During the first half of the gospel we have seen the disciples asking, 'Who is this?' From Caesarea Philippi onwards, however, when Peter at last recognises Jesus as the Christ, Mark focuses on Jesus as the suffering Messiah and Son of God, who is followed by his Messianic people, who in like manner will also suffer, but march through their suffering to glory.

QUESTIONS ON MARK 8:27-9:1

1. What symbolism is implied by *Caesarea* Philippi (8:27) as the venue for Peter's confession?
2. How does Peter's confession (8:29) mark a turning point in the disciples' faith (cf 8:17-21)? What is the significance of the location of the miracle (8:22-26) between these two episodes?
3. Why *must* the Son of man suffer (8:31)?
4. Why was the idea of a suffering Christ a problem to Peter (8:32)?
5. What is the significance in Jesus bracketing loyalty to him with loyalty to the gospel (8:35; 10:29) and to his words (8:38) from this point on? Discuss how 'disciple' becomes 'discipleship' post-Easter?
6. When does the kingdom of God 'come with power' (9:1)?
7. What is the path to glory for the Messiah? for his followers?

17

The mountain and the valley 9:2-29

If there will be suffering with Jesus, there will also be triumph, though it will be different from that expected by many Jews of his time, including the Twelve. Jesus now permits his followers to see the glory which will soon be his, after his sufferings are complete. People's typical expectations of political Messiahs — whether ancient or modern, Gentile or Jewish — is that glory will arise from power and success. Jesus, however, uniquely teaches and demonstrates by what happens to him that, with God, glory arises out of faithful and non-violent endurance in the face of evil.

(1) Transfiguration (9:2-8)

Jesus has spoken to his disciples about the glory of the Son of Man (8:38); now, pulling back the veil of suffering which will characterise his death and be the mark of his people's life in the world in his absence, he shows them what that glory will be like. The Twelve are given a preview of the triumphant, post-Easter Jesus, crowned with glory.

Why should *Elijah and Moses* be present with Jesus? Just as Jesus would be taken up to heaven with his humanity intact, so Elijah had been taken directly to heaven (2 Kings

176

2:11-12) and, in the belief of many, Moses also (cf Deuteronomy 34:5-7). Moses and Elijah were great prophetic leaders from Israel's past, with whom it would have been easy for people at that time to associate Jesus. Was not Jesus a prophet of the soon-to-appear kingdom of God?

But it was important for the Twelve to understand both the difference in kind and also the infinite superiority of Jesus to these two great prophets; they could hardly be compared with Jesus or even spoken of in the same breath. Jesus was *transfigured,* or glorified, before the disciples and *his clothes became dazzling white*; no details are given about the appearance of Moses and Elijah. The voice of the Father declared of Jesus, *'This is my Son, whom I love. Listen to him!'* (The voice had also spoken to Jesus at his baptism, assuring him that he was the beloved Son — 1:11.) The voice addressed the Twelve and demanded that they listen to Jesus and in particular, to what he had said about the suffering of the Messiah and his people (8:31-9:1). But the voice was silent about Moses and Elijah.

In the second half of the gospel it is important that the Twelve — and the readers — understand who Jesus is. From now on, Mark reminds us that Jesus is not merely the Messiah of Israel, but the Son of Man who is the Son of God (12:6-7; 13:32; 15:39). This becomes the central belief in the creeds of Christianity.

Some scholars have asked, is this narrative factual? The alternatives are that the story arose from a legend, that Mark composed it himself or that it is historically true. In favour of its historicity we should note the many specific details in the narrative: the time — *after six days*; the people — *Peter, James and John,* who are typically present with Jesus at critical moments (see 5:37; 14:33); and the place — *a high mountain,* almost certainly snow-capped Mount Hermon, adjacent to Caesarea Philippi. In addition, we should note the homely

177

analogy of *bleach* brightness for Jesus' clothes, Peter's customary address to Jesus as *'Rabbi'* and also his typically vacuous comment, *'It is good for us to be here'* (cf 8:33). Peter, for his part, later remembers the transfiguration more profoundly: 'We were eyewitnesses of his majesty [when] he received honour and glory from God the Father ... We heard this voice that came from heaven when we were with him on the sacred mountain' (2 Peter 1:16-18). For these reasons we should regard the narrative as historical.

(2) Elijah has come (9:9-13)

During their descent from the mountain, Jesus makes it clear to the three disciples that they must say nothing of what they have seen *until the Son of Man had risen from the dead.* They were not to refer to Jesus as a glorified person until he had entered into that glory by his resurrection from the dead. He must first obediently run the course laid down by his Father, a course which would involve suffering, rejection and death. Messiah he truly was, but his kingdom would be marked by resolute fidelity to the will of God.

Here we note once more the opposing views of Jesus and the Twelve. The disciples did not understand *what 'rising from the dead' meant.* Having rejected Jesus' prediction of the suffering and death of the Messiah (8:32), they are baffled by this mention of resurrection. Couldn't he go straight to glory, as Elijah had, without undergoing death and resurrection? But Jesus knew that glory would arise out of his obedience, death and resurrection.

Speaking of Elijah, the disciples want to know where he is. Based on Malachi 4:5, *the teachers of the law* taught *that Elijah must come first* to prepare the people for the great and dreadful day of the Lord. If the glory of Jesus was to appear any minute, as his transfiguration suggested, why hadn't Elijah appeared to prepare the people for it?

Jesus' reply is double-barrelled. First, he reaffirms to the disciples that *the Son of Man must suffer*. There must be no misunderstanding: it is so *written* in the Scriptures. Second, Elijah's coming would not be in the future, but was in the past. *'Elijah has come* already,' he says, 'as John the Baptist, and Herod and Herodias *have done to him everything they wished.'* Despite great pressure from the tetrarch and his wife, John's faithfulness to God and faithful proclamation of his kingdom had restored *all things*. This 'Elijah' had prepared a repentant people for the coming of Jesus the Messiah (1:2-8), and the Twelve were among their ranks.

Not only was suffering the portion of the Messiah, it was the portion also of his forerunner, and it would also be the way of the disciples. They needed to know that, from beginning to end, even from the appearance of 'Elijah' the restorer, the Messianic age would be marked by suffering. This proves to be a difficult lesson for the Twelve to learn.

(3) The demon-possessed boy (9:14-29)

Jesus and the three disciples descend from the glory of the high mountain to the darkness of demon possession in the valley beneath. The contrast could not be more striking. The world, darkened by evil and pain, does not automatically or easily become bright with the glory of God. The initiative lies with God alone, and the darkness of evil must be faced full on, experienced in all its magnitude, and defeated before the light can come. As Jesus once more faces cosmic evil here, we cannot doubt that he sustained a measure of suffering himself. But even this is nothing compared to the darkness that awaits him in Jerusalem. If ever more reason was needed why the Messiah and his people must undergo suffering before the glory of God comes, this episode beneath the mountain provides it.

This is a remarkable drama played in four vivid scenes with no less than seven groups of players — Jesus, the nine disciples, the teachers of the law, the father, his son, the crowd and the unclean spirit. It is one of the most astonishing stories in Mark's narrative.

In the first scene, Jesus arrives back from the mountain with Peter, James and John, to the amazement and *wonder* of a *large crowd* which had gathered. Was there something about the appearance of the recently transfigured Jesus that aroused this reaction, as there had been with Moses when he returned from the mountain of God centuries earlier (Exodus 34:29-35)? The crowd was gathered around *the other disciples* and *the teachers of the law* who were *arguing with them.*

Were these teachers of the law from Galilee or from Jerusalem (cf 3:22; 7:1)? Possibly they were scholars located in Galilee to give instruction to the Pharisaic brotherhoods in the region, who kept in close contact with their leaders in Jerusalem concerning the troublesome prophet from Nazareth whom they followed to Caesarea Philippi.

The matter in dispute — the casting out of demons — is not new (cf 3:22). What is new, though, is that the teachers are arguing with the disciples and not with Jesus. Therefore, Jesus asks, *'What are you* [the disciples or the teachers?] *arguing with them* [the teachers or the disciples?] *about?'* Neither party replies.

Instead, *a man in the crowd* speaks up. This is the second scene. Addressing Jesus reverently as *'Teacher'* (= rabbi), he explains that he had *brought [his] son* to Jesus for help. In Jesus' absence he had asked the disciples to drive out the spirit possessing the boy, *but they could not.* (For other examples of relatives who sought help from Jesus, see 1:30; 5:22-23; 7:25-26.)

The father then tells Jesus that the spirit has not only *robbed [his son] of speech* (and also hearing — 9:25), it also *seizes* the boy and *throws him to the ground* so that *he foams at the mouth, gnashes his teeth and becomes rigid.* Here is dark, destructive evil confronting Jesus and the three disciples after the bright glory of the mountain.

Who are the people Jesus now addresses as *'O unbelieving generation'?* Clearly Jesus includes the father (9:24) and the teachers of the law, but equally clearly he is addressing the nine disciples. They above all are unbelieving, and have been throughout Mark's narrative. In words reminiscent of those he spoke to the disciples when crossing the lake (8:17-21), Jesus exclaims, *'How long shall I stay with you? How long shall I put up with you?'* Let them now see his God-given power: *'Bring the boy to me.'*

The third scene is very dramatic. Jesus and the spirit confront each other, as Jesus and the spirits have done on previous occasions (1:23-26; 3:11; 5:6-7). This is no earthly confrontation but a cosmic one. It is between Jesus and Satan, 'the strong man' with a household or community of unclean spirits which takes up destructive residence within human lives (3:27). *When the spirit saw Jesus,* Mark tells us, *it immediately threw the boy into a convulsion.* The symptoms resemble a severe epileptic fit (*he fell to the ground and rolled around, foaming at the mouth*) though the cause in this case was not organic or natural, but supernatural and demonic: the spirit was out to destroy the boy.

We should notice that Mark distinguishes illness from demon possession here and throughout his narrative (1:34; 6:13). Various illnesses — fever (1:29-31), leprosy (1:40-42), paralysis (2:1-3), a shrivelled hand (3:1), haemorrhaging (5:25), deafness (7:32) and blindness (8:22) — are described in natural and not supernatural terms. These illnesses and disabilities were not caused by unclean spirits. But this boy is different: his disability is attributed to an unclean spirit — *'You deaf and mute spirit ... come out'.*

Instead of immediately addressing the spirit, Jesus asks the father, *'How long has [the boy] been like this?'* His question reveals once again the personal interest he showed towards people in need (cf 5:40; 7:33; 8:23). Jesus healed in the context of deep concern for the individual and his or her family.

'From childhood,' answers the father, who then describes the destructive power which has been at work in his son: 'It has often thrown him into fire or water to kill him.' His desperation is revealed by his request, 'But if you can do anything, take pity on us and help us.' The man's low opinion of the disciples — 'they could not' (verse 18) — and his high hopes focused on Jesus — 'if you can do anything' — should not be missed.

Jesus immediately picks up the man's words, 'That saying of yours — "If you can"' (literally 'If you have power'), then states the critical words in this whole incident, 'Everything is possible [literally 'everything is powerful'] for him who believes.'

The disciples lacked the strength to help the boy (verse 18). Had they become blase about casting out demons due to their ministry during the mission? Had they reduced the expulsion of unclean spirits to a mere technique, something mechanical? Had they omitted the most important factor in the whole equation — God himself? Jesus is saying that *God* is not powerless even in this tragic situation. *All* things are possible for us when we believe because all things are possible for *the one in whom we believe*. Believing, namely that God is powerful and unlimited, is the means by which his power is released in our lives.

The climax of this third scene is the father's pitiful cry, 'I do believe; help me overcome my unbelief!' This man unknowingly represents many of us: he is an unbelieving believer, whose mixture of faith and doubt we easily identify in our own lives.

At this point Jesus sees *a crowd running* towards them. As on a number of earlier occasions he prefers a situation of relative privacy in which to heal or, in this case, cast out

182

demons (cf 5:40; 7:33; 8:23), so his dialogue with the father is concluded. *He rebuked the evil spirit, 'You deaf and mute spirit ... I command you, come out of him and never enter him again.'* And at this *the spirit shrieked, convulsed [the boy] violently and came out.* However, by this stage the boy *looked so much like a corpse* that the bystanders said, *'He's dead.'* So Jesus, as he had frequently done to others (1:31,41; 3:5; 5:23,41; 6:5; 7:33; 10:16), *took him by the hand and lifted him to his feet, and he stood up.*

The description resembles the healing of Jairus' daughter at this point (cf 5:39-43). The girl was dead; the boy appeared to be dead. Both children were raised up (Greek *egeirin*) by the hand of Jesus, then stood up (Greek *anastenai*) by themselves. The conjunction of the vocabulary of death and resurrection in both episodes is probably not accidental, especially since Caesarea Philippi when Jesus began to refer repeatedly to his own death and resurrection (8:31). Mark may be deliberately showing that these healings foreshadow the great coming resurrection, when the dead will be raised by the hand of Jesus.

The fourth and final scene occurs somewhere *indoors* away from the crowd: Jesus is alone with the Twelve (cf 3:31-35; 4:10; 7:17; 10:10). As on other such occasions, he must explain what they did not understand, signifying, on the one hand, their slowness of comprehension and, on the other, the special place he gave to them.

The English translation here, and indeed elsewhere in this incident, masks the critical word 'power' as it occurs in the original. The disciples ask, *'Why couldn't we drive it out?'* or, more literally, 'Why weren't we *powerful* enough to drive it out?' Jesus' reply, *'This kind can come out only by prayer,'* or, more literally, 'This kind is *empowered* to come out only by prayer,' echoes their question and picks up the key word *power.* When we remember that the idea of strength, ability or power (verses 18,22-23) has been prominent in the story so far, we can see the force of Jesus' words here.

The other key word in the incident is *belief*. The disciples are *unbelieving* (verse 19), whereas all things are possible to the one who *believes* (verse 23). The father declares that he believes and pleads for help in his *unbelief* (verse 24). How is belief to be expressed? The answer is *by prayer*, that is, by calling out to God for help.

The disciples had not prayed, had not invoked God's help, in seeking deliverance for this boy. Perhaps their efforts had been only on the level of exorcism by the use of some kind of formula (which was common among the Jews at that time). Our conclusion is that we must not omit God from our reckoning.

As we pray, as we exercise faith in God — for whom everything is possible and nothing is impossible — there is a new horizon of hope. That is not to say that he will always heal or deliver within a fixed time or space. It may not be his purpose to do so, in which case we must accept his will, as the apostle Paul did (2 Corinthians 12:8-10). However, it is always his will to heal and deliver in an ultimate sense all those who give themselves in repentance and faith to enter the kingdom of God through Jesus Christ.

QUESTIONS ON MARK 9:2-29

1. Why did Moses and Elijah appear with Jesus on the mountain (9:4)?
2. What reasons are there for thinking that the transfiguration is historically based?
3. Why was it important that the Twelve were reinforced at this time in their belief that Jesus was the Son of God?
4. Why did the disciples have trouble with the idea of Jesus' death and resurrection (8:32; 9:10)?
5. How did Jesus correct their views on Elijah (9:13)?
6. Describe the manner of Jesus' approach to the father of the boy with the evil spirit (9:21-24). What does it teach us?
7. How is the power of God to be appropriated today (9:23,29)?

18

Journey through Galilee 9:30-50

The critical time in the north is complete. The Twelve have recognised Jesus as the Messiah, a role which he has redefined as a *suffering* Messiah. Glory awaits him — and them — but only at the end of the path of suffering. The journey from Caesarea Philippi to Jerusalem (9:30-11:1) symbolises that way of suffering, which reaches its climax in the city of Jerusalem. Therefore, Jesus will often speak to the disciples 'on the way' about what it will mean for them to follow him in the period when he will no longer be with him.

It is shortly before the Feast of Tabernacles (see John 7:2) — about six months before the fateful Passover — when Jesus turns to head for Jerusalem.

(1) Into Galilee (9:30-32)

Jesus and the Twelve retrace their steps down the upper Jordan Valley and cross again into the tetrarchy of *Galilee*, moving towards Capernaum on the north-west shore of the Sea.

Possibly they made the day-long trip by night to avoid attention; *Jesus did not want anyone to know where they were* on account of the *teaching* he was giving the *disciples* about his betrayal, death and resurrection. This was not teaching for the crowds, but only for his followers.

A further reason for the secret journey was to evade the unwelcome attention of the Pharisees and the Herodians, whose bad intentions Jesus knew well (8:15; cf 3:6). The attempt of the Galileans to force the kingship on him after the feeding of the five thousand (see John 6:14-15) was a virtual death sentence; who could forget the fate of John the Baptist at the hands of Herod Antipas (6:17-29)?

Jesus' teaching to the Twelve repeats his surprising prophecy of the fate which awaited him in Jerusalem (8:31). He says again that *men ... will kill* him — *the Son of Man* — but that *after three days he will rise.* The earlier emphasis had been on his rejection — by the major factions of the Sanhedrin. Now, however, he emphasises that he will be *betrayed,* or 'handed over' (Greek *paradidonai*). Judas Iscariot, one of the Twelve, was identified as his betrayer when he was first mentioned — 'Judas Iscariot, who betrayed him' (3:19). And, after Jesus comes to Jerusalem, we will witness the chain of his 'handing over': from Judas to the chief priests (14:10-11,18,21,41-46), from the chief priests to Pilate (15:1,10), and from Pilate to the soldiers who crucify him (15:15). Rejection from the religious establishment was something for which Jesus had long prepared himself; betrayal by a friend whom he saw every day must have been exceptionally hard to bear.

Before Caesarea Philippi the disciples did not know who Jesus was. After Caesarea Philippi they continually misinterpret both his role and theirs in the kingdom of God which is soon coming. Typical of their lack of comprehension of Jesus' role as suffering Messiah, it is once again reported that *they did not understand what he meant and were afraid* (cf 8:32; 9:6; 9:10; 10:32).

(2) The greatest (9:33-37)

Now Jesus and the disciples are in *Capernaum,* which had been the centre of the Galilean ministry (chapters 1-6). Specifically they are *in the house.* This must again be Jesus' adopted home, the house of Peter (1:29; 2:1; 3:20,31; 7:17).

Two factors suggest that this is an occasion for important teaching to the Twelve. First, Jesus asks a question: *'What were you arguing about on the road?'* — his questions often preceded teaching (2:9,19,25; 8:27,29). Second, he is *sitting down* when he calls the Twelve and speaks to them: rabbis customarily sat to teach (see Matthew 5:1; cf 23:2).

On the way from Caesarea Philippi the disciples *had argued about who was the greatest* among them. Jesus' statements about 'glory' (8:38) and 'the kingdom of God come with power' (9:1), followed by his transfiguration (9:2-4), had convinced them that the age of God's Messiah was about to dawn. But what would be their place in the kingdom of God? Who would be the greatest? Their argument is revealing. Clearly they understand neither Jesus' role nor theirs in the Messianic community. The radical nature of the kingdom, as taught by Jesus, has not yet been glimpsed; existing practices and values still dominate their thinking.

The desert community of Qumran (the disciples' contemporaries) had a strict sense of place, an order of hierarchy in anticipation of the coming of the Messiah:

And then the Messiah of Israel shall come and the chiefs of the clans of Israel shall sit before him, each in order of his dignity, according to his place in their camps and marches (*The Messianic Rule,* II).

In mainstream Jewish life there was also a preoccupation with status and position. As Jesus comments in Matthew:

'The teachers of the law ... love the place of honour at banquets and the most important seats in the synagogues; they love to be greeted in the marketplaces and to have men call them "Rabbi"'. (Matthew 23:2,6-7)

It should be added that nor have Christian clergy been slow to accumulate honorific titles and ceremonial vestments which can tend to elevate them above their brothers and sisters in the Messianic community.

Jesus teaches about greatness in the kingdom of God by means of a saying, then an enacted parable followed by another saying.

Jesus' first saying reverses all expectations of greatness: *'If anyone wants to be first, he must be the very last.'* This he explains as being *'the servant of all'*. In that society (and others since then) the one who serves or waits on others was regarded in lowly terms, as inferior. But Jesus is saying that in God's new order the one who serves is the greatest, the 'first'.

The deliberate action that follows is an enacted parable. (The earlier healing of the paralytic in that very house is another example; see 2:8-12). Jesus *took a little child —* possibly belonging to one of the Twelve *— and had him stand among them;* then, as a separate deliberate action, he took him *in his arms.* By picking up the child, Jesus had symbolically received and welcomed him. Jesus, the first and the greatest, had made himself the last by serving the child. (Jesus cared deeply for children; see 5:40-43; 7:24-30; 9:19-27; 10:13-16.)

In the second saying there is a shift of meaning. The focus moves from giving service to receiving ministry. With the child in his arms, Jesus says, *'Whoever welcomes one of these little children in my name welcomes me'.* Who are these *little children* who are to be welcomed in Jesus' name? They are Jesus' disciples, as sent out by him in ministry. So close is the relationship between Jesus and the disciples that to welcome them is to welcome him. So close is the relationship between God and Jesus that he says, *'Whoever welcomes me does not welcome me but the one who sent me.'* God sent Jesus, who in turn sends these 'little children', his missionaries. To welcome them is to welcome Jesus; to welcome him is to welcome God who sent him (cf Matthew 25:31-46).

The words *the one who sent me* (Greek *apostello*; literally 'apostled me') give us a precious insight into Jesus' sense of identity. He is an *apostle* of God (cf 12:6 – 'He had.... to *send*, a son, whom he loved. He *sent* him last of all'). Jesus' sense of identity is closely connected with his sense of purpose as revealed in his 'I came to ...' sayings (eg 'to call ... sinners', 2:17; 'to give his life as a ransom', 10:45). Jesus *came* to do particular tasks on earth as God's beloved Son, because he was *sent* by God for those purposes.

Thus, the child in Jesus' arms was used as a living parable of both sayings. The child in his 'littleness' was both the symbol of a person to whom service should be given (verse 35) and a 'little one' (9:42) who comes in Jesus' name whose ministry is to be received (verse 37). Giving service to a child and going like a child in Jesus' name clearly reversed the disciples' existing notions of greatness. Much time has passed since this teaching but self-centred notions of greatness remain.

Both sayings point to the future life of the Twelve when, as a result of his death and resurrection, Jesus would no longer be with them. The first saying anticipates the *serving* nature of the Messianic community, based on the loving example of their master. The second saying foreshadows the community's *sending* character. God had *sent* his Son, who in turn *sent* the Twelve – first into Galilee, then into all the world – to gather the multiracial people of the Messiah. This theme of mission, of being 'sent', continues into the next episode.

(3) The Messiah's people (9:38-41)

The Twelve's misunderstanding about the Teacher's will is again seen here. Still in the house of Peter in Capernaum, John, speaking for the Twelve, declares, *'Teacher* [Greek didaskalos, *literally 'Rabbi'*], *we saw a man driving out demons in your name and we told him to stop, because he was not one of us'*. Perhaps the disciples were especially annoyed because of their own recent failure to cast out an evil spirit (see 9:18).

Had this man seen the disciples casting out demons during the their mission six months earlier? We should note that the casting out of demons was by no means unknown among the Jews. Josephus reports that, while campaigning in Palestine in AD 67, the Roman general Vespasian had witnessed an exorcism by a Jew named Eleazar:

[Eleazar] put to the nose of the possessed man a ring which had under its seal one of the roots prescribed by Solomon, and then as the man smelled it, drew out the demon through its nostrils, and, when the man fell down, adjured the demon never to go back into him, speaking Solomon's name and reciting the incantations which he composed. Then, wishing to convince the bystanders and to prove to them that he had this power, Eleazar placed a cup or foot basin of water a little way off and commanded the demon, as it went out of the man, to overturn it and make known to the spectators that he had left the man (*Antiquities of the Jews,* viii.46-49).

Unlike Jesus, the exorcist Eleazar appears to have regarded possession as some kind of illness, to be treated by a combination of natural and supernatural means. To Jesus, demon possession was visible evidence of the invisible cosmic and supernatural kingdom of the Evil One, which

191

he had come to assault and defeat as a sign that the age of the kingdom of God had dawned (see Luke 11:20).

Jesus himself acknowledges that other people also cast out demons (Matthew 12:27; Luke 11:19) and that even false prophets performed miracles (Matthew 7:15-22). Jesus neither commends nor condemns such miracle workers. Clearly the performing of a miracle on its own was no final seal of approval from God. What shows that Jesus had the endorsement of God was the effortless performance of numerous indisputable miracles of many kinds — healings, resurrections, nature miracles — matched by his call to repentance arising out of his impeccable life.

John the disciple requests Jesus to *stop* other men performing miracles in the name of Jesus. But Jesus does not concur. Surprising though it may be to the Twelve, the Messiah's people are more numerous than his immediate circle. Jesus then adds this proverb, *'For whoever is not against us is for us'* — if someone performs a miracle in Jesus' name, he will not say anything bad about Jesus in the next moment. These words serve as a warning against the practice of hastily 'unchurching' others, something to which believers have been prone throughout history.

Jesus now gives an example of what it means to be *not against* him. As with the previous matter (the question about 'who was the greatest', 9:34) Jesus turns this discussion also to the future, when he would no longer be present with them. It is typical of his teaching 'on the way' from Caesarea Philippi to Jerusalem that Jesus directs the disciples' thoughts to the time after Easter.

Speaking with the authority of one sent by God (cf 9:37) Jesus introduces the saying with the solemn *'I tell you the truth'* (Greek *amen;* cf 3:28; 8:12; 9:1; 10:15,29; 11:23; 12:43; 13:30; 14:18,25,30). Let the disciples listen carefully! The saying that follows — *'anyone who gives you a cup of water in my name because you belong to Christ'* — implies that the

The Servant King

disciples will be sent out by Jesus and that they will be welcomed (cf 9:37). The gift of water in a desperately dry climate was tangible welcome to the visitor standing at the door. More important, it honoured the Messiah, the *Christ,* in whose name the visitor had come.

Peter has declared Jesus to be 'the Christ' (8:29), and Bartimaeus of Jericho will call him 'Son of David' (10:47-48). In Jerusalem the high priest will demand to know if he is 'the Christ' (14:61), and the chief priests ridicule the crucified man as 'this Christ, this king of Israel' (15:32). Jesus never denied that he was the Christ. But this (verse 41) is the only occasion in the Gospel of Mark when Jesus speaks directly of himself as the *Christ* or Messiah.

The word *Christ* is used in the original in the possessive case: '*of* Christ' (Greek *Christou*). The disciples *belong to Christ*; he owns them. They bear his name and they come in his name. Fifteen years later, in the Gentile metropolis of Antioch in northern Syria, the locals would mockingly call the disciples 'messiah-men' (Greek *christianoi*); this is the origin of the word 'Christian' (see Acts 11:26). The task of being sent/going in Jesus' name (verse 41) began with the Twelve — first in their mission to Galilee (6:12-13), then in the decades after Easter; but it is to be continued in every succeeding generation by all who, like them, *belong to Christ.*

But the *reward* of God is not only for those who, like the Twelve, *go* in the name of Jesus; it is also for those who *welcome* them *in [his] name* (verse 41). Here again is the chain of sending and receiving which stretches from God, through Jesus, through the Twelve, to those who receive them. To receive them is to receive Jesus, and to receive Jesus is to receive the Father who sent him.

Jesus expands upon this in the story of the 'sheep' and the 'goats' (Matthew 25:31-46), which is set in the context of persecution. There, the suffering emissaries of the King are hungry when they arrive, but are fed by those who receive

193

them. In the same way they are thirsty but given a drink; homeless but given shelter; naked and given clothes; sick but cared for; and imprisoned but visited. The King rewards those who thus received his representatives, because he had come in their persons. Jesus is saying that to welcome those who come in his name — to care for those persecuted ones who represent the King — is to care for the one who sent them. Jesus the King (= the Christ) would suffer death through crucifixion. His messengers would suffer hunger, homelessness, poverty and prison. To receive such people, to be identified with them in a hostile environment, would involve suffering (cf Hebrews 10:33-34; 13:3) as well as reward.

(4) Warnings against sin (9:42-50)

Still set in Peter's house in Capernaum, Mark records a series of sayings of Jesus which are strung together by common themes.

Mindful of the child he has held in his arms (9:36), Jesus now warns against *anyone [causing] one of these little ones who believe in me to sin* (Greek *skandalizein* = to cause to stumble). The *sin* in the first instance is falling away from Jesus (as Peter would). The *little ones* refers to those who believed in Christ through the missionaries who had come to them, but who are now under presssure to apostasise. These new believers are precious to Jesus, as they would be to his apostle, Paul (see 1 Corinthians 8:13 and 2 Corinthians 11:29 where the verb *skandalizein* is also used). Jesus uses the incredible image of *a man thrown into the sea with a large millstone tied around his neck* to indicate the severity of the punishment which awaits those who destroy the faith of new believers. While Jesus originally directed this warning to persecutors of believers, unbelieving theologians and false pastors should also take note!

Jesus continues the twin ideas of 'causing to sin' and the dire punishment of God on account of sin. But he now warns his disciples, not other people, about the consequences of their actions. Disciples then and now are warned that a *hand*, a *foot* or an *eye* can *cause ... sin* (Greek *skandalizein*), sin which will consign a person to *hell*. Hell is a place of eternal punishment: there the *'worm does not die and the fire is not quenched'*. Hell is to be avoided at all costs — even to the point of cutting off the offending hand or foot or plucking out the offending eye. *Better* by far, as Jesus says, *to enter* eternal *life* — or *the kingdom of God* (the terms are synonymous) — *crippled than to ... be thrown into hell* with all your body parts intact. Jesus is not advocating self-mutilation; that would be to misunderstand his manner of teaching. He is pointing out the terrible and eternal nature of hell and the reality that sin will take us there.

The idea of *fire* leads on to Jesus' words: *'Everyone will be salted with fire.'* It is not clear what this brief statement means. Most likely it refers to the persecution that all believers will face (cf verse 42) to a greater or lesser degree. Persecution will create a depth of Christian character, 'saltiness', in believers (cf Matthew 5:13).

Jesus strongly encourages this saltiness among believers: 'Salt is good'. This speaks of the need for Christian distinctiveness, as opposed to an undifferentiated blandness. In our modern liberal secular societies Christians win praise aplenty for social action and good works; but those who spread the gospel or take a stand on the doctrines of the creed are labelled as 'literalists' or 'fundamentalists'. Once the distinctive saltiness is lost from believers, Jesus asks, *'How can you make it salty again?'* Finally he adds, *'Be at peace with each other,'* reflecting perhaps on the quarrel between the disciples over greatness, which began this Capernaum episode (9:34).

This string of teachings relates to the post-Easter life of the followers of Jesus and is typical of his teaching 'on the way' to Jerusalem. He has warned severely against causing sin in others and in ourselves, and he has called for clear salt-like testimony to the Christian faith and for peace among his people.

QUESTIONS ON MARK 9:30-50

1. Why were the disciples interested in greatness (9:34)?
2. What did Jesus teach them by picking up the child (9:36)?
3. How did Jesus, as compared with other Jews of the period, view demon possession?
4. Why are people rewarded for welcoming or receiving those who come from Christ?
5. What, according to 9:42-43, are the consequences of causing sin in others? in ourselves?
6. How seriously do we take Jesus' warnings here (9:43-47)?

19

The Journey to Jerusalem 10:1-52

The journey to Jerusalem continues, Jesus leading and the disciples following. Jesus gives further teaching about what it will mean to follow him in the period when he will no longer be with them. Sacrifice lies at the heart of the way of the Messiah and of his followers.

(1) Jesus in Perea (10:1)

Jesus now leaves Capernaum for the last time. According to Mark, he travels *into the region of Judea* and from there *across the Jordan*. Once again we note Mark's knowledge of *regional boundaries* (Greek *ta horia tes Ioudaias*; cf 5:17; 7:24,31).

This journey is probably to be identified with Jesus' visit to Jerusalem at the Feast of Tabernacles, as noted by John (John 7:2,10). According to John, Jesus remained in Jerusalem from Tabernacles (October) until the Feast of Dedication (December), whereupon he went back to Perea (John 10:22,40-42). Mark, however, deliberately structures his gospel so that Jesus goes only once to Jerusalem, for his death. In keeping with this, Mark does not refer to Jesus' extended visit to Jerusalem at this time.

198

But Mark (here in verse 1) and John (John 10:41) agree that large *crowds* [from Judea and Jerusalem?] *came to [Jesus], and as was his custom, he taught them.* This is the first occasion for many months that Jesus has taught in public. Not since the feeding of the five thousand almost a year earlier has Jesus publicly taught a crowd (6:34). John specifically identifies the location as 'the place where John had been baptising in the early days' (John 10:40), which he had earlier identified as 'Bethany on the other side of Jordan' (John 1:28).

It will be remembered that the tetrarch Herod Antipas had arrested John in Perea on account of the large crowds which followed him and because he had said it was not lawful for Herod to marry his brother's wife after divorcing his own wife (see comments on 6:14-29). Once more, therefore, Jesus is vulnerable to the malevolence of the tetrarch of Galilee.

(2) Is divorce lawful? (10:2-12)

The *Pharisees came* [from Jerusalem?] *and tested him by asking* a question on divorce. John the Baptist had been arrested in Perea because he had declared Herod's divorce and remarriage 'not lawful' (Greek *ouk exestin*, 6:18). Now, the Pharisees pointedly ask Jesus, *'Is it lawful for a man to divorce his wife?'* They place him in a precarious position: Herod Antipas would be very interested in his reply.

Customarily, Jesus responds with another question, *'What did Moses command you?'* Their reply — *'Moses permitted a man to write a certificate of divorce and send her away'* —suggests they were in favour of a man divorcing his wife by this means. Jesus, however, immediately shows his disagreement with the current interpretations of Mosaic law: 'You imply that Moses commanded you to divorce your wives! But *it was because your hearts were hard that Moses wrote this law.'*

The passage in question, Deuteronomy 24:1, provided a measure of protection for women by requiring that 'hard-hearted' husbands certify in writing that they were, in fact, divorcing their wives. Jewish men of Jesus' time, however, were using the text to sanction easy divorce (cf Matthew 5:31-32).

Even more important, such men had forgotten the original intention of God in his creation of men and women for a permanent union. Referring to *the beginning of creation* in Genesis 1, Jesus declares that God *'made male and female.'* He then quotes Genesis 2: *'For this reason'* —that is, because God created sexuality — *'a man will leave his father and mother and be united to his wife, and the two will become one flesh.'* And then he gives his interpretation of these texts: the oneness of the man and the woman in marriage arises directly from God's creation. *So they are no longer two, but one. Therefore, what God has joined together, let man not separate.*

There Jesus leaves the matter, with the Pharisees' specific question unanswered, though with the principle of the permanency of marriage clearly stated. He does not give his teaching on a plate: as with his teaching to the crowds in parables (4:11), the Pharisees must work out what he really means.

But, as he often does with his teaching, Jesus now explains to the Twelve in private (we do not know the exact location of *the house*) what he has just said in public (cf 3:31; 4:11; 7:17; 9:28; 10:23). In reply to the disciples, Jesus declares that *any* [man] *who divorces his wife and marries another woman commits adultery against* [his wife]. *And if* [the wife] *divorces her husband and marries another man, she commits adultery* [against him].

Jesus' statement is noteworthy for two reasons. First, Jewish women at that time had no authority to divorce their husbands. By allowing the possibility of divorce to women, Jesus tacitly corrects the balance of justice in their favour.

He also anticipates the conversion of Gentile peoples, such as the Romans, among whom it was possible for women to initiate divorce.

Second, Jesus declares the act of remarriage to be adultery against the original spouse, an opinion unheard of among the rabbis. This, then, is Jesus' answer to the Pharisees' question as to whether it is 'lawful' to send a wife away in divorce. The act of remarriage, to which the divorce has led, is 'unlawful'. It breaks the commandment of God which says, 'You shall not commit adultery' (Exodus 20:14). In so teaching, Jesus sought the protection of women against their husbands' desire to be rid of them. In antiquity, women without husbands were generally destitute.

Despite the Pharisees' preoccupation with questions of the law and their repeated accusations that Jesus did not observe it, the truth is that it is Jesus, not they, who is solidly committed to upholding the law of God as set forth in the Ten Commandments. Earlier in the Gospel of Mark, Jesus upheld the commandment to honour mother and father, while showing that the Pharisees encouraged its avoidance (7:9-13). Now he demonstrates his endorsement of the commandment about adultery which they, in fact, had overturned. It is not the law of God that Jesus opposes but the traditions of the Pharisees which obscured that law.

As with his other teaching 'on the way' from Caesarea Philippi to Jerusalem, we note Jesus' concern for the lifestyle of the disciples in the post-Easter period. The Messiah's people were not to live by the easy divorce and remarriage practices of the Jews or, even worse, of the Gentiles of that time. Rather, disciples of Jesus were to observe life-long commitments to their spouses, showing loyalty and love towards them.

Paul, the apostle to the Gentiles, upheld the teachings of Jesus in the churches he established. The wife was not to withdraw from her husband; the husband was not to divorce his wife (1 Corinthians 7:10-11). Situations arose, however, which were not directly covered by Jesus' words. What was a Christian to do when the unbelieving spouse withdrew from the marriage? Paul declares that in those circumstances the remaining spouse is not bound by the obligations of the marriage (1 Corinthians 7:15).

According to Matthew 19:8-9, the other circumstance in which a partner is free to remarry is in the event of the spouse's *porneia*, a Greek word referring to sexual practice outside the bond of marriage and including such aberrant activities as adultery, homosexuality and bestiality.

These exceptions establish the principle that insofar as it is up to the individual, he or she must be committed to his or her spouse 'till death do us part' and must do nothing to damage the marriage. Yet if the other partner withdraws from the marriage or commits *porneia*, thereby breaking the marriage covenant, the remaining partner is free to remarry.

(3) A kingdom of children (10:13-16)

The teaching on the sanctity of marriage is now followed by Jesus' blessing of children. The thematic connection is obvious. Note once more the importance of the instruction which Jesus is giving 'on the way' to Jerusalem. He gives very clear teaching about the home life of his people: husbands and wives are to stay together; children are to be highly valued.

This teaching would be particularly important as the gospel spread among the Gentiles. Roman society, for example, was noted for its high divorce rate and for its lack of concern for small children. Abortion was perfectly legal, as well as infanticide, especially by the 'exposure' of children. A father was at liberty not to bring up his new-born child, in which case the child was 'exposed' —left in the open to die or be taken by whoever wanted it (often for prostitution or begging). In the middle of the second century, the Christian writer Justin Martyr commented:

> We have been taught that to expose newly born children is the part of wicked men ... we see that almost all so exposed (not only girls, but also the males) are brought up to prostitution ... some are openly mutilated for the purpose of sodomy. (*First Apology*, xxvii)

Parents today should feel no superiority in this. In modern societies there are almost as many homicides and acts of violence committed against children as against adults, often by their own parents.

The children in Mark's story are *little* — Jesus takes them *in his arms* — and are presumably brought by their parents to Jesus so that he might *touch them*, that is, bless them in prayer and by the laying on of his hands.

That *the disciples rebuked them* (the parents?) and, by inference, tried to hinder them (verse 14) once again, shows how much at odds they were with their Teacher (cf 9:33-35; 9:38-41).

There are two reasons the disciples might have shown this attitude towards the children. First, it is known that small children were not permitted to belong to the Qumran sect (*Damascus Rule*, xv) and this may reflect a patronising attitude towards children among Jews at large. Second, the disciples' preoccupation with their greatness has already been noted and will surface again (9:33-34; 10:35-37); probably the disciples see these children as too unimportant to warrant Jesus' interest in them.

Jesus, however, was *indignant*, a word denoting anger (for other strong emotions of Jesus, see 1:41,43; 3:5: 7:34; 9:19; 14:34). '*Let the little children come to me,*' he demands, *'do not hinder them.'* Then he expresses his point in a parable, verbal and enacted.

'The kingdom of God,' says Jesus, referring to the community over whom God will rule as King, *'belongs to such as these [children]. I tell you the truth [Greek* amen – see comment on 8:12], *anyone who will not receive the kingdom of God like a little child will never enter it.'* The disciples were preoccupied with greatness (9:33-37), but, says Jesus, only those who are childlike in dependence upon God can belong to the people ruled by him. Here is a powerful challenge to the wealthy, the highly qualified and the highly accomplished. As we stand before God, unless we admit that we are utterly dependent upon him as small children are on their parents, we will never enter his kingdom.

In a living parable which demonstrates the manner of entry into the kingdom of God, Jesus then *took the children in his arms, put his hands on them and blessed them.* God, in his human representative Jesus, received into his kingdom the children who came in simple trust to him. One implication is obvious: If God receives children and if his kingdom is composed of those who are like children, then a high value must be placed on children by their parents, by their churches and by the community.

(4) Riches and the kingdom (10:17-31)

Having left the house (10:10), Jesus and the Twelve set out once more on the *way* (Greek *hodos*; cf 8:27; 9:33,34; 10:32,46,52) to Jerusalem. As with other incidents on their journey between Caesarea Philippi and Jerusalem, the focus is on the distinctively sacrificial behaviour of those who follow Jesus (8:34-38; 9:33-37) and on the kingdom of God which is rapidly approaching (9:1,42-50).

This well-known story is told in two parts: a public event followed by Jesus' private teaching to the disciples. (For other public/private stories, see 3:31; 4:11; 7:17; 9:28; 10:10; 10:42.)

In his public persona Jesus is perceived by the questioner to be a rabbi (*'good teacher'*) and is asked a question which a rabbi could be expected to answer (*'what must I do to inherit eternal life?'*). The rabbi's reply is formally consistent with the layman's enquiry (*'You know the commandments: "Do not murder, do not commit adultery, do not steal, do not give false testimony, do not defraud, honour your father and mother"'*) and also consistent with the high view of the commandments which Jesus had expressed earlier (7:9-13,21-22; 10:11-12).

The conversation continues along these formal lines, the questioner declaring, *'Teacher, all these [commandments] I have kept since I was a boy.'* According to the Mishnah a boy was 'fit for the scripture' at five years of age and 'fit for the commandments' at thirteen (*Aboth*, 5.21). That Jesus *looked at him and loved him* expresses his approval of the care with which the man had been educated in the scriptures and the commandments.

Doubtless other anxious men of the time had asked other rabbis questions about their eternal destiny. This rabbi, however, is different. He is the herald and bearer of the kingdom of God and himself the source of the *eternal life* about which he is being asked. Yet even within this formal conversation Jesus is building a bridge from the public world of Judaism to the private world of the kingdom of God, which at this point Jesus and the Twelve alone share.

Jesus had corrected the man, *'No one is good – except God alone,'* intending him to include himself humbly as one who lacked goodness before God. But there is no such admission: he answers that he has kept the commandments since boyhood. Jesus then makes public the private and hidden world of the kingdom of God and invites the questioner to enter and receive the eternal life which he seeks. *'Come, follow me,'* he says, *'and you will have treasure in heaven.'*

Eternal life in the kingdom of God (the two are synonymous) is found in Jesus. To follow him is to fulfil the law of God; Jesus is God with his people (Matthew 1:23). But Jesus must be seen as deserving to be followed radically. The Twelve had to be prepared to die as his followers (8:34-38). This rich man must be prepared to *'go, sell everything ... and give to the poor.... Then come, follow me.'* Eternal life in the kingdom of God, which is found in Jesus, must be valued above life itself — to say nothing of riches — if a person is to lay hold of it.

The rich man seeks eternal life, but how badly does he want to find it? The answer is, not badly enough. The fishermen were prepared to leave their nets and families, the customs collector his booth, and Bartimaeus his beggar's cloak (1:16-20; 2:13-14; 10:50). But this man was not prepared to leave his property and possessions; at Jesus' words his *face fell*. Contrast his approach with his departure: *He ran up to [Jesus] and fell on his knees* but *he went away sad.* When the crunch came his *great wealth* meant more to him than eternal life.

No one can take comfort from this story; it is profoundly disturbing. Jesus challenged the disciples: did they prefer their lives and their livelihoods to him? And the rich man he challenged – did he prefer his wealth to eternal life? What is his challenge to us? One thing is clear, we cannot be believers unless we are also disciples.

In private Jesus now instructs the disciples about this incident. Earlier 'on the way' he had spoken to them about the priority of serving one another and of mission to the outsider (9:35-37,41-42), of the permanence of marriage and the value of little children (10:1-12; 10:13-16). Now he speaks to them about wealth.

Jesus looked around (Greek *periblepomai* = looked around in a circle, as he often did at dramatic moments; see 3:5,34; 5:32; 11:11), then he declared, *'How hard it is for the rich to enter the kingdom of God!'* He illustrates his saying with a wry parable about the impossibility of a camel, the largest animal in Palestine, struggling though the eye of an needle.

Because wealth brings security against the unexpected, power over others and the possibility of a self-indulgent lifestyle, it is much sought after by those who believe that this world is all there is to human existence. It is, therefore, the most subtle and powerful of false gods, as Jesus knew well. How hard it is to put riches to one side so as to lay hold of Jesus and eternal life in the kingdom of God.

The disciples are *amazed* (verses 24,26) at this teaching of Jesus. The Old Testament implied that righteousness was rewarded by a greatly prolonged life (note the ages of the righteous ones in Genesis 5) and by riches; righteous Job had all his riches and family restored to him as well as a lengthened life as his reward for faithfully enduring his ordeal (Job 42:12-17). But Jesus teaches that the reward of earthly prosperity and a life 'full of years' under the old covenant is now to be seen as eternal life in the kingdom of God and is of infinitely greater value (cf 8:36-37).

If the rich can't enter the kingdom of God, the disciples wonder, *'Who then can be saved?'* (Note the use of synonymous phrases: to be saved = to enter the kingdom of God = eternal life.) Jesus replies, 'With man salvation is impossible; it is only possible with God.' Left to ourselves we would never desire the kingdom of God more than riches. By God's grace, however, we are given the passion to seek eternal life above everything else.

The disciples' amazement is followed by resentment, as expressed by their spokesman Peter (cf 8:29,32-33; 11:21; 14:29,70-71). *'We have left everything* — fishing nets, parents, wives — *to follow you!'* he declares, no doubt remembering the day Jesus had called them by the seashore (1:16-20). This reaction reveals the bitterness in the disciples' minds. Even though they were not wealthy like the rich man they had just met, following Jesus had indeed been very costly to them. They had left homes, brothers, sisters, mothers, fathers, children and fields for the sake of Jesus and the gospel (verse 29). Following the Teacher had meant the dislocation of their lives and separation from their loved ones.

For us in the post-Easter period it is not possible to follow Jesus physically since his body is not here. But the gospel is here; it is now the focus of our discipleship and we are to proclaim it to the whole world (8:35,38; 13:10; 14:9).

Jesus reassures his disciples that although following him means being willing to give up — and indeed the reality of giving up — *everything*, God will nonetheless provide for them *a hundred times* over. In obedience to the Master they may indeed lose their homes, but they will be received into the homes of those to whom they come in Christ's name (9:41). They may be disowned by natural brothers, sisters, mother and father on account of Jesus, but God will give them in his own family close and caring brothers, sisters and parents (cf 3:34-35). They may indeed lose their fields, but God will supply whatever material resources they need to serve him — and *persecutions* as well. Most important of all, they will also receive *eternal life* in the kingdom of God. There *the first* — the rich in this world who, like the enquiring man, reject Jesus — *will be last, and the last* — the persecuted poor of this world like the disciples — will be *first*. There will be a reversal of this age's scale of values.

Here are two powerful challenges. Not only must we be prepared to lose everything — life and riches included — for Jesus and the gospel; we are also to be brothers, sisters and parents to those who have been disowned by their own siblings and parents on Jesus' account. We must not fail them.

(5) On the way to Jerusalem (10:32-34)

Once more, Mark refers to the *way*, or journey, of Jesus from Caesarea Philippi *up to Jerusalem* (Greek *hodos;* cf 8:27; 9:33,34; 10:17,46,52). Jesus speaks to his disciples of his own sufferings and about theirs. Thus, the journey of Jesus to his death in Jerusalem symbolised both his 'way' as well as that 'way' in which his disciples must walk in the future. That the early Christians were known as people who belonged to 'the Way' (Acts 9:2; 24:14,22) probably arose from Jesus' walk to Jerusalem and the teachings he gave as he went.

Mark's description of Jesus as he speaks here is both detailed (more than earlier prediction passages) and dramatically symbolic. Appropriate to his role as their Messianic leader, *Jesus* is *leading the way.* Typical of their bewilderment since Caesarea Philippi, and in contrast with Jesus' clear sense of purpose, *the disciples were astonished, while* [others] *who followed* (the women from Galilee? see 15:41) *were afraid.* Mark has painted a powerful word-picture of the brave leader walking ahead of his bewildered and fearful followers.

Mark will make two further references to Jesus 'going ahead' (Greek *proagein*); both will be of the risen Lord 'going ahead' of his disciples to Galilee (14:28; 16:7). Implicit in this word is the image of Jesus the shepherd walking ahead of and being followed by his sheep. (Shepherds in Palestine *led* their flocks; see John 10:3,4, 27.) As Jesus walks to his death in Jerusalem and through to his victory over death, we his disciples follow him. In similar vein, he is referred to elsewhere as the 'forerunner' (Greek *prodromos*, Hebrews 6:20) and the 'file-leader' (Greek *archegos*, Acts 3:15; 5:31; Hebrews 2:10; 12:2). Jesus' example and his words beckon us to follow him, whatever the cost.

From the wider group who followed, Jesus *took the Twelve aside.* As we have seen, Jesus has a special relationship with the Twelve, whom he often teaches in private (3:31; 4:11; 7:17; 9:28; 9:35-37; 10:10-12;10:13-16, 23-31). Then he makes his third prediction, while on his way to Jerusalem, of his death and resurrection. In the first he had emphasised the verdict of 'rejection' or 'unworthiness' which would be passed against him by the religious leaders (8:31), while in the second he had focused on his 'betrayal' or 'handing over' (9:31).

Much of this third prediction is new; only the theme, *the Son of Man will be betrayed to the chief priests and teachers of the law,* is repeated (cf 9:30-31). Now, the destination, *Jerusalem,* is mentioned. A trial is implied by the words *they will condemn him to death.* His judges, having condemned him, will also betray the Son of Man and *hand him over to the Gentiles, who will mock him and spit on him, flog him and kill him.* Here again is serial betrayal – from Judas to the chief priests, from the chief priests to the Gentiles (see comment on 9:30-32).

Throughout history many have condemned the Jewish people for the death of Jesus. Let us be quite clear that no race of people as such but *individuals* were responsible for Jesus' terrible fate. One of his own disciples betrayed him to the chief priests who themselves belonged to a small elite known as the Sadducees. They in turn handed him over to the Roman prefect whose soldiers finally carried out the execution. Individuals, both Jewish and Gentile peoples and thereby the whole of humanity – contributed to Jesus' ordeal, just as both groups ('many') would have access to the benefits of his redemptive death (see comments on 10:45; 14:24).

(6) Greatness in the kingdom (10:35-45)

The insensitivity of the Twelve to Jesus' impending death and their blindness to his teaching about sacrifice is again highlighted. As on an earlier occasion, immediately after

Jesus has spoken of his death the disciples are found arguing about superiority.

On the way from Caesarea Philippi to Capernaum the disciples had been disputing this question among themselves (9:33-34). Now two of their number — *James and John, the sons of Zebedee* — bring their request directly to Jesus. *'Teacher,'* they say, *'we want you to do for us whatever we ask.'* And when Jesus invites them to make their request, they reply, *'Let one of us sit at your right and the other at your left in your glory.'* How inconstant the Twelve are! One moment they stumble along behind Jesus astonished at his determined march to death (8:32). The next, when Jesus speaks to them about going up to Jerusalem, James and John want to know about his glory and the pre-eminence they might enjoy. (For the Jews' interest in status see comments on 9:33-35.)

This sudden change may be attributed to Jesus' reference to Jerusalem, since it was believed that the Messiah's arrival in the holy city would be the dramatic moment when the kingdom of God would arrive. Luke comments that 'because [Jesus] was near Jerusalem ... the people thought that the kingdom of God was going to appear at once' (Luke 19:11).

Jesus declares that they *don't know* what they are requesting. He asks them parabolically if they can *drink the cup* he must drink or face the *baptism* he must undergo. The 'cup' regularly symbolised judgment in the Old Testament (eg Jeremiah 49:12); 'baptism' was apparently Jesus' own metaphor for his passion (Luke 12:50).

Doubtless the Twelve had some idea that suffering and death were implied by these metaphors. It is a measure of their superficiality that they reply, *'We can.'* In fact they could not. Jesus' *cup* and *baptism* were eternal in character, bringing 'a ransom for many', as he will soon announce (verse 45). He will refer with deep horror to the 'cup' before

211

his betrayal in the Garden of Gethsemane, when he asks his Father that he might be spared drinking from it (14:36). His reference to the 'baptism' he was about to undergo is also expressed in terms of deep foreboding (Luke 12:50). But James and John do not understand this at all.

Nonetheless, Jesus says, they *will drink [his] cup ... and be baptized with [his] baptism,* thus foreseeing Herod Agrippa's execution of James in Jerusalem ten years later (Acts 12:2) and the tribulation of John on Patmos sixty years later (Revelation 1:9). Despite their shallow grasp of his teaching at this point, Jesus perceives that in the years to come these two men will become faithful Christian leaders who will suffer as they follow the Master. But theirs would be physical suffering, lacking the eternal dimension of separation from God which Jesus' cup and baptism will entail (see 15:34).

Yet, Jesus adds, to sit at his *right or left* hand is not for him *to grant,* because those *places* are for *those for whom they have been prepared,* that is, by the Father (cf Matthew 20:23). Jesus is implying limits to his own sovereignty. Only the Father knows the time of the coming of the Son of Man (13:32); only the Father may grant the highest place in the kingdom of God.

James' and John's lust for status now provokes an *indignant* reaction among the remaining *ten:* Why should these two make a preemptive bid for power? We can imagine the unseemly dispute which probably erupted among the Twelve at this moment, with the disciples dividing into warring factions. So *Jesus called them together.* Natural ambition divided them; unity was restored as they focused again on Jesus.

The kingdom of God was imminent. The dispute provided an appropriate moment for Jesus to give the criteria by which members of the kingdom would be judged 'great' or 'first'.

Again, Jesus' words must be understood against the background of Daniel 7. The first part of that chapter is an account of a dream in which four terrifying beasts in turn conquer the earth. But finally God gives his everlasting dominion not to any beast, but to a human figure, 'one like a son of man' (Daniel 7:13). In the second part of the chapter the dream is interpreted. The four great beasts are 'four kingdoms that will rise from the earth' and conquer it, but the 'saints of the Most High will receive the kingdom and will possess it forever' (Daniel 7:17-18). Notice the virtual equation between those who will inherit God's everlasting kingdom: 'one like a son of man' and 'the saints of the Most High'.

Clearly Jesus was influenced by Daniel 7. He is that 'Son of Man', and the 'saints of the Most High' are his Twelve disciples, at least in embryo. Jesus and the Twelve are the everlasting kingdom of God which will replace the kingdom of the beast-like empires.

Jesus sets the 'beast empires' in stark contrast with God's kingdom. *'You know,'* he says, appealing to their knowledge of the ways of men, *'that those who are regarded as rulers of the Gentiles lord it over them'*. God is the only real ruler (see John 19:11); all others are mere pretenders. The Romans were the current 'rulers'; before them there had been Greeks, Persians and Babylonians. But these diverse rulers and their satraps had in common their *tyranny* over other nations, including Israel *(rulers...lord it over,...their high officials exercise authority over)*.

Certainly, as Jesus and the Twelve knew well, Roman rule in Judea — then current for 25 years — was repressive. The uprising in AD 7, led by Judas and Saddok over direct Roman taxation, was brutally put down. Roman governors of provinces like Judea were cynically likened by the Emperor Tiberius to blood-sucking flies gorging themselves on a wounded man. For the past seven years in particular,

Judea had been under the heel of Pontius Pilate, whom a contemporary describes as 'a man of inflexible disposition, harsh and obdurate' (Philo, *Embassy to Gaius*, 302). Pilate had repeatedly outraged Jewish religious scruples; the blood of many Jews flowed in the streets of Judea during his prefecture. More recently, the patriot Barabbas had led an unsuccessful uprising against Roman rule. He and some of his supporters were in custody in Jerusalem at this very time, awaiting crucifixion at the Passover (15:7-11,15,27).

But the 'rule' of the Twelve would not resemble that of the Gentiles; indeed it would be the very opposite. *'Not so with you,'* Jesus says, adding this parable,

> *Whoever wants to become great among you*
> *must be your servant, and*
> *whoever wants to be first*
> *must be slave of all.*

To become *great* in the Messianic community, to be *first* (as the Zebedee brothers wanted to be), required a complete inversion of Gentile values, to say nothing of current Jewish values (see comment on 9:33-35). Servants in all societies are looked down upon as inferior. But Jesus declares that the *great* one in the community of the kingdom of God, the *first* of all, is the one who is the *servant*, the *slave of all.*

Who is this *great...first* member of the Messianic community? Jesus. As we well know, he is speaking of himself in this parable. He exemplifies his words. *For even the Son of Man* — Jesus — *did not come to be served, but to serve.* As the servant *par excellence*, Jesus is *great* among 'the saints of the Most High'; he is their leader, their *first* man. To date, the disciples have not understood Jesus' radical canon that greatness is measured by service. Their successors, the Christian leaders of the years to come, would easily forget it too.

214

Jesus is the exemplar servant. But his words have an even deeper meaning, as implied by *'the Son of Man did ... come'*. If we ask, *'When* did the Son of Man come?' we must answer, 'When he began his ministry three years earlier.' But more fundamentally we must answer, 'When he was born.' And if we ask further, *'Where* did he come from?' our answer must be, 'From God.' Jesus' incarnation, when he assumed humanity from a higher plane of existence, is to be inferred from his words *'the Son of Man ... did come'*.

Moreover, Jesus' coming was marked by great humility, as implied by his words *for even*. According to Daniel 7:14, the 'one like a son of man' would receive from God 'an everlasting dominion that will not pass away, [a] kingdom ... that will never be destroyed'. Yet *even* this man who would be so great, who was destined to inherit the universe, *did not come to be served, but to serve*. The humility of Jesus' coming and serving (cf Philippians 2:6-8), rather than the ambition and tyranny of the Gentile rulers, must be the model for relationships within the community of the new covenant.

How did the Son of Man *serve*? By what action was he *slave of all*? Jesus says that the end-point and goal of his coming is *to give his life a ransom for many*. On three occasions Jesus has declared his impending death (8:31-32; 9:31; 10:32-34), but without explaining why he 'must' die (8:31). Now he gives the reason: his death will be *for many* (cf 14:24).

The background for these words is Isaiah's poem of the suffering servant (Isaiah 52:13-53:12), where the word 'many' occurs on a number of occasions, for example:

> ... my righteous servant will justify *many*,
> and he will bear their iniquities....
> For he bore the sin of *many*,
> and made intercession for the transgressors.
> (Isaiah 53:11b-12)

Jesus thus welds together the prophecies of Daniel 7 and Isaiah 52-53, both of which share the idea of one focal figure and the group to which he belonged. Just as the Son of Man in Daniel 7 is the first member of the 'saints of the Most High' so Isaiah's servant justifies and bears 'the sin of many'.

But who is this group, the *many*? Offensive as it must have been to Jews of Jesus' time — the disciples included — Isaiah's 'many' included the hated 'nations' or Gentiles (Isaiah 52:15). Jesus often spoke of the Gentiles, or the 'many', who would share in the blessings of the kingdom of God (see Matthew 8:11-12; 22:1-10; Luke 4:25-27). 'The saints of the Most High' (Daniel 7) and the 'many' (Isaiah 52-53) are to be drawn not just from the historic people of God, the Jews, but from the 'nations' as well. Humanity in all its racial and social diversity will be represented in the community of the new covenant, sharing in the ransom of the Son of Man.

Jesus will donate *his life as a ransom [Greek* lutron = *a means of liberation] for [Greek* anti = *in place of] many*, his multinational people. Hitherto, humanity had been imprisoned by 'the strong man' Satan (3:27). As part of Satan's 'house' or 'kingdom' (3:24-25), in servitude to him they shared their leader's revolt against God. But Jesus was about to give his life to liberate the Twelve (and others who in the course of years will join them) from the kingdom of Satan, and bring them into his own 'house', the kingdom of the Son (cf Colossians 1:13-14). Release from Satan's prison is purchased by Jesus' gift of his life.

(7) The healing of a blind man (10:46-52)

Jericho, a mere 30 kilometres from Jerusalem, marks the last stop on the journey that had begun at Caesarea Philippi in the extreme north of Palestine. It is quite possible that Jesus and the disciples broke their travels on a number of occasions, for example, at Ephraim which was to the north-east of Jericho (John 11:54; cf 12:1). The *large crowd* to which Jesus and the Twelve apparently now belonged were probably Galilean Passover pilgrims who, to avoid contact with Samaritans, came up to Jerusalem via the Jordan valley and Jericho.

It is not clear whether the city they were leaving was the older Jericho or Herod's new city. A *blind* beggar, *Bartimaeus* (= son of Timaeus — the Aramaic, as elsewhere, is translated for Mark's Gentile readers), was positioned at the exit from the city, doubtless hoping for alms from those going up to Jerusalem for the Passover. The preservation of the name of this blind beggar — as compared to the rich man whose name, ironically, is unrecorded — suggests that Bartimaeus was known to the members of the Jerusalem church.

As soon as the blind man *heard that it was Jesus of Nazareth*, he began to make a commotion. He keeps on shouting to Jesus, *'Son of David [= Messiah], have mercy on me!'* and despite the efforts of bystanders to silence him, he only ceases when Jesus addresses him.

Bartimaeus' cry to Jesus, *'have mercy on me'*, is the same invocation frequently made to Yahweh in the Psalms (eg Psalm 4:1; 6:2; 41:4,10; 51:1; 109:26; 123:3) and implies that Bartimaeus ascribed divinity to the Messiah. How did this blind beggar of Jericho know that the man passing by him was the Messiah, for that in truth is who he declared Jesus to be (cf Peter's confession, 8:29)? It is probable that every blind person in Israel, Bartimaeus included, had heard of Jesus' miraculous healing of the blind man in Bethsaida (8:22-26). And blind people, more than most others, must have been eagerly awaiting the coming of the Messiah since he was the one who would open the eyes of the blind (cf Isaiah 35:5).

Jesus stopped, having at last heard Bartimaeus' cries, and called the blind man to him. The bystanders had to calm the now distraught man: *'Cheer up! On your feet! He's calling you'* they said. Then, dramatically *throwing his cloak aside* — his receptacle for alms — *he jumped to his feet and came to Jesus.*

As with other encounters with sick or disabled people, Jesus' approach here is personal and directed to the whole man, not merely to his disability. *'What do you want me to do for you?'* Jesus asks. To which Bartimaeus replies, *'Rabbi, I want to see.'* 'Then,' says Jesus, *'go, your faith has healed you.'* And *immediately he received his sight and followed Jesus along* the way.

This story is remarkable: on one hand, for its detail suggesting an eyewitness as the source, and on the other, for the evocative language used by the narrator. The names of both the city and the blind man seated at its exit, together with the circumstances of the blind man's begging and the persistence of his cries to Jesus, combine to assure modern readers that this story is based securely in history.

In addition, even the casual reader cannot fail to notice the carefully chosen words with which Mark tells the story. Bartimaeus is the man of faith whose healing from a physical affliction also speaks of the faith which is the source of God's ultimate salvation; his faith not only heals him, it saves him in the post-Easter sense. Bartimaeus also recognises Jesus as 'Son of David', the Messiah, in a manner which we sense shows more discernment than that of the Twelve (cf 8:27-33). As the blind man, who was given sight at Bethsaida, marks the beginning of a long sequence where 'eyes' are opened to the identity of Jesus as Messiah (8:22-26), so the now sighted Bartimaeus represents the end of that sequence. The eyes of the blind have indeed been opened to recognise in Jesus the arrival of the Messiah and the Messianic age.

But Bartimaeus also becomes a disciple, a follower of Jesus. Three times in verse 49 a *call* is issued to the man, indicating at one level a simple invitation to come forward, but at a deeper level the Messiah's invitation to join him 'on the way'. Bartimaeus casting aside his cloak, his physical means of support, clearly parallels the fishermen leaving their nets and family, and Levi leaving his toll-booth, and contrasts with the rich man failing to leave his estate. As the original five disciples 'followed' after Jesus (1:16-20; 2:13-14), so now Bartimaeus follows Jesus *along the road*. This latest mention of 'the way' to Jerusalem, so prominent since Caesarea Philippi, completes the pattern of following Jesus which had commenced with the calling of the first disciples (1:16-20).

Bartimaeus, as presented to us by Mark, is the believer-disciple *par excellence*: he believes in the Messiah; he follows him in the way. Fittingly, Mark locates this story at very end of the first part of his narrative, before the Jerusalem sequence begins.

QUESTIONS ON MARK 10:1-52

1. How is God the source of oneness in marriage (10:6-7)?
2. What is the objective effect of remarriage on the spouse left behind (10:11-12)?
3. What is the significance of the teachings on children being located next to those on marriage (10:6-16)?
4. What is the relationship between children and the kingdom (10:14-15)?
5. Why are Jesus' words to the rich man (10:21) so challenging to him? to us?
6. In what ways does God compensate those who have left much for him (10:29-30)?
7. What new elements are found in Jesus' third prediction of his death (10:32-34)?
8. How is greatness measured in the Messianic community (10:43-44)? Why is Jesus the greatest and the first (10:45)
9. Why is the Bartimaeus incident so important in Mark's Gospel (10:52)?

20

Jerusalem: The Lord in his temple 11:1-12:44

Mark's account of Jesus' arrival in Jerusalem and his days there is dominated by four closely related themes — Jesus' kingship, the destruction of the temple, the death of the 'king of the Jews' and the victory of God. The author skilfully and movingly weaves these strands together as he unfolds the tragic story of the final week of Jesus' life.

The theme of kingship goes back to the beginning of the gospel, to Jesus' announcement of the arrival of God's kingdom (1:15). The themes of the death of the Son of Man and the victory of God through the Son of Man's resurrection and triumphant coming began explicitly at the gospel's mid-point, at Caesarea Philippi (8:31-9:1). Although the temple has not been named before now, it is virtually identifiable with Jerusalem, which is referred to earlier as a source of danger and death (3:22; 7:1; 10:32,33); moreover, in two of the three predictions of those who would bring about his death, Jesus specifically mentions the 'chief priests' of the temple (8:31; 10:33).

Mark teaches theology not in an abstract way, but through a sequence of stories in which these themes are to be found. Of course, he does this in the earlier part of his gospel, too, but he reaches his greatest heights as a theologian-storyteller in these last chapters.

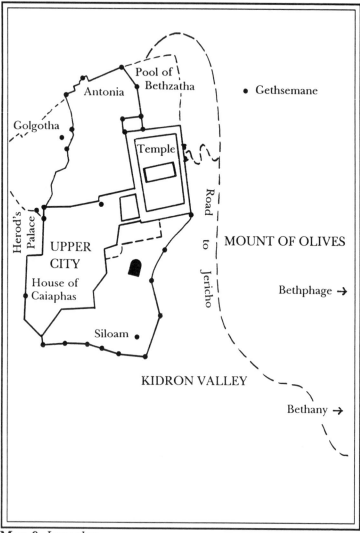

Map 9 *Jerusalem*

(1) The king arrives in Jerusalem (11:1-11)

By his dramatic arrival in *Jerusalem*, Jesus now publicly declares himself to be the Messiah, the king of the Jews. Up to this point Jesus has kept his Messiahship secret; now he announces it clearly, for everyone to see.

Jesus enters Jerusalem carefully and deliberately so as to fulfil two oracles from the Old Testament. The first is found in Genesis:

> The sceptre will not depart from Judah,
> nor the ruler's staff from between his feet,
> until he comes to whom it belongs....
> He will *tether* his donkey to a vine,
> his *colt* to the choicest branch;....
> (Genesis 49:10-11a)

Mark refers repeatedly to the *untying* of a *colt* which was *tied* (verses 2-5). Clearly Jesus wanted his followers to understand that this Old Testament oracle was being fulfilled by him. He is the 'ruler' who has now 'come'; his is the 'sceptre' which 'will not depart from Judah.'

The second oracle is from Zechariah:

> Rejoice greatly, O Daughter of Zion!
> Shout, Daughter of Jerusalem!
> See, your king comes to you,
> righteous and having salvation,
> gentle and riding on a donkey,
> on a colt, the foal of a donkey.
> (Zechariah 9:9)

By *untying* a 'donkey' that had been *tied* and 'riding' it up to Jerusalem, Jesus thus fulfils these two oracles and is saying, 'Jerusalem, I am your king! Receive me!'

Indeed, Jesus is acclaimed as he rides up to Jerusalem, but not by the Jerusalem people. In just a few days they will reject him in favour of Barabbas, calling for the crucifixion of Jesus, the so-called 'king of the Jews' (see 15:1-15). It was, rather, the Galilean Passover contingent (cf 10:46) who *shouted,*

> *Hosanna!* [='Save!']
> *Blessed is he who comes in the name of the Lord!*
> *Blessed is the coming kingdom of our father David!*
> *Hosanna in the highest!*(Psalm 118:25-26)

By speaking these words and spreading *branches* and *their cloaks on the road,* these Galileans were identifying Jesus as the Son of David, the Messiah. Had he not opened the eyes of a blind man — a sign of the Messianic age — in Jericho only a few hours earlier? They identified him as 'David', coming to David's City to receive David's kingdom (cf 2 Samuel 5:9; Isaiah 9:7).

But how do these Galileans view Jesus' kingship? And does Jesus see his kingship in the same way? Recalling their earlier attempt to force Jesus to become a king after the feeding of the five thousand and Jesus' subsequent withdrawal (6:45-46; John 6:14-15), we are reminded that their view of kingship was nationalistic and his was not.

As Jesus rode up to Jerusalem he was unambiguously and openly laying claim to the throne of Israel. But it was as a prince of peace, not a warrior-king, that he came. The king in Zechariah's oracle was 'righteous' and 'gentle'. As a result of his rule,

> [God] will take away the chariots from Ephraim
> and the war-horses from Jerusalem,
> and the battle bow will be broken.
> [The king] will proclaim peace to the nations.

His rule will extend from sea to sea
and from the River to the ends of the earth.
(Zechariah 9:10)

The goal of Jesus' triumphant entry was not the city as such but its *temple*. Mark, now introducing his second theme, writes that *Jesus entered Jerusalem and went to the temple*. Characteristically, *he looked around [Greek* periblepomai, *literally 'in a circle'; see comment on 3:5] at everything*. Clearly Jesus had come for a purpose, which we shall soon discover. *But since it was already late, he went out to Bethany with the Twelve*. Simon the Leper and Lazarus, Martha and Mary were all from Bethany (14:3; John 11:1), which was about five kilometres down the Jericho road; Jesus and the Twelve may have been billeted with these families while they were there.

(2) The clearing of the temple (11:12-19)

The temple theme continues.

The next day, on the way back to Jerusalem, *Jesus was hungry* and, *seeing a fig tree in leaf, he went to find out if it had any fruit.* Finding none, *he said to the tree, 'May no one ever eat fruit from you again.'*

Curiously, Mark adds that *it was not the season for figs*. Why, then, does Jesus seek fruit from a tree in the full leaf of spring — it was Passover — when he knew that summer was the time for figs? It so happens that fig trees do produce a few early figs before the spring leaves appear. Jesus may have been displeased at finding no such early fruit. A better suggestion is that Jesus is addressing the leafy but fruitless fig tree prophetically, as if addressing the temple which was also all show but no substance. (The fig tree was a known symbol for Israel, eg Jeremiah 8:13.) By speaking this word against the fig tree Jesus was, in fact, pronouncing the doom

225

of the temple. (Prophets in the Old Testament often conveyed their God-given messages by dramatic action, eg Isaiah 20:1-6.)

The incident is followed immediately by Jesus' arrival in Jerusalem, whereupon he *entered the temple area*. Notice that Jesus' presence in Jerusalem is focused not on the city but on the temple. Now he will do what there was no time to do the previous evening.

A violent scene erupts as Jesus comes into the outer court — the vast space surrounding the temple proper, where Gentiles were permitted to enter. Until AD 30 the sellers of animals and doves for temple sacrifice, and the men who changed money from Gentile to Jewish coinage for unblemished donations, had been located some distance from the temple, on the Mount of Olives. But Caiaphas, the present High Priest had recently permitted these traders access to the outer court of the temple. In an instant Jesus *began driving out those who were buying and selling there. He overturned the tables of the money changers and ... of those selling doves,* and he blocked the path of those who sought to *carry merchandise through the temple courts.*

In taking this action Jesus probably had a cluster of five closely related intentions.

First, he perhaps was protesting against the recently introduced corruption of the temple court by Caiaphas, the incumbent High Priest.

Second, by referring to the temple as *'a den of robbers'*, as Jeremiah had done before him (Jeremiah 7:11), Jesus, like Jeremiah, may have been criticising the near superstitious trust of the people in the temple. Did they think that because the temple was in Jerusalem no harm could befall them (see Jeremiah 7:1-8)?

Third, by purging corruption from the court of the Gentiles Jesus may have been signalling his great concern for their salvation. He quoted Isaiah 56:7:

My house will be called
a house of prayer for all nations [= Gentiles].

By his action Jesus was declaring that the 'nations', or Gentile peoples, must be given access to the temple of God — which they soon would gain, by means of his death. When the Gentile centurion acknowledges Jesus to be the 'Son of God', the temple curtain would be destroyed (15:38-39). That the curtain would be torn from top to bottom signifies that it was *God* who destroyed it. But God would provide a *new* temple in place of the old — the risen body of Jesus, where Gentiles and Jews may worship God together (cf John 2:19-22).

Fourth, Jesus took this action mindful of Malachi's oracle: 'Then suddenly the LORD you are seeking will come to his temple.... But who can endure the day of his coming?... For he will be like a refiner's fire....' (Malachi 3:1-2). Here the theme of kingship surfaces once more. Just as the ride up to Jerusalem was Jesus' open statement of his Messiahship, so, too, is his 'coming' into the 'temple' to 'refine' it. Jesus is now loudly declaring himself to be the Messiah.

Fifth, the action in the temple court is in close relationship with the cursing of the fig tree and its death, the events which immediately precede and succeed it. By sandwiching the clearing of the temple between the sign and the fact of the destruction of the fig tree, Mark is saying to the readers, 'Just as the fig tree is destroyed, so will be the temple.' Bystanders may well have interpreted Jesus' violent action in the temple precincts as his intention to destroy the temple himself. The accusation which would be later made before the Sanhedrin, that Jesus himself had threatened to destroy the temple (14:57-58), was a clever twist of the facts. Nonetheless, it reflects Jesus' suggestion here that the temple will be destroyed, though not in truth by him.

Mark now introduces into the Jerusalem narrative a third theme, the death of 'the king of the Jews'. Jesus' prophetic action against the temple struck a blow at the heart of Israel. The economy of Jerusalem was dependent on the thousands of pilgrims who came there for the great feasts. Numerous hostel owners, money changers and vendors of sacrificial animals, whose livelihoods depended on the thousands of pilgrims coming to the feasts, would be put out of business if anything happened to the temple. Moreover, the wealth and power of the incumbent High Priest and the chief priestly family were integrally connected with the temple. Not surprisingly *the chief priests and teachers of the law ... began looking for a way to kill him, for they feared him* (cf 8:31).

This is the first of three Jerusalem references to the chief priests' and teachers of the law's intention to kill Jesus (cf 12:12; 14:1-2). They appear to match the three predictions of his impending death which Jesus made as he travelled between Caesarea Philippi and Jerusalem (8:31; 9:31; 10:33-34). The problem for the temple authorities was how to remove Jesus privately. They feared the public's support for him, knowing that *the whole crowd was amazed at his teaching.* And, indeed, the Roman governor usually brought in extra troops to Jerusalem at Passover on account of the great number of pilgrims who were notoriously volatile and capable of massive disturbance (Josephus, *Jewish Antiquities,* xx.106-107).

(3) Have faith in God (11:20-25)

The fourth theme – the victory of God – now appears.

It is now *the morning* of Jesus' third day in Jerusalem. Again he and the disciples make their way from Bethany to the temple. Once more they see the fig tree, but now it is dead, withered from its roots. Mark's sequence of references – the fig tree, temple, fig tree – makes his message unmistakable. Yesterday the disciples heard Jesus speak to the tree (11:14), after which he cleared the temple (11:15-18). Today they see *the fig tree withered from the roots*, whereupon Peter remembers Jesus' words to the tree. They *heard, saw* and *remembered*. Peter says, '*Rabbi, look! The tree you cursed has withered!*' For Peter and the Twelve this meant only one thing — Israel's temple was doomed.

But Jesus' reply in verses 22-26 is a kind of mirror image of what has just occurred. The theme of the victory of God now rises to the surface. '*Have faith in God,*' Jesus says, implying that God will still provide a temple. The temple must go, but there will be another temple to replace it. In place of the temple he has condemned there will be 'a house of prayer for all nations' (11:17). The purposes of God will not be overturned by the wickedness of men.

Some scholars suggest a connection between the 'house of prayer' and Mark's numerous references to Jesus being alone with the Twelve in a *house* or some other private location (see 3:31; 4:10; 7:17; 9:28; 10:10). Perhaps such intimate meetings prefigure the epoch where the temple as a house of prayer is replaced by Christian houses of prayer, the congregations of believers meeting privately which begin to arise after the first Easter (cf Acts 2:42-47)?

The new temple — the living congregation of Christian believers — is to have two characteristics: *faith,* expressed as believing prayer, and *forgiveness.*

Faith as prayer is no new theme in Mark. In the incident at Caesarea Philippi where the disciples had been unable to cast out a demon from a boy, Jesus first said, 'Everything is possible for him who *believes,*' (9:23) then added, 'This kind can come out only by *prayer*' (9:29).

Jesus now gives this same teaching in the brief parable of the *mountain* cast *into the sea*. If *this mountain* refers to Mount Zion, which would have been in view as they approached the city from Bethany, this may be another example of Jesus' prediction of the end of the temple. Again Jesus uses outrageous imagery to make a point (cf 10:25).

Jesus defines *faith in God* as prayer which believes that nothing is impossible for God. Just as small children naively believe that their fathers can do anything in the world, so, too, those who belong to the household of faith believe, with calculated naivety, that their heavenly Father can do anything and everything. Practical trust in the omnipotence of God, expressed in intercession, is the mark of true faith. Therefore, Jesus adds, *'Whatever you ask for in prayer, believe that you have received it, and it will be yours.'* Faith is not defined by Jesus as orthodox belief in a creed (this is presupposed) but as the undoubting confidence of the children of God expressed in prayer for life's daily needs.

The second mark of the new temple is forgiveness. As far as we can see, forgiveness was not greatly in evidence within Judaism in Jesus' time; in fact, it seems to have been quite the reverse. New members of the Essene community at Qumran near the Dead Sea were required to 'hate the sons of darkness', that is, the Gentiles (*Community Rule,* 1.9); the various bands of freedom fighters demanded loyalty to fellow members and hostility to opponents; and in the *Twelfth Benediction,* composed about AD 80 and directed at Christians, the members of a synagogue were to pray, 'may ... the Nazarenes ... perish as in a moment and be blotted out of the Book of Life.'

But, said Jesus, *'When you stand praying'* — in the 'house of prayer' which he would establish — *'if you hold anything against anyone, forgive him, so that your Father in heaven may forgive you your sins.'* Forgiveness was, and remains, fundamental and revolutionary in the teaching of Jesus. Whether in the politics of a 'primitive' tribe or the Middle East or Northern Ireland, life is dominated by an ethic of 'paying back', often for generation after generation. But Jesus' teaching and example powerfully break the cycle of vengeance. Revenge can have no part in the lives of his people either. 'Do not expect your Father to forgive you,' says Jesus, 'if you are holding anything against anyone.'

(4) The temple authorities confront Jesus (11:27-12:12)

The third theme — the death of 'the king of the Jews' — now reappears (cf 11:18).

Jesus enters the temple area for the third time (cf 11:11,15) and finds the authorities ready for him. They had been put on alert by the dramatic incident the previous day which led to their decision to kill him (11:18). It was just as Jesus had predicted at Caesarea Philippi, when he said that the *elders* (= lay aristocracy), *the chief priests* (= senior temple priests) and *the teachers of the law* (= leading Pharisaic scholars) would reject him and he would be killed (8:31).

Representatives of these three groups (which constituted the Sanhedrin) now stand ominously before Jesus demanding answers to two questions: *'By what authority are you doing these things?... And who gave you authority to do this?'* Their questions related to Jesus' clearing of the temple the previous day.

Fundamental to these questions is the word *authority* (Greek *exousia,* meaning the legal right to do something). Jesus' interrogators wanted to know who had authorised him to act the way he had within the temple. There was a sinister intent to their questions: If Jesus were so foolish as to say directly that he was the Messiah or that he was on an errand from God, they would then be able to ridicule him or in some way discredit him.

Till 150 years before, all high priests had been descendants of Zadok the priest (1 Kings 1:8). The Hasmonean family, however, had broken with the Zadokite succession and appointed themselves as high priests. At least, descended from Aaron, they were still a priestly family.

231

But Herod, followed by the Romans, did not appoint the high priests from priestly families; now they were chosen for nakedly political reasons. Caiaphas, the current High Priest, owed his appointment to the Roman Prefect, Gratus, acting on behalf of the Roman Emperor, Tiberius. Doubtless Caiaphas would have claimed that *his authority* flowed from God, but in reality it flowed from a man, the Gentile emperor of the Roman occupying forces.

How does Jesus answer these loaded questions? Customarily, he meets question with question (cf 2:9; 2:19; 2:25; 3:4; 10:3; 12:15; 12:24): *'Answer me, and I will tell you by what authority I am doing these things.'* His question relates to the authority of John the Baptist, and by inference Jesus' own authority: *'John's baptism – was it from heaven, or from men? Tell me!'*

Many people from Judea and Jerusalem had travelled the short distance to the Jordan to hear John (1:5); his teachings must have been well known by the temple authorities. After discussion, they reply, *'We don't know.'* Jesus' question had put them in an impossible position. If they answered that John derived his authority *'from heaven'* they knew that Jesus would press with a further question: *'Then why didn't you believe him?'* But nor did they say *'from men'* since *everyone held that John really was a prophet.*

This was a deadly game. Jesus' question about John was really about himself, as his interrogators must have known. John and Jesus each linked himself with the other. John had spoken of Jesus as the 'one more powerful than I' who would come after him (1:7). Jesus identified John as 'Elijah', the one who had come to 'prepare the way of the Lord' (9:12-13; cf Malachi 3:1; 4:5). Moreover, both John and Jesus were popularly recognised as prophets. Jesus' question about John's authority, and implicitly his own, was unanswerable. So he replies, *'Neither will I tell you by what authority I am doing these things.'*

But that is precisely what Jesus proceeds to do, though obliquely, through a parable. By this means his reply will be sufficiently indirect to avoid open arrest. The passage which follows — the parable of the wicked tenants — contains the most important teaching which Jesus gives about himself in the Gospel of Mark (verse 6 is especially significant).

Jesus' parable about a man who *planted a vineyard ... put a wall around it, dug a pit for the winepress and built a watchtower* is based on Isaiah 5:1-7. There God is the owner and his people the vineyard. The vineyard does not yield the good grapes of justice and righteousness but the bad fruit of bloodshed and distress. According to Isaiah, God announces that he will therefore destroy the vineyard and make it a wasteland.

Into Isaiah's framework Jesus adds details about the owner being *away on a journey* and the various agents who are *sent ... to collect* the rent from the tenants. Some were badly beaten; none were paid any rent. (It is possible that Jesus is relating a notorious incident that had occurred in real life on one of the large vineyards in Galilee.) Finally the owner sends his own *son* to receive the rent, in the belief that the tenants will *respect* the heir to the property. Quite the contrary: they decide to kill the son and grab the inheritance for themselves. The owner was abroad and possibly well advanced in years, and there was a custom that ownerless property fell into the hands of the tenants. So they kill the heir and throw his body *out of the vineyard.* But they had not calculated on the resolution of the owner. Despite the distance, he comes, kills the tenants and gives the vineyard to others.

What does Jesus teach by this parable? As in Isaiah's allegory, the owner in Jesus' parable is God. The vineyard is Israel, in particular her leaders. The servants who are sent are God's prophets, including John the Baptist about whom

233

Jesus has just been speaking. But the critical verse is verse 6, where Jesus reveals who he is:

(i) He, too, has been sent (literally 'apostled'), as a *servant* of God, as one of his prophets;

(ii) But he has also been sent *last of all* (Greek *eschaton*), the end of the sequence of God's prophets. Jesus ends the old and begins God's new age;

(iii)He sees himself as God's *son, whom he loved*. This is not so much Messianic language as deeply filial and personal. It is consistent with the way he calls God 'Abba' and 'dear Father' (14:36). Here in Jerusalem not only the Messianic secret but also the filial secret is made public.

Verse 6 should be read alongside 1:15 where Jesus earlier declared the finality of the times — 'the time has come'. Now 'the kingdom of God' which had drawn 'near' is focused on the man who reveals himself to be God's *servant*, the one *sent ... last of all*, the *son, whom he loved*. God's kingdom is the kingdom of his dear Son (cf Colossians 1:13).

But the theme of divine self-revelation is here joined by another, the killing of the beloved son. With chilling foresight Jesus has announced what his hearers would soon do, *'So they took [the son] and killed him, and threw him out of the vineyard.'* The Messianic king, the Son of God, would be killed.

But to these two themes — the self-revelation of the Messiah, the Son of God, and his death in Jerusalem — Jesus adds a third: the victory of God. The owner *will come and kill those tenants and give the vineyard to others*. The vineyard is not lost; its tenancy is transferred. So, too, the temple authorities will be made to relinquish their leadership of the people of God and it will be given to others, that is, the Twelve. Jesus heralds the victory of God, quoting from Psalm 118:

The stone the builders rejected
has become the capstone;
the Lord has done this,
and it is marvellous in our eyes. (Psalm 118:22-23)

In Caesarea Philippi (8:31) Jesus had foretold that he would be 'rejected' (Greek *apodokimazein* = tested and found wanting). Now he says, despite this, God will triumph. Despite Jesus' rejection by the temple authorities, there will be a new temple and he will be its capstone. Peter captures this same sense of triumph when he later declares that Jesus is 'the living Stone — *rejected* by men but *chosen* by God and precious to him'. Peter adds 'you also, like living stones, are being built into a spiritual house' (1 Peter 2:4-5a). God reverses the rejection of Jesus by the creation of a new temple made up of living stones — people who come to Jesus.

The chief priests, the teachers of the law and the elders *knew* that Jesus *had spoken the parable against them*. But though they sought to arrest him (cf 11:18; 14:1-2), they were still unable to do so because they feared the possible reaction of the Passover *crowd*. Accordingly *they left him and went away*. Their opportunity would come later from an unexpected quarter.

(5) The attempt to trap Jesus (12:13-17)

Jesus faces another loaded question — this time from *some of the Pharisees and Herodians* sent by the upper echelon of the Sanhedrin in order *to catch him in his words*. They were the same unlikely alliance of antagonists from Galilee (see comment on 3:6) who obviously have been having some contact with the Sanhedrin about Jesus. The theme of the death of Jesus continues relentlessly.

Addressing Jesus as *'Teacher'*, and clothing their words in ironic flattery — *'you are a man of integrity ... you teach the way of God in accordance with the truth'* — they pose a menacing question: *'Is it right to pay taxes to Caesar or not? Should we pay or shouldn't we?'* For Jesus to give the wrong answer would mean certain death.

When Augustus had brought Judea under direct Roman rule 27 years earlier, a patriotic leader named Judas came from Galilee to Judea and led a revolt. Roman rule had meant a Roman census, which in turn meant Roman taxes which the Jews had to pay directly to the Gentile emperor in Rome. (Latin *census*, transferred into Greek as *kensos* in verse 14, means 'head tax'.) But, to Judas, the payment of such taxes had meant that God's people were no longer under the rule of God, but under the rule of a man — and a Gentile man at that! Ten years later, in AD 17, the Jews again sought relief from such taxes. This question to Jesus reveals that payment of taxes to Rome was still a lively issue in the thirties.

The question, literally *'Is it lawful?'* (Greek *exestin*), is put to Jesus on a number of occasions in the course of the gospel by the teachers of the law and the Pharisees (cf 2:24; 3:4; 10:2). It reflects their concern with the Sabbath, remarriage and, in this case, the payment of taxes to the Gentiles.

It would have been easy for Jesus' enemies to portray him as a rebel like Judas the Galilean. Indeed, the Sanhedrin later accuse Jesus to Pilate as a man 'subverting our nation [who] opposes ... payment of taxes to Caesar' (Luke 23:2). Like Judas, Jesus was a Galilean and a popular teacher of the people, who had now come from Galilee to Judea.

This was a very dangerous moment for Jesus. To reply 'No, don't pay the tax to Rome' would identify him as a new Judas and bring his immediate arrest on the charge of treason against Rome. But to reply, 'Yes, pay the tax' would imply his support of Rome against Israel and therefore against God. This would seal Jesus' fate with the Passover crowd. Either way the chief priests' worries would be over: Jesus would be removed from the scene — and by his very own words. We can imagine the stillness as they awaited his reply.

But Jesus discerned their *hypocrisy* and the *trap* they had laid for him. Matchless teacher that he was, he called for *a denarius,* a Roman coin which was the rate of pay for a day's work (see Matthew 20:2). When he asked his questioners whose *portrait* and whose *inscription* appeared on the denarius, they replied, *'Caesar's'.*

Jesus' reply saved his life, at least for that moment, as well as giving the guidelines for a proper relationship with God and Caesar. *'Give to Caesar what is Caesar's ...'* he began, signifying the payment of taxes. Unlike the freedom-fighter Judas the Galilean, Jesus recognised that there was a place under God in human society even for a Gentile ruler. Influenced by this teaching, the apostle Paul later writes that a ruler is 'God's servant for [our] good' and that we must 'pay ... taxes to whom taxes are due' (Romans 13:4,7 RSV). Peter, too, calls for submission 'for the Lord's sake' to the emperor and 'every authority instituted among men' (1 Peter 2:13). Clearly Jesus and the apostles distanced themselves from any process of violent action against ungodly rulers as advocated at that time by Judas the Galilean and others.

The contemporary denarius bore Tiberius' image and was inscribed with the words 'son of the deified Augustus' which implied that the deceased Augustus was now a god to be worshipped. But Jesus' concluding words, *'Give ... to God what is God's'* mean that God alone must be the object of our worship.

So in one brief sentence Jesus gives a structure of thought to guide his people: we must render civil obedience and the payment of taxes to 'Caesar' but worship and conscience may only be given to God. 'Caesar', too, is told what his limits are: he must not encroach into the holy place reserved for the worship of God.

Two groups — the chief priests, the teachers of the law and the elders, and the Pharisees and Herodians — have now confronted Jesus, seeking a justifiable reason for his arrest, and both have been unsuccessful (11:27; 12:13).

(6) The Sadducees' question (12:18-27)

Now *the Sadducees ... came to [Jesus] with a question.* Who were the Sadducees? They appear to be a small group of families in whose hands most of the land was concentrated, who had gained control of the Sanhedrin and who stood to gain most from the continuing Roman occupation of Judea. The incumbent high priests were drawn from this elite group. According to Josephus, who came from this circle, 'There are but few men to whom this doctrine has been made known, but they are men of the highest standing' (*Jewish Antiquities,* xviii.17). But Josephus also speaks badly of them, commenting on their rudeness to one another, their harshness as judges in the Sanhedrin and their lack of support by the people at large. The people preferred the Pharisees.

Mark's comment, *'[they] say there is no resurrection'* is confirmed by Josephus: 'As for the persistence of the soul after death, penalties in the underworld, and rewards, they will have none of them' (*Jewish War,* ii.166). Their rejection of resurrection probably arose from a deliberate disagreement with any belief held by their rivals, the Pharisees (who did believe in resurrection, Acts 23:8), from their strict adherence to the written text of the Scriptures (where resurrection is only found a few times) and from the influence of Greek teaching about God's remoteness from the world.

The Sadducees' reason for approaching Jesus was doubtless malicious. As the group which controlled the Sanhedrin they had despatched the two previous groups which had confronted him. Their question to him now, about the *resurrection*, was designed to elicit from Jesus an answer which would discredit him in the eyes of the resurrection- believing multitude. Cleverly, they appeal to *Moses*, universally venerated among the Jews as the giver of the law of God. Their question relates to Deuteronomy 25:5-10; Moses required that a man marry his deceased brother's wife to preserve his brother's name through their offspring. Jesus' questioners ask, hypothetically, what will happen in the resurrection after seven brothers, each of whom the same woman has married under this arrangement, have died and been raised. *Whose wife will she be, since the seven were married to her?*

Again Jesus turns the question back on his interrogators. Unlike the Pharisees, who based their teaching in the living tradition of the rabbis (see comment on 7:4), the Sadducees claimed to confine their teachings to the Scriptures alone. *'Are you not in error,'* Jesus pointedly asks, *'because you do not know the Scriptures or the power of God?'* And are their assumptions correct? Jesus teaches that *when the dead rise* in the resurrection *they will neither marry nor be given in marriage.* Resurrection will bring us into close relationship with God, which will mean the dissolution of marital ties. The resurrected dead will be *like the angels,* Jesus adds — another wickedly pointed remark since the Sadducees did not believe in angels either (Acts 23:8).

Jesus turns to the Scriptures which, he says, they *'do not know'.* Deliberately restricting himself to the Pentateuch — the first five books of the Old Testament, and the only Scriptures the Sadducees accepted — he asks, *'Have you not read in the book of Moses, in the account of the bush, how God said to him ...'* — Jesus then quotes God's words to Moses — *'"I am the God of Abraham, the God of Isaac, and the God of Jacob"?'* (Exodus 3:6).

These words can be taken in two ways, depending on your view of God. For the Sadducees, who see God as uninvolved with the world, who, according to Jesus, *'do not know the power of God'*, Abraham, Isaac and Jacob were long dead when God spoke to Moses. But for Jesus, when God says of himself, *'I am'*, he is also saying, 'I was and I always will be the God of these three men.' Jesus' commentary on Exodus 3:6 is: 'He is not the God of the dead but of the living.' The Sadducees were badly mistaken. God is the living God and these deceased patriarchs are and will always be alive to him. The resurrection of the dead is due to the power of God, which the Sadducees denied.

(7) The greatest commandment (12:28-34)

Throughout this chapter Jesus is at the centre of a series of disputes within the temple precincts – first with the chief priests, the teachers of the law and the elders, then with the Pharisees and Herodians, and finally with the Sadducees. But now, *one of the teachers of the law,* who had *heard* Jesus *debating* with the Sadducees, approached him with a genuine question. The rabbis had added up the various laws in the Old Testament and found there were 613 altogether. This teacher's question, *'Of all the commandments, which is the most important?'* was often discussed by experts in the law. What would Rabbi Jesus say?

In answer Jesus points not to one but to two commandments from the Old Testament, both of which are characterised by love. The most important commandment according to Jesus was Deuteronomy 6:4-5: *'Hear, O Israel, the Lord our God, the Lord is one. Love the Lord your God with all your heart and with all your soul and with all your mind and with all your strength.'* This was an uncontroversial reply.

240

What is unusual is the way Jesus joins to it a second commandment, based on Leviticus 19:18: *'Love your neighbour as yourself'*, adding, *'There is no commandment greater than these.'*

Each of the disputes in this chapter serves to show how God-centred Jesus is. To him, God is to be given the worship he is due (12:17); he is to be recognised as powerful (12:24) and he is to be loved with a person's whole being (note the fourfold *all*). Yet Jesus does not let the command to love God stand alone; he adds to it the command to *'love your neighbour as yourself.'* These commandments are complementary. Love for God is expressed by love for neighbour. Love for neighbour is perfected by love for God.

It is not just that these two are the most important of the 613 laws found in the Old Testament. Rather it is that these 'love' commandments summarise and interpret the remaining 611 laws. The remaining laws no longer stand in their own right; they must now be qualified by these two. Paul later calls this 'the fulfilment of the law' and 'the law of Christ' (Romans 13:8-10; Galatians 6:2), and James calls it 'the royal law' (James 2:8). Love is to be the total expression of our lives; it is the principle of all godly behaviour.

The teacher agrees entirely with Jesus' endorsements that God is *one,* that he is to be loved with all of our being and that our neighbours are to be loved as ourselves, and he unexpectedly adds that these are *more important than all burnt offerings and sacrifices.*

Once again the theme of the temple comes to the surface. When God and the people are loved, the sacrifices and the temple become irrelevant. This was a controversial comment to make in the shadow of the temple where the sacrifices were made. And the Sadducees, from whose small numbers the high priest was appointed, were presumably still in earshot. Any approval by Jesus of this sentiment would be added to the list of his crimes against the Temple. Yet Mark's words, *Jesus saw that he had answered wisely,* imply that Jesus approved of the teacher's comment. Nonetheless, Jesus' actual reply, *'You are not far from the kingdom of God'* indicates that the man was not in the kingdom of God — only by personal attachment to the king, Jesus, does a person come into the kingdom of God. The teacher's insight and attitude had brought him *close to* the kingdom of God, but he was not yet *in* that kingdom.

(8) How is the Christ the son of David? (12:35-37)

The theme of Jesus' kingship now reappears. It will be remembered that Jesus had kept his Messiahship secret throughout his ministry, only declaring it dramatically to the Galilean pilgrims when he rode, king-like, up to Jerusalem at the Passover. The next day he publicly expelled the traders from the temple precincts — another Messianic action. Now he asks a question, the answer to which will also point to himself as Messiah.

Jesus asks first, *'How is it that the teachers of the law say that the Christ* [= the Messiah] *is the son of David?'* The scholars had good reason for this opinion. Centuries earlier God had told David: 'I will raise up your offspring to succeed you, who will come from your own body, and I will establish his kingdom. He is the one who will build a house for my Name...' (2 Samuel 7:12b-13). Other prophecies also pointed to the Messiah being a son of David (eg Isaiah 9:2-7; 11:1-9).

Jesus knew himself to be this *son of David* who would build a house (= the Church) for the name of God (Matthew 16:16-18). The gospel genealogies (Matthew 1:1; Luke 3:31), as well as Paul's gospel summary (Romans 1:3), further establish that he was the 'son of David'. At the time he asked this question, Jesus knew he was the 'son of David' (cf 10:47-48).

But Jesus raises a problem: How can someone be the *son of David* and at the same time be *David's Lord*? In one of David's own psalms, God (*'The Lord'*) speaks to someone whom David calls *'my Lord'*. He says to David's 'Lord', who is the long-awaited one, the Messiah: 'Sit at my right hand until I put all your enemies under your feet' (Psalm 110:1). Since *'David himself calls him "Lord"'* when he wrote Psalm 110, *'how then can he be his son'* at this present time?

No immediate answer is given to this riddle, either by the teachers of the law or by Jesus. But the answer will soon be given when Peter preaches that the risen and ascended Jesus is 'both Lord and Christ' (Acts 2:36). This is the answer to the riddle. Psalm 110:1 prophesied the time when David's 'son' would become David's 'Lord' through his resurrection and ascension. Jesus' unanswerable question prepares his hearers, especially the Twelve, for what will happen in a few days' time. Then the riddle will become clear: Jesus will be proclaimed as both 'Lord', the risen son of David, and 'Christ' (Acts 2:29-31; 13:22-23; Romans 1:2-4; 2 Timothy 2:8; Revelation 5:5).

(9) Jesus' warning about the teachers of the law (12:38-40)

One of the four main themes running through these Jerusalem chapters is the destruction of the temple. It was introduced obliquely in chapter 11:12-19 when Jesus cursed the fig tree and expelled the traders from the temple, and in chapter 13 Jesus will specifically predict the destruction of the temple. In this brief passage and the one following, Jesus speaks to his disciples about temple-related matters. The theme of the destruction of the temple and the death of Jesus the Messiah are very closely connected: Jesus' pronouncements about the end of the temple brought about his death.

It is clear that Jesus engaged in more teaching in the temple at this time than is recorded by Mark in 11:20-12:44. At his arrest Jesus said, 'Every day I was with you, teaching in the temple courts...' (14:49).It is during one of these extensive teaching sessions that he warns his hearers, *'Watch out for the teachers of the law'*. They were one of the three groups whom he said would be responsible for his death (8:31; 10:33; cf 11:18,27; 14:1,43,53; 15:1,31).

Josephus tells us that the Pharisees, whose leaders were the teachers of the law, were 'extremely influential among the townsfolk and all prayers and sacred rites of divine worship were performed according to their exposition' (*Jewish Antiquities*, xviii.15). But from Jesus we gain a rather less attractive perception, of men who sought recognition — *'They like to walk around in flowing robes and be greeted in the marketplace'* — and pre-eminence — *'They like to ... have the most important seats in the synagogues and the places of honour at banquets.'* In this vivid picture Jesus sketches the religious ostentation of many, though not all, of the teachers of the law in his time (cf Matthew 23:1-12).

A particularly sinister note is sounded by his criticism, *'They devour widows' houses and for a show make lengthy prayers.'* The teachers of the law were often dependent on hospitality and it is possible that Jesus is referring to specific examples of abuse current at that time. It will be remembered that Jesus had complained earlier that, through the influence of the teachers of the law, some elderly parents were not being provided for by their children (7:11-12).

(10) The widow's offering (12:44)

Mark does not allow us to forget that Jesus is still within the temple precincts (cf 11:27; 12:35; 13:1,3). In and around this temple we meet people who are contributing to its corruption: sellers of sacrifices and changers of money, murderous chief priests, sycophantic Pharisees and Herodians, cunning Sadducees, hypocritical teachers of the law and insincere rich people. All justify Jesus' pronouncements against the temple which will follow (13:1-31). Jesus' arrival in the temple as a godly teacher serves to reveal the darkness of others who strode these courts every day.

But there was at least one exception. The temple served in part as a bank, and money was placed into one of 13 trumpet-shaped receptacles for various kinds of gifts (Greek *gazaphylakion*; the Mishnah's *Shekalim*, vi.5 also refers to this). As Jesus *sat there he watched the crowd putting their money into the temple treasury*. He saw *rich people* putting in *large amounts* and *a poor widow* putting in *two very small copper coins*.

This scene encapsulates all that was wrong with the temple system. Like the fig tree which Jesus cursed because it was all leaves but no fruit, service and sacrifice in the temple was all show but no substance. The rich gave large amounts but the true sacrifice was the offering made by the poor widow. Introducing his words with *'I tell you the truth'* (= Amen), Jesus teaches his disciples that this poor widow had put *'into the treasury more than all the others'*, though her gift had been so small. Others had given *'out of their wealth'*; but she, *'out of her poverty [had] put in everything – all she had to live on'*. It has been well said that the measure of true sacrifice is not what we give but what we keep. The wealthy – who exemplified the spirit of temple service – did not measure up very well by this canon, despite the greatness of their contribution. But the poor widow was singled out by Jesus as a true worshipper of God; she gave to God what was God's (cf 12:17).

QUESTIONS ON MARK 11:1-12:44

1. How does Jesus' ride into Jerusalem reveal him publicly to be the Messiah (11:1-11)? Why does he do this now?

2. How does the 'sandwiching' of the clearing of the temple between the cursing and death of the fig tree help us understand Jesus' actions there (11:12-21)?

3. Why was Jesus' presence in Jerusalem during Passover a problem to the authorities (11:18; 14:1-2)?

4. Why is Jesus' parable of the tenants so important (12:1-11)?

5. How does God triumph (11:22; 12:9-11) despite what is about to happen to Jesus?

6. Why was the question about taxes so dangerous to Jesus (12:14-15)?

7. In what ways does Jesus' reply to the Sadducees bring comfort to us (12:27)?

8. How can the Messiah be the son of David? Why is this important?

9. How do the scenes which Mark describes (11:15-17; 12:38-40; 12:41-44) contribute to our overall view of the corruption of the temple?

21

The end of the temple 13:1-37

Jesus now explicitly speaks of the destruction of the temple. Nonetheless, at the end there will be a new 'temple' — God's chosen ones — who will be gathered to the Son of Man.

(1) The setting (13:1-4)

Jesus' third day in Jerusalem (see 11:20,27) was characterised by disputation with the temple authorities. Jews of the time believed that the temple would become the world centre of the kingdom of God; but Jesus said that the temple would be destroyed (cf John 2:13-19).

Now Jesus and the Twelve leave the temple area, probably from the eastern side, with the intention of returning to Bethany a few kilometres down the Jericho road.

Fifty years earlier, Herod had begun work on his greatest building, the temple in Jerusalem. In order to provide a level base in the steep ravines of Jerusalem, Herod's builders constructed a marble platform of great size — approximately 250 metres (south) by 450 (east) by 300 (north) by 500 (west) — about 35 acres in area. The platform was supported by massive walls of carefully chiselled masonry, some stones being 13 metres in length. Even today the traveller can walk beneath part of the platform and marvel at the size and skill of the construction. This great marble podium was enclosed on all sides by roofed porticos. Within this enclosed space, and occupying less than one quarter of the whole, was the temple itself. The open space on the platform between the porticos and the temple was called the Court of the Gentiles, where many hundreds of thousands of pilgrims assembled for the great feasts. According to Josephus, the whole complex was 'more noteworthy than any under the sun' (*Jewish Antiquities*, xv.p411).

The grandeur of this scene provokes one of the disciples to say to Jesus, '*Look, Teacher! What massive stones! What magnificent buildings!*' For the Jews the greatness of the temple was not merely its size, but its significance as the place on earth where Yahweh, the God of Israel, chose to dwell. The temple had a Messianic significance for the people of God; it was almost the incarnation of God on earth. Along with the Law, the temple was the great symbol of Yahweh's election of his people. Jews readily gave their lives to defend the sanctity of both. Jesus' response, therefore, is very surprising, '*Do you see all these great buildings? Not one stone here will be left on another; every one will be thrown down.*'

Jesus and the Twelve now walk down into the Kidron ravine to the east of the temple and up the steep slopes of the Mount of Olives. There Jesus sits with Peter, James, John and Andrew, looking across the ravine to the radiant marble temple which must have presented a dazzling sight. Once more, a disciple (Peter, their usual spokesman; cf 8:29; 9:5; 10:28) opens the conversation: '*Tell us, when will these things happen? And what will be the sign that they are all about to be fulfilled?*'

The dramatic setting of this episode must not allow us to forget that the whole passage of the gospel from the time of Jesus' arrival in Jerusalem has been dominated by the theme of the destruction of the temple (11:11, 12-14, 15-17, 20-21, 22-25). The climax to this theme is about to be reached.

(2) The sign of the destruction of the temple (13:5-23)

Peter's question to Jesus is expressed in classically biblical terms. First, he asks about the *sign* (Greek *semeion*) which would in turn herald *these things,* the destruction of the temple. We are reminded that the plagues in Egypt were 'signs' pointing to the great salvation event, the Exodus (Exodus 10:1-2; Deuteronomy 7:19). So, what is the 'sign' here and when will 'these things' be fulfilled?

Jesus answers the question in the same end-time terminology, referring to *the end* (verses 7,13) and to *the birth pains* which precede the end (verse 8). 'The end' will be the birth of God's new age. 'The sign' of 'the end' will be *'the abomination that causes desolation' standing where he does not belong* (verse 14). This speaks of the desecration of the temple; this desecration will be the sign pointing to the temple's destruction. As to when 'the end'/'these things' would occur, Jesus' answer is: 'Very soon — *this generation will certainly not pass away until all these things have happened'* (13:30).

But Jesus is not content merely to answer Peter's questions. The thrust of his teaching here on the Mount of Olives is to warn the disciples about the dangers to their faith which they would face in the immediate future, in the time leading up to the destruction of the temple. Three times he warns them, *'Watch out ...'* (though regrettably the force of the original is lost in the NIV as the thrice-repeated Greek *blepete* is not translated uniformly — 'watch out' in verse 5; 'be on your guard' in verses 9,23).

First (verses 5-8), the disciples must *watch out* lest they be deceived by the many who will come in Jesus' name, each in imitation of him, claiming to be the deified returning Christ — '*I am he*' (Greek *ego eimi*). These deceivers will be active during times of war, earthquake and famine.

Second (verses 9-13), they must *be on ... guard* against persecution. During the time before *the end* (verse 13), when *the gospel must ... be preached to all the nations* (verse 10), *all men will hate* the followers of Christ (verse 13). There will be floggings, trials before governors and kings, and betrayals by members of the disciples' own families. (Strange as it may seem to us who see the world as yet unevangelised, the apostle Paul believed that the gospel had been proclaimed to the world within his lifetime. See Romans 10:18; Colossians 1:6.) Third, and most important of all (verses 14-23), they must be on their guard when they see '*the abomination that causes desolation*' (cf Daniel 9:27; 11:31; 12:11, where the phrase relates to the desecration of the temple) *standing where he does not belong*. Since the word 'abomination' is neuter gender the text ought to continue 'standing where *it* does not belong'. But Mark has changed the grammar to read 'standing where *he* does not belong' and added '*let the reader understand*'. This was an instruction to the 'lector' or public reader of the gospel to explain to the listeners what was meant. So what did Mark mean?

On August 30, AD 70, after the temple had finally been captured by the Romans and set on fire, the Roman general Titus entered the Holy of Holies. According to Josephus, 'Caesar [Titus] therefore led his staff inside the building and viewed the Holy Place of the Sanctuary with its furnishings'. Later that same day,

> As the [Jewish] partisans had fled into the City, and flames were consuming the Sanctuary itself and all its surroundings, the Romans brought their standards into the temple area, and erecting them opposite the East Gate, sacrificed to them there, and with thunderous

acclamation hailed Titus as Imperator. (*Jewish War,* vi.260,316)

Many suggest that Mark has put prophecy into Jesus' mouth after the event. But this cannot be true. While Jesus accurately prophesied the *general fact* of the desecration and destruction of the temple, *in detail* things happened differently from the way he said they would. Jesus said that the desecration would precede and be the sign of the destruction of the temple (verses 7,14). But, in fact, desecration and destruction occurred on the same day, on August 30, AD 70, and in reverse order.

Moreover, although Jesus said that the sufferings of the people of Judea and the appearance of various false Christs and false prophets (verses 19,22) would occur *after* the desecration of the temple, historically they occurred *beforehand.* The desecration/destruction of the temple on August 30 was the climax of, not the prelude to, the crisis in Judea.

These differences between Jesus' general prophecy and the precise order of the events as they occurred are evidence that Jesus' prophecy was not created by the events and then put into his mouth later by Mark.

Mark's alteration of 'it' to 'he' and his words 'let the reader understand' are, however, editorial comments. In the opinion of many scholars they also refer to Rome's desecration of the temple and are, therefore, evidence of a post-AD 70 date for this Gospel. This, however, is an unnecessary conclusion. In AD 40 the emperor, Caligula, decreed that a statue of himself should be erected inside the temple, bringing the Jews to the brink of war with Rome. Paul may have been referring to this when in AD 50 — twenty years before the desecration of the temple — he wrote about 'the *man* of lawlessness ... [who] sets himself up in God's temple, proclaiming himself to be God' (2 Thessalonians 2:3-4).

It is likely that Mark's "'the abomination that causes desolation" standing where he does not belong' and Paul's 'man of lawlessness ... in God's temple' are each author's way of repeating Jesus' original prophecy. Mark's editorial remarks, therefore, make perfectly good sense if written in anticipation of the desecration of the temple. Moreover, because the actual sequence of events which occurred in Judea turned out to be different from Jesus' prophecy, there is good reason to believe that Mark was written *before,* not after, the desecration and destruction of the temple in AD 70.

(3) The coming of the Son of Man (13:24-27)

The events to this point prophesied by Jesus – assaults on believers, the desecration of the temple, the rise of pseudo-Messiahs and dreadful suffering in Judea – are recognisably historical. We can read about them in the Acts of the Apostles and Josephus' histories. But now Jesus' prophecy becomes 'cosmic', *supra*-historical:

In those days following that distress [sufferings in Judea],

> *'the sun will be darkened,*
> *and the moon will not give its light;*
> *the stars will fall from the sky,*
> *and the heavenly bodies will be shaken.'*

'At that time,' adds Jesus, distinguishing it from the time of the desecration of the temple, *'men will see the Son of Man coming in clouds with great power and glory.'*

Previously Jesus had said to his hearers, 'You [will] see ...' (13:14); but now he says (literally), *'They* will see ...' This suggests that the cosmic coming of the Son of Man may not be in the lifetime of those who will witness the desecration of the temple.

This is the second of three references in Mark to the second coming of Jesus. As there are three predictions of Jesus' death and resurrection in Jerusalem (8:31; 9:31; 10:32-34), so there are three cosmic predictions of his coming with 'great power and glory' (8:38; 13:26; 14:62). The humiliation of the Son of Man within history will be matched by his return in glory to gather his elect. The death, resurrection and return of Jesus should be thought of together as the kingdom of God. The bridge between Jesus' humiliating death and triumphant return is his resurrection (which occurred historically at the time of his death); it is the *risen* Son of Man who will return.

This will be the great climax of the ages, to be described only in other-worldly, cosmic language, as in the Book of Revelation. As we who are bound within time and history hear these words of Jesus and contemplate the frontiers of time and eternity when God's kingdom will appear in fullness and radiance, we are confronted with both majesty and mystery. Prosaic words fail us.

When the Son of Man appears, *he will send his angels and gather his elect from the four winds, from the ends of the earth to the ends of the heavens.* Here finally is the 'new temple' of God's gathered people. The old is gone; the new is come. The theme of the destruction of the Jerusalem temple and its replacement with another, which has dominated the Gospel since Jesus' arrival in Jerusalem, is now complete.

What is the relationship between these two great events — the desecration/destruction of the temple in the immediate future and the coming of the Son of Man in the remote future — which Jesus foresaw as he sat on the Mount of Olives?

Both events are preceded by a *sign*. The desecration of the temple is the sign of the destruction of the temple, and the destruction of the temple is the sign of the coming of the Son of Man. The first event is the sign of the second.

And the desecration/destruction of the temple (13:2,14,) which is the sign of the cosmic coming of the Son of Man to gather his elect (verses 24-27), marks *the end* (verses 7,13). However, it is a good end — the Greek word *telos* means 'perfection' (cf 1 Peter 4:7) — and the 'birth' of the coming age (verse 8).

Jesus spoke these words a long while ago. His non-appearance so far raises doubts in some minds that he will ever return. But those who doubt that Jesus will return would do well to reflect that the sign of his coming, the destruction of the temple, took place as he said it would. *All* the other prophecies of Jesus — his death and resurrection, the coming of the Holy Spirit, the persecution of his followers, the rise of Jewish 'sign' prophets, the desecration and destruction of the temple and the sufferings in Judea — have been fulfilled in history. Only his prophecy of his second coming awaits historical fulfilment.

Jesus now gives two parables in regard to the future, the first relating to the destruction of the temple, the second relating to the coming of the Son of Man.

(4) The parable of the fig tree (13:28-31)

You do not need a calendar if you have a fig tree: when *its twigs get tender and its leaves come out,* it is obvious that *summer is near.* 'So,' says Jesus, '*when you [the disciples] see these things happening, you know that it [the destruction of the temple] is near, right at the door.*' The phrase 'these things' (verses 4,29-30) refers uniformly to the events preceding the destruction of the temple — the rise of pseudo-Messiahs, the spread of the gospel, the persecution of believers. 'These things' are the tender twig and the budding leaf that will tell of the nearness of the coming crisis.

And they would occur very soon. *'I tell you the truth'* (literally Amen, I say to you'; see comment on 3:28), Jesus says, *this generation will certainly not pass away until all these things have happened.'* He adds, 'Even *heaven and earth will pass away, but my words will never pass away.'* As such, Jesus' words are on a par with 'the *word of our God* [which] stands forever' (Isaiah 40:8). The words spoken by this man are true and authoritative, more permanent than the universe, and they control history. Here is another implied claim to deity by Jesus.

(5) The parable of the absent householder (13:32-37)

This second parable relates to the coming of the Son of Man, and its meaning is opposite to the first. It declares that, unlike the destruction of the temple, there will be no warning of *that day or hour.*

There can be no warning because neither *the angels* nor Jesus know when it will take place. Although Jesus is *the Son* he does not know the time of his coming. He knew about the nearness of the destruction of Jerusalem and the events which would precede it, but only *the Father* knows the secret of the return of the Son of Man. Thus, there will be no prior warning.

We should note in passing the absolute way Jesus refers to himself ('the Son') and to God ('the Father'). As in the parable of the wicked tenants (12:6), we hear an echo of Jesus' own view of himself in relationship to God. The various confessions of the New Testament (eg Galatians 4:4-6; Romans 1:2-4), and ultimately of the Church's creeds, go back to and depend on Jesus' own view of his identity and his filial relationship to God. Nonetheless, although the Son belongs to the Father and shares fully in his deity, some element of subordination is implied by the Father's knowledge and the Son's ignorance about the day and hour of the coming of the Son of Man.

Jesus' parable tells of a man of substance who goes away for a significant period of time. Concerned for the proper operation of his house the master delegates important duties to his servants, including the task to *keep watch* for his return so that he can be appropriately welcomed. The servant who was to keep watch had to be alert because it was not known when the owner of the house would return — *whether in the evening, or at midnight, or when the rooster crows, or at dawn* (the four watches which Roman soldiers were rostered to keep). If the absent owner came suddenly, he must not find his servants *sleeping!*

The parable begins and ends with sharp challenges. At the beginning (verse 33) Jesus says, *'Be on guard!'* (Greek *blepete*, see 13:5,9,23) and *'Be alert!* (Greek *agrupneite*; literally 'sleep in the open fields', implying alertness to danger); and at the end, *'Watch!'* (Greek *gregoreite*).

And once more Mark's hand can be seen applying Jesus' original spoken words to the readers (cf 13:14): *'What I say to you,* the disciples, *I say to everyone,* the readers: *"Watch!"'*. Mark and his readers, then and now, have the destruction of Jerusalem behind them and the return of the Son of Man ahead. The former stands as a permanent sign that the Son of Man will return and gather together his elect. Mark has taken the original words of Jesus to the four disciples on the Mount of Olives and written them in ministry to his readers, then and now, in a challenging and applicable manner.

A wife separated from her husband for months misses him desperately and longs to be with him. She can talk to him by phone, but only briefly because of the cost. She looks longingly at his letters and photographs, counting the days until his return. We, the Church, are that bride. We read the Gospels; we reflect upon the broken bread and the outpoured cup, as reminders of his dying love for us; we are one with him in the Spirit. But we watch longingly and expectantly for his return. One day we can dispense with photos and phone calls. We will be together again, forever.

QUESTIONS ON MARK 13:1-37

1.   What is the relationship between the destruction of the old temple and the appearance of the new temple (13:1-2,26-27)?
2.   What is the 'sign' of the destruction of the temple and the coming of the Son of Man?
3.   Has Mark put prophetic words into the mouth of Jesus?
4.   After all this time, why should we still believe in the second coming of Jesus?
5.   What is the point of the parable of the fig tree (13:28-29)?
6.   How does the parable of the absent householder (13:32-37) apply to us?

22

The night he was betrayed 14:1-72

From Caesarea Philippi to Jerusalem, Mark's Gospel has been dominated by the paradox of a Messiah who will be killed by the temple authorities. Mark now brings us to the dark night when Judas Iscariot, one of the Twelve, betrays Jesus to the chief priests for money. The remaining eleven, however, also emerge without credit: in contrast to Jesus' courage and determination, the central three sleep while he prays, the eleven run off while he stands firm, and Peter denies while he confesses.

(1) The chief priests' dilemma (14:1-2)

Once again, Mark draws aside the curtain to let us see the religious authorities plotting the death of Jesus (see 11:18; 12:12). Jesus' activities in the temple since his arrival in Jerusalem have provoked their implacable hostility.

But *the chief priests and the teachers of the law* have a dilemma. It is now only two days before the greatest of the Jewish festivals — *the Passover and the Feast of Unleavened Bread* — when Jews would commemorate God's deliverance of them from Egypt more than a thousand years earlier (Exodus 12:1-20). According to Josephus,

259

they celebrate it with gladness, and it is their custom to slaughter a greater number of sacrifices at this festival than at any other, and an innumerable multitude of people come down from the country and even from abroad to worship God. (*Jewish Antiquities,* xvii.214)

Hundreds of thousands of pilgrims were pouring into Jerusalem for Passover. The authorities, therefore, said, *'Not during the Feast, or the people may riot.'* They knew from history that a tiny spark could ignite a mighty explosion in Jerusalem (see comment on 12:12), and any such riot would call into question their competence to govern. The Romans might sack the incumbent High Priest, Caiaphas; or worse, bring Judea under even more direct Roman rule. Moreover, as the authorities were acutely aware, there was already tension over the insurrection which had occurred in the last few days. A number of those involved, including Barabbas, were being held in custody by the Romans and were awaiting execution during the Passover (see 15:7). The last thing the Jewish leadership wanted was a Jesus-inspired insurrection.

(2) Anointed for burial (14:3-9)

With a fine sense of contrast, Mark frames this bright picture of a woman's loyalty to Jesus between the chief priests' dark plans to kill Jesus (verse 1-2) and their conspiracy with Judas Iscariot to betray him (verse 10).

The incident — the same as that recorded in John 12:1-8 — occurs in *Bethany* where Jesus and the Twelve were billeted and to which they returned each evening after spending the day at the temple (cf 11:11-12,19-20). *Simon the Leper,* in whose house Jesus and the Twelve were *reclining* for the meal — not at a literal table, but on the floor, supported by cushions (cf 14:18) – is not otherwise known to us. (Was he a former leper whom Jesus had healed?)

The *woman* who came bringing *very expensive perfume, made of pure nard,* was Mary, sister of Martha and Lazarus (see John 12:2-3; cf John 11:1). To retain its fragrance the ointment was kept in sealed alabaster flasks which had to be broken to release the contents. This flask may have been an heirloom which had passed from generation to generation.

While anointing was common at feasts, the extraordinary value of Mary's perfume – it was worth *more than a year's wages* – prompted those present to demand, *'Why this waste of perfume?'* Passover was by custom an occasion for making gifts for the poor (see John 13:29); reckless extravagance at such a time was frowned upon. So *they* [probably the disciples] *rebuked her harshly.*

The sensitivity and loyalty of this *woman* of Bethany is very different from the uncomprehending hostility of the male disciples, who at this point stand symbolically with the conspirators. They are indistinguishable from Jesus' opponents and outsiders. When Jesus is arrested the disciples will desert him (14:50), and no disciple will be at hand to bear his cross or take him down from it to lay him to rest. Only the women of Galilee stand by him at the crucifixion and visit the tomb to anoint his body once the Sabbath is past (15:40-41; 15:47-16:1).

'She has done a beautiful thing to me,' says Jesus, expressing a deep thankfulness with which we can readily identify. Then, knowing that in the next few days he would be facing death with its heart-breaking separations, he says, *'The poor you will always have with you, and you can help them any time you want,'* adding significantly, *'But you will not always have me. She did what she could.'* Jesus endorses the ongoing obligation to care for the poor (with an allusion to Deuteronomy 15:11); but he would soon be gone from them.

The greatness of Mary's gift was a measure of her gratitude to the Teacher. In a significant departure from Jewish prejudice which declared, 'May the words of the Torah be burned rather than handed over to a woman' (*y.Sota*, 8,10a), Jesus had taught her (see Luke 10:38-42). And, moreover, he had brought her brother Lazarus back from the dead (John 11:32-44). Her instincts are correct: the blessings of God flow to us through his Son Jesus, our Lord.

But does Mary's audacious generosity encourage, for example, lavish expenditure on church architecture, which some justify on the basis of Jesus' observation that 'the poor you will always have'? Such a conclusion is incorrect. Jesus' actions in the temple and his pronouncements against it represent a severe warning that Christians are not to make the same mistakes as the Jews in venerating any 'this-worldly' shrine. Besides, Jesus confirmed, rather than denied, the Deuteronomic obligation to provide ongoing care for the poor.

Mary's action prompts Jesus to make the fourth prediction of his death (cf 8:31; 9:31; 10:32-34). But to his death, he now adds an explicit reference to his burial: '*She poured perfume on my body beforehand to prepare for my burial.*' Whether or not she knew what she was doing, says Jesus, this in fact is what she has done.

And he concludes with the solemn words, '*I tell you the truth* [literally 'Amen, I say to you ...'; see comments on 1:22; 3:28], *wherever the gospel is preached throughout the world, what she has done will also be told, in memory of her.*' Before Easter, Jesus and the Twelve *preached* (Greek *keryssein*) the gospel in Galilee (1:14-15,39; 3:14; 6:6,12). But subsequent to his death and burial, the gospel will be preached throughout the world, to all nations (13:10).

Mary's powerful and loving action in anointing Jesus' *body* highlights and adorns the very important fact of Jesus' *burial*. The burial of Jesus is crucial to the *gospel* because, on one hand, it confirms the fact of his death, and on the other, it is the necessary precondition of an empty tomb, which in turn is a precondition of bodily resurrection. The burial of Jesus is the vital bridge between his death and his resurrection.

That there is a gospel to be proclaimed rests upon the reality of the resurrection, the step beyond the burial. Clearly there can be no gospel proclamation to the world without the resurrection. Thus, this episode draws attention, by inference at least, to the historical events which are fundamental to the gospel — the death, the burial and the resurrection of Jesus (cf 1 Corinthians 15:3-5).

(3) Judas and the chief priests (14:10-11)

The dilemma for the temple authorities, that Jesus must not be arrested during the Feast for fear of riot (14:2), is about to be resolved. By what must have seemed an incredible gift from God to them, Judas Iscariot — *one of the Galilean's own followers* — approaches them, offering to hand him over.

To this point, Mark has said nothing about Judas except to list him last as one of the Twelve apostles — 'Judas Iscariot, who *betrayed* him' (3:19). This theme of betrayal, or 'handing over', also appeared in Jesus' second and the third predictions of his death, as he made his way to Jerusalem (9:31; 10:32-34).

This tragic story is told with Mark's typical restraint. He simply states that *Judas Iscariot, one of the Twelve, went to the chief priests to betray Jesus to them.* And naturally, *they were delighted to hear this.*

Why did Judas betray Jesus? The suggestion that he was disillusioned with Jesus' ineffectual idealism, preferring a leader of violent action, is speculative. We are told elsewhere that Judas was a thief (John 12:6), and this general picture is confirmed by the chief priests' promise to give him money. A desire for money appears to have been his motive: basically he preferred 30 pieces of silver to Jesus (Matthew 26:15). The name 'Judas' now stands for someone who would betray a friend; this Judas betrayed the Messiah. *So he watched for an opportunity to hand him over* (Greek *paradidomi* = betray; see comment on 9:31).

(4) Preparation for the Passover (14:12-16)

We come now to the black night when Jesus was betrayed, deserted and denied by his friends, the Twelve.

Mark describes the preparation for the Feast at length for several reasons. First, he shows that Jesus was in fact handed over *during* the Passover, despite the potential problem of an ensuing upheaval (14:2). Thus he commences, *'On the first day of the Feast of Unleavened Bread ...'* adding by way of explanation for Gentile readers, ' *... when it was customary to sacrifice the Passover lamb.'* Strictly speaking, the Passover was celebrated on the fourteenth day of the month of Nisan; the week of Unleavened (= yeast-free) Bread followed, beginning on the fifteenth. Mark's words would have been sufficient for Gentile readers, however, who were not very interested in the finer details of Jewish feasts.

Second, by quoting the disciples' question, *'Where do you want us to go and make preparations for you to eat the Passover?'* Mark reveals that Jesus used the powerful symbolism of the Passover meal to teach his disciples about the fact and the meaning of his death.

Third, Mark allows us to see that despite the powerful forces gathered against Jesus, he is quietly in control of events, including even his arrest. Jesus had arranged in advance for *a man carrying a jar of water* (women usually carried water) to meet the two disciples in the city and lead them in secrecy (no words would be exchanged with him) to *the owner* of a house with a *guest room — a large upper room.* When the disciples went into the city they found everything just as Jesus had told them.

The easily missed detail of the 'guest room' confirms the truth of this story. It was required under Jewish law at the time that Passover be eaten within the city of Jerusalem (Mishnah, *Pesahim*, 7.9,12). Jesus and the Twelve could not eat the Passover in Bethany where they were billeted; it was necessary for them to come 'into the city' and eat it inside the walls of Jerusalem. The specific reference to a 'guest room' is consistent with a synagogue inscription dating from that era which mentions 'a guest house and the rooms and water supplies as an inn for those who have need when they come from abroad' (C.K Barrett, *New Testament Background*, Document 50). Large numbers of Jews from abroad, including Galileans, who came into Jerusalem for the great feasts, necessitated the provision of the kind of 'guest house' mentioned in the inscription and 'guest room' as described by Mark.

(5) The upper room (14:17-25)

When evening came — which in Jewish reckoning marks the beginning of a new day — *Jesus arrived with the Twelve* for the Passover meal. The Greek practice of *reclining* to eat, that is, of eating in a semi-prone position on the floor supported by cushions, had been gaining wider acceptance for several centuries and was now thoroughly established among the Jews.

A third century work, the Mishnah (*Pesahim*, 10), shows us what happened on a typical Passover night in Jesus' time. The Passover meal was (and still is) a religious service led by the father of the household. The food — bitter herbs, unleavened bread and roasted lamb — would be prepared and ready on the table, but would not be eaten until the pronouncement of the blessing for the first of four cups of wine which would be drunk during the course of the service. The father would then explain that the bitter herbs symbolised the bitterness of the Jews' life in bondage in Egypt, the unleavened bread their escape in haste, and the roast lamb the lamb's blood which the Jews had daubed on their doors, causing the angel of death to 'pass over' their households prior to the exodus (see Exodus 12:1-13). The meal was punctuated throughout by the singing of Psalms 113 to 118 and the reading of other Scriptures.

Good storyteller that he is, Mark does not recount the Passover liturgy in full, but only mentions those elements which highlight the unfolding drama of Jesus' death. He fixes our attention on the dovetailing details of the betrayal of Jesus and Jesus' explanation of his imminent death.

The theme of betrayal goes back almost to the beginning of the Gospel and runs like a thread through the whole story (3:19; 9:31; 10:33; 14:10-11). Mark undersupplies details here, not giving Judas' name at this critical stage nor mentioning his withdrawal from the room to go to the temple authorities (cf John 13:30). Rather, he highlights the deep pathos of Jesus' betrayal *by a friend*. Jesus says that his betrayer is '*one who is eating with me ... It is one of the Twelve*' (cf 14:10), adding — with reference to the eating of the bitter herbs at the Passover meal — '*one who dips bread into the bowl with me*' (cf Psalm 41:9).

According to Daniel 7, the Son of Man is both head over and physically part of the saints of the Most High, as if he and they are indistinguishable. The gospel story, however, distinguishes sharply between the bright faithfulness of Jesus the Son of Man and the dark treachery and cowardice of the Twelve. Jesus' betrayal by his friend Judas will soon be added to in the desertion of his remaining friends (14:50) and the denial by one of his special friends, Peter (14:66-72). The Twelve are merely the saints of the Most High in embryo. Their unworthiness represents the unworthiness of us all; given the same circumstances we would also betray, desert and deny our Master. The death of the Son of Man was brought about *by* the sins of his people, as well as *in substitution for* them.

In what Jesus now says, we see the divine and human outworkings side by side. *'The Son of Man will go just as it is written about him,'* he says, referring to the will of God set out in Scripture (Isaiah 53:8,9,12; Psalm 22:1-7; Daniel 7:21,25; and see comment on 9:12). But referring to the agency of Judas, he says, *'Woe to that man who betrays the Son of Man!'* We should draw comfort from the fact that God works out his purposes even through wicked men like Judas who disobey him. God is not thwarted by evil; indeed he brings good out of evil. Nonetheless, the sovereign will of God in no way eliminates human accountability for actions like those of Judas.

While they were eating, Jesus spoke of the meaning of his death, using the symbolism of the Passover meal. At the point in the service where the unleavened loaf was broken and shared among the household members, *Jesus took the bread, gave thanks and broke it, and gave it to his disciples,* adding the critical words, *'Take it; this is my body.'* Following his words about betrayal, there can be no doubt that Jesus, by breaking the loaf, was dramatically portraying his death.

Then he took the cup, that is, the third cup in the Passover meal, *gave thanks and offered it to them,* as a father would do at the Passover, so that *they all drank from it.* Once again, Jesus' words are critical: *'This is my blood of the covenant.'* After the exodus, God made a covenant with his people at Mount Sinai and gave them the Ten Commandments. The covenant was sealed with blood — the blood of young bulls — which was sprinkled on the covenant people (Exodus 24:5-8). Later, the prophet Jeremiah, conscious that the people had not kept faith with God, promised a new covenant which would be based on the forgiveness of God and in which God's law would be written within the hearts of the people (Jeremiah 31:31-34). On the eve of his death, Jesus now institutes God's new covenant, sealed not with the blood of an animal, but with his own blood. The blood is not sprinkled on an unworthy people but sprinkled, as it were, on Jesus himself — the only Israelite who truly kept the covenant with God.

Jesus continues, 'My blood of the covenant *is poured out for many.*' The words to notice here are *for* and *many*. The use of the preposition *for* (Greek *hyper* = on behalf of/in place of) means that Jesus' *blood* or death is 'on behalf of or in place of' others. Just as the blood of the firstborn lambs spared the covenant people and made possible their escape from Egypt, so the blood of God's beloved Son will be shed for the protection and liberation of the people of God under a new covenant. By his sacrificial death, Jesus the Messiah dedicates himself to God as the righteous sufferer *on behalf of* his people for their exodus, not now from Egypt, but from the judgment of God on their sins (cf 1 Corinthians 15:3-5; 2 Corinthians 5:21).

Many refers to the people of God under the new covenant, who henceforth will be composed of Gentiles as well as Jews (Matthew 8:11-12; see comment on 10:45). From now on, the people of God will be drawn from all races, nations and tribes of people, not just from Israel. God's ancient promise to Abraham that one day 'all peoples on the earth will be blessed through you' (Genesis 12:3) is about to be fulfilled by the death of Jesus.

In other words, Jesus' offering of himself at this Passover Feast superseded the annual sacrifice of the Passover lamb. Jesus' words as he took the bread and the cup into his hands, followed by his death the next day, profoundly influenced the thinking of the apostles. As Paul declares, 'Christ, our Passover lamb, has been sacrificed' (1 Corinthians 5:7).

Peter, too, writes of 'the precious blood of Christ, a lamb without blemish or defect' (1 Peter 1:19). And John, in Revelation, portrays the Messiah, the Lion of the tribe of Judah, as 'a Lamb, looking as if it had been slain' (Revelation 5:5,6). In each case the unimaginable paradox of Christ crucified — foreshadowed privately at Caesarea Philippi, signified publicly by his majestic entry into Jerusalem, and powerfully reiterated at the Passover meal — has passed on into the imagery of the apostolic writings.

But a striking omission makes Mark's account distinctive. Why is there no institution of the Lord's Supper, no injunction by Jesus (as recorded by Luke and Paul) to 'Do this in remembrance of me' (Luke 22:19; cf 1 Corinthians 11:24-25)? The answer must be that Mark is so focusing the readers' attention here on Jesus' imminent death (as he does in every other incident 'on the night he was betrayed') that he omits any detail which would distract us from it. It is reasonable to assume also that the institution of the Lord's Supper at the Last Supper was so well known that it was not necessary for Mark to include it.

This is the last occasion in his earthly life that Jesus drinks *the fruit of the vine,* the everyday beverage of the Jews. He knows that he will be betrayed before the night is out. Not until *the kingdom of God,* the heavenly banquet of the Messiah, would Jesus drink wine again. But it would not then be ordinary wine but 'new' (verse 25, RSV; Greek *kainos*), as appropriate in the 'new heaven' and 'new earth' where God makes everything 'new' (Revelation 21:1,5). Humiliation will be followed by consummation.

The Passover meal concluded, Jesus and the disciples sang a *hymn* — that is, one of the Psalms set for the occasion — and went out of the city on the east side, down across the Kidron ravine and up the steep slopes of the *Mount of Olives,* a journey of about one hour. Once more Jerusalem lay before them across the valley (cf 13:3), though now in darkness; once more Jesus is going to make predictions about the future.

(6) The Mount of Olives (14:27-31)

At the Passover, Jesus made the dramatic announcement that one of the Twelve would betray him. Equally dramatic is this prediction, *'You will all fall away.'* Jesus' point is that there is a qualitative difference between him and his disciples — *all* of them, without exception. He illustrates this from Zechariah 13:7, *'[God] will strike the shepherd and the sheep will be scattered.'* He, their shepherd, will remain resolutely faithful to the call of God, come what may; but they, his sheep, will be scattered from his presence (cf John 16:32).

This would be true, not only on the black night of their desertion, but right through until his return, as Zechariah 13:8-9 prophesied. Against Augustine's view that the Church is the continuing incarnation of Christ in the world, it must be said that the flock of Christ, like its original Twelve members, is permanently prone to faithlessness and cowardice, constantly depending upon the loyalty and forgiveness of the Good Shepherd.

Alongside the theme of his death which runs unremittingly through every episode on this, the night of his betrayal, Jesus now reintroduces the theme of the victory of God (cf 11:22-25). His words, *'after I have risen',* focus once more on his resurrection, which he has been speaking of since Caesarea Philippi and during his journey to Jerusalem (8:31; 9:9-10,31; 10:34; cf 16:6). The themes of the humiliation and glorification of the Son of Man have been closely woven together from that time.

In the manner of shepherds (who led their flocks — see John 10:3,4,27), Jesus, the Risen One, will go ahead of the disciples to Galilee. At Jerusalem he will be killed and the faithless sheep scattered; but, risen, he will lead them to Galilee where he will mercifully reconstitute them as his flock. Three times Mark writes of Jesus 'going ahead' of his disciples as a shepherd-leader — once on the way to his death in Jerusalem (10:32), and twice on the way to Galilee as their risen Master (14:28; 16:7). Jesus leads his people through humiliation to glory, the path he himself trod (see comment on 10:32).

But Peter has no ears for this. He has not been able to listen beyond Jesus' prediction, which he rebuts vehemently, *'Even if all fall away, I will not.'* Jesus answers that *before the rooster crows twice* before morning, Peter *will disown* [him] *three times.* Peter insists he will not, *and all the others said the same.* But Jesus knows that Peter will soon speak for them all and *disown* him (Greek *aparneomai,* cf 8:34). They *will all fall away,* just as he says.

(7) Gethsemane: Jesus' prayer vigil (14:32-42)

Returning from the Mount of Olives towards Jerusalem, Jesus and the disciples come back down the steep slope, through the olive groves to *a place called Gethsemane* (Hebrew 'oil press'; cf John 18:1).

There have been many earlier references in Mark to Jesus' death. Those which speak of his rejection, betrayal and denial (8:31; 9:31; 10:33; 14:18,30) paint the human portrait of his death. Those which speak of 'the ransom for many' and 'my blood of the covenant ... poured out for many' (10:45; 14:24) paint the divine portrait. The two portraits converge here.

Taking Peter, James and John along with him, Jesus instructs the remaining disciples, *'Sit here while I pray.'* These three men, who had been present with Jesus on earlier significant occasions (5:37; 9:2), will exercise

271

important leadership in the future (see Acts 3:1,11; 4:1,3,7,13,23; 8:14; 12:2; Galatians 2:9).

Mark has only mentioned Jesus praying on two previous occasions — when he faced the challenge to heal rather than proclaim the kingdom (1:35), and when the men attempted to make him king after the feeding of the five thousand (6:46; John 6:14-15). Now, facing death the next day, he prays again. Each time Jesus' solitude is recorded, he is being tempted to turn aside from the servant-ministry God had given him.

Moreover, this is the only occasion Mark describes Jesus suffering (*he began to be deeply distressed and troubled*), and, apart from his cry from the cross, the only occasion we hear from the lips of Jesus the pain which he felt (*'My soul is overwhelmed with sorrow to the point of death'*). Mark's extraordinarily strong language anticipates the horrors of the next day, when Jesus will be abandoned in death by both man and God.

Jesus tells the three disciples, *'Stay here and keep watch,'* that is, they were to adopt a spirit of watchfulness and prayer in view of the great trial they would face that night. And, for the disciples of Jesus, it would mark the beginning, not the end, of the need for watchfulness. Indeed, they must continue to 'watch' throughout the age until his return (13:35-37).

Meanwhile, Jesus went *a little farther ... fell to the ground and prayed that if possible the hour might pass from him.* At the beginning of the Gospel, Jesus said, 'The *time* [Greek *kairos*] has come ... The kingdom of God is near' (1:14-15). Now at last the *hour* (Greek *hora*) has struck. The 'time' which had been 'near' is finally *here* : God's special 'hour', the moment of his direct intervention in history to establish his kingdom. This is Mark's signal that the kingdom of God is about to eventuate — in Jesus' death. Mark refers only once to Jesus' 'hour', but it is a common theme in the Gospel of John (John

2:4; 4:21,23; 5:25,28,35; 7:30; 8:20; 12:23,27; 13:1; 17:1). But so awesome will this 'hour' be that Jesus prays that he might not have to face it.

Now Mark lets us hear Jesus praying. His words are extremely important, being addressed to God as *Abba,* an Aramaic word meaning *Father,* which Mark translates for his Gentile readers (cf 5:41; 7:34; 15:22,34). In praying, *Abba,* Jesus was speaking to God like a child saying 'dadda' to his father, thus expressing the intimate, simple and exclusive relationship he enjoyed with God (cf Matthew 11:27). But for the Jews to call God *Abba* was unthinkable, even blasphemous (cf John 5:16-18). Jews of that time prayed to *Abinu* (= 'our Father') — a remote God, separated from them by intermediaries such as angels.

Jesus' private revelation to the Twelve about *'Abba, Father'* was passed on to Paul, who later reminds the Gentile churches to regard God as *Abba* too (Galatians 4:6; Romans 8:15). God as Father, as taught by Jesus and passed on to the apostles, became fundamental to Christian belief (eg 2 Corinthians 1:2-3; James 1:17; 1 Peter 1:17).

But the God whom Jesus addresses as *'Abba,* Father' is also powerful. *'Everything is possible for you,'* he says. With God there is intimate relationship but, at the same time, unlimited power.

Jesus' prayer is, *'Take this cup from me.'* In biblical thought, the *cup* symbolises suffering and humiliation (see comment on 10:38). Who could have guessed that when God's 'hour' finally struck to bring in the kingdom, his anointed King would have to drink the cup? Here is the Son of Man as he contemplates the offering of his own life as a 'ransom' (10:45) to release others from the grip of 'the strong man' (3:27), the outpouring of his blood 'for many' (14:24).

Jesus saw death and hell like a bottomless pit yawning before him, and he naturally shrank from it. Nonetheless, as the faithful and obedient Son of God, he bent his will without compromise to the will of God: *'Yet not what I will, but what you will.'* As the man who obeyed God and gave himself to serve others, Jesus is the role model we imitate, the Master we follow.

But Jesus' courageous obedience to God is immediately contrasted with the weakness and cowardice of the Twelve whom, when he returned, he found *sleeping.* Jesus asks Peter, *'Could you not keep watch for one hour?'* And knowing Peter as he did, he admonishes him, *'Watch and pray so that you will not fall into temptation.'* Jesus' own temptation was to abandon the servant ministry which God had given him; the temptation of his disciple will be to deny Jesus. He continues, *'The spirit is willing* — referring to Peter's impulsiveness in verses 29-31 — *but the body is weak'* . Peter's weak character will soon be exposed in verses 66-72. Jesus, however, is ready in both his spirit and body for the demands of the 'hour'. The disciples have slept; he has prayed.

Once more he went away and prayed the same thing; once more *when he came back, he again found them sleeping.* Doubtless the disciples were very tired after the Passover meal and the steep climb up the Mount of Olives. But Mark is saying to us that, typical of the spiritual weakness they have shown consistently throughout the Gospel, the disciples do not even stay awake at this time of extreme spiritual danger. Once more *they did not know what to say to him.*

But now the moment of crisis is coming. The light of torches can be seen and the sound of voices heard. Judas Iscariot and a squad of men are closing in, coming down the Kidron ravine towards Jesus. He returns to the three men for a third time and asks ironically, *'Are you still sleeping and resting? Enough! The hour has come.'* The time for sleeping — literally and metaphorically — is passed. They have slept enough. Jesus' time of watching is passed. From now on, it is time for the disciples to be both wakeful and watchful.

Jesus declares, *'Look, the Son of Man is betrayed into the hands of sinners.'* Mark, in his narrative of these events, is also teaching us their ultimate meaning. *Sinners* like Judas and the chief priests bring about the death of the Son of Man; at one level, Jesus dies *because* of their wickedness. And more profoundly, though they don't know it, he dies *for* their wickedness, for their redemption (cf 2:17; 10:45).

This, at last, is the 'hour' of cosmic conflict between Satan and the Son of Man. Finally, Jesus tells Peter, James and John, *'Rise! Let us go! Here comes my betrayer.'* Would they go with him? If he led a Zealot rebellion, yes. But to fulfil his Father's will, to die for the salvation of sinners? No, they will desert him and flee.

(8) Gethsemane: The betrayal of Jesus (14:43-52)

Even before Jesus finishes speaking, *Judas ... appeared; one of the Twelve,* Mark adds, as if to underline the shamefulness of his treachery. How did Judas know where to come? According to John's version of the incident, 'Judas ... knew the place, because Jesus had often met there with his disciples' (18:2).

Accompanying Judas was a large arresting party, *armed with swords and clubs, sent from the chief priests, the teachers of the law, and the elders,* the three parties which composed the Sanhedrin (cf 11:27; 15:1).

John's account speaks of 'a detachment of soldiers' with a 'commander', and 'officials from the chief priests and Pharisees' (18:3,12). So possibly this was a mixed group, with a Roman *commander* (Greek *chiliarchos*) and *cohort of soldiers* (Greek *speira*) bearing swords, and Jewish officials bearing clubs. Foreseeing the possibility of serious trouble at Jesus' capture, the high priest must have asked the Roman military governor for soldiers to arrest him. Neither high priest nor prefect would have wanted a Barabbas-like uprising, especially at Passover time. It is a measure of Jesus' political significance that so large a force was sent to take him into custody.

To ensure no mistake was made, *the betrayer*, as Mark now bitingly calls him, *had arranged a signal* with the authorities (cf 14:11): *'The one I kiss is the man; arrest him and lead him away under guard.'* Mark's tragic irony — a betrayer who kisses — should not be missed. Outwardly there is affection; inwardly there is treachery. Although the NIV uses the name of Judas in verse 43, the last reference Mark makes to him is in verse 44, where he is 'the betrayer'.

Thus, the betrayer went *at once to Jesus,* addressed him with the familiar Aramaic title, *'Rabbi'* (cf 9:5; 11:21), and *kissed him.* Immediately, *the men seized Jesus and arrested him.*

We are startled to learn that *one of those standing near* (= Peter; cf John 18:10) not only *had a sword* with him, but used it to attack *the servant of the high priest,* successfully *cutting off his ear.* Why does Peter have a sword? To ward off wild beasts? Or because he and the other disciples were, like many Jews of their day, committed to violent revolution?

If Jesus himself had offered resistance at this moment, indicating that he, too, was committed to violence, fighting between the disciples and the soldiers might have ensued. But Jesus asks, *'Am I leading a rebellion* [literally 'Am I a revolutionary?' — Greek *lestes*] *that you have come out with swords and clubs to capture me?'* And he adds, *'Every day I was with you, teaching in the temple courts, and you did not arrest me.'* Whatever the hopes of his followers, Jesus was a teacher not a revolutionary. Notice that it is only when he offered no resistance that the disciples *deserted him and fled* (thus fulfilling Zechariah 13:7). Their desertion was inspired by ideological disillusionment, not fear.

Not all, however, fled at that moment. Now follows the unusual account, found only in this Gospel, of the *young man* who, as the soldiers *seized* him, ran off *naked, leaving his garment behind.* Various attempts to find some deeper meaning behind these words have failed. Most probably this was the author's 'signature' to his work, for those with inside knowledge. The original hearers of the gospel knew that the young man who fled naked into the night was Mark: had he not told them the story many times?

(9) The high priest's house: Jesus (14:53-65)

The events of this night — the provision of a detachment of Roman soldiers, the successful arrest of Jesus on the slopes of the Mount of Olives, and now his trial in the palace of the high priest — bear all the marks of careful planning and coordination. Witnesses against the Nazarene and the judges of the Sanhedrin had been alerted and were at hand for the trial when the prisoner was brought to the house. With the Passover now in full swing, a Galilean uprising was a real possibility. This man must be dealt with and the matter concluded swiftly.

While the trial proceeded indoors, *guards* had been placed in the *courtyard* where a *fire* had been lit to give warmth against the chill of the night. *Peter* had *followed* the Teacher — not at close quarters so as to be associated with him, but, as Mark ironically says, *at a distance.* Noting *he sat with them and warmed himself at the fire,* the author portrays Peter identifying himself with the captors rather than with the prisoner. Jesus' call to follow him on his own terms has failed (see 8:34): Peter takes up a sword, but not a cross.

In recent years, archaeologists have discovered the remains of a palatial mansion in the south-western quarter of the old city of Jerusalem, overlooking the temple. Within this large complex there is a central courtyard as well as a spacious reception hall. Professor Avigad, the chief archaeologist, believes this was the house of a high priest. Whilst it cannot be proved to be *this* high priest's house, the restored buildings do at least give us some idea of the scale and grandeur of the kind of house to which Jesus was taken and the general area in which Caiaphas' house was located.

Many claim that the Jewish trial of Jesus that now follows in Mark's narrative could not have actually occurred, that it was invented by Christians to blame the Jews for the death of Jesus and to absolve the Romans of the chief responsibility. They point to the Mishnah (*Sanhedrin*, 4-7), which states that capital trials must take place during the daytime in the meeting house of the Sanhedrin, that they must not occur on the eve of either a feast or the Sabbath, and that sentencing must occur on a subsequent day. But this trial occurs at night, in a private house, during the feast of Passover.

These objections are based on two assumptions, namely that the provisions of the Mishnah (AD 200) were in force at the time of Jesus and that the Sanhedrin always strictly followed those provisions.

The first assumption is reasonable. Indeed, the rejection of witnesses whose statements did not agree (verse 56) and the holding of a second hearing on the morning of the next day (15:1) both correspond with prescribed trial procedures.

But the second assumption is open to question. The illegal actions of the High Priest Annas II in the trial and execution of James, the brother of Jesus, in AD 62 (Josephus, *Antiquities*, xx.200-203) warn us that the temple authorities ignored the proper procedures when the need arose.

The extreme urgency of the Galilean's arrival in Jerusalem at Passover explains why a meeting was held at night, during a feast and in the house of the high priest. The implacable opposition of the chief priests and other members of the Sanhedrin to Jesus is deeply rooted within Mark's Gospel and can scarcely be doubted. The danger to the public order, and hence to the high priest's tenure of office, would have been sufficient to justify some bending of the rules.

As the high priest knew well, Roman annexation of Judea had deprived the Sanhedrin of its power to execute (by stoning) blasphemers and other capital offenders. The Sanhedrin could convict, but only the Roman prefect was allowed by the emperor to enforce the sentence (cf John 18:31). The high priest had to establish the guilt of the prisoner for a crime or crimes, on account of which the Roman prefect would then carry out the execution. Thus, *the whole Sanhedrin was looking for evidence against Jesus.*

Normal procedure was that individual witnesses were brought in one by one to be cross-examined by the judges (of whom the minimum number was 23 and the maximum 71). Evidence was allowed provided it was first-hand and there was no discrepancy of detail between the witnesses. But in this case *many testified falsely against* Jesus and *their testimony did not agree.* These witnesses had been hastily assembled and gave ill-coordinated versions of events. But at least some of the judges must have stood out against the majority of the Sanhedrin and asked searching questions (as Nicodemus had done earlier; see John 7:50-51). So far, the trial proceedings were in disarray.

The next line of attack was closer to the mark. Several witnesses in turn *stood up and gave this false testimony against him,* namely that they had heard Jesus say, *'I will destroy this temple ...'.* This telling accusation was false and yet, to the casual listener, true. Jesus had indeed said that the temple would be destroyed and that he would re-build it after three days (11:12-21; 13:2; John 2:19). But to allege that Jesus had said *he* would destroy the temple himself was to twist the evidence deliberately against him. The high priest knew that even a Gentile governor with no love for the temple would be alarmed at the thought of civil upheaval resulting from its destruction. Establishing that Jesus posed a threat to the temple, and therefore to public order, would make him guilty of the kind of crime for which Pilate might order his execution.

Accused persons were obliged to defend themselves before the judges, as the high priest now commands Jesus to do. But on this occasion the accused declines to offer any rebuttal; *Jesus remained silent and gave no answer.* This was a show trial, altogether lacking integrity.

The high priest now leaves his seat and stands before them. The chief judge becomes the chief accuser. This is the climax of the trial. The conviction for a crime which the Romans will execute must now be secured. The temple destruction charge was serious but something else, something stronger, was needed.

So the high priest asks Jesus, *'Are you the Christ, the Son of the Blessed One?'* He had good reason to ask this question. Exactly a year before, a mob of Galileans had attempted to force the Messiahship on this man (John 6:14-15). And just a week ago Jesus had ridden up to the City of David as a king, deliberately fulfilling a well-known oracle (Zechariah 9:9). The next day he had caused a serious disturbance in the temple. The high priest knew that if Jesus of Nazareth admitted to being the Messiah he was as good as dead. 'Christ', when translated for the Romans, meant 'king of the Jews' — in Roman eyes, this was treason, a direct challenge to the authority of the Roman emperor.

The high priest could not believe his good fortune: not only did Jesus reply, *'I am'*; he blasphemously added, *'And you will see the Son of Man sitting at the right hand of the Mighty One'.* This man — about to be crushed by the authorities — is claiming that he will be seen universally as the heavenly

Son of Man, a divine figure, sitting in the place of highest honour at God's side, directing the course of history (Daniel 7:13-14). Moreover, they will see him *coming on the clouds of heaven* as their judge, vindicated by God (cf 8:38; 13:26).

The high priest tore his clothes as a ceremonial sign that blasphemy had been uttered in his hearing. Since only God could appoint the Son of Man, this man Jesus was a blasphemer, in addition to being a temple destroyer and Messianic pretender. This man Jesus was an upstart, a threat to the good order of Jerusalem, dangerously deluded. *'Why do we need any more witnesses?'* the high priest asks. *'You have heard this blasphemy. What do you think?'* They all condemned him as worthy of death.

Jesus was doomed. Nothing could save him now. Within a few hours he would be killed and the potential crisis averted. Only a few formalities remained.

Now it was time for some entertainment at the expense of this foolish man. *Some began to spit at him,* showing their utter contempt. Others preferred mockery so *they blindfolded him, struck him with their fists, and said, 'Prophesy!'* Surely the one who would sit at God's right hand would know who hit him! There was also a belief that the Messiah had special powers of smell so that he could identify people. And when they wearied of this, the humiliated man was given to *the guards* who *took him and,* with feet, knees, fists, elbows and clubs, *beat him.*

(10) In the courtyard: Peter (14:66-72)

The awful scene inside the palace is matched by this one outside, where Peter has been sitting with the guards *warming himself* by the fire. Now he faces a crisis. *One of the servant girls of the high priest* has recognised him as a companion of Jesus. She tells Peter, *'You also were with that Nazarene, Jesus.'* Then she tells the guards, *'This fellow is one of them.'* Finally, the guards recognise Peter's northern accent and say to him, *'Surely you are one of them, for you are a Galilean.'*

Three times Peter is accused and three times he denies knowing Jesus. In Gethsemene, he had fallen asleep three times instead of praying. Now, that threefold sleeping is matched by this threefold denial, though he had said he would stand by Jesus, regardless what others might do (14:31). The spirit was willing, but the flesh has indeed proved weak (14:38). Though Jesus would prophesy nothing to his tormentors (14:65), he had prophesied this to the Twelve (14:30).

No sooner had Peter denied knowing Jesus than the rooster crowed the second time, bringing immediately to mind the words Jesus had spoken. Studies in the crowing habits of roosters suggest that the time would have been between 2.00am and 3.00am.

Why does Mark include this sorry story? He wants his readers to understand that Jesus the Teacher, the man inside the house, is steadfastly faithful to God in contrast with the morally weak follower outside. Jesus is utterly alone as the faithful servant of God. An absolute qualitative difference exists between him and his disciples. With the passing of the years the disciples will become famous as Christian leaders, but no one is to forget that Jesus is uniquely obedient to God, prepared to suffer the baptism and drink the cup (see 10:38). The disciples are men with grievous flaws, with feet of clay; but Jesus is the heroic Son of Man. Only he is worthy to die for others.

QUESTIONS ON MARK 14:1-72

1. Why would the religious authorities have been nervous about disturbances in Jerusalem centred on Jesus (11:18; 14:1-2)?
2. How is the burial of Jesus (14:3-9) a significant part of the gospel?
3. How might Jesus have felt about Judas' actions (14:10-11,18-22)?
4. What is the meaning of Jesus' words as he breaks the bread and gives thanks for the wine (14:22-25)?
5. Why are Jesus' words in Gethsemane important in relationship to his announcement of the kingdom of God (14:41; cf 1:14-15)?
6. Why did the disciples desert Jesus (14:46-50)?
7. What were the aims of the high priest at the trial of Jesus (14:55-64)?
8. How is Peter's denial instructive to us as followers of Jesus today (14:66-72; cf 14:38)?

23

King of the
Jews 15:1-47

The dominant theme running through this chapter is 'the king of the Jews'. Jesus revealed himself in public as such for the first time by his mounted entry into Jerusalem (11:1-11). But, ironically, it is in his crucifixion on a trumped-up charge of high treason that Jesus ultimately reveals himself to be 'the king of the Jews'.

Although Jesus has announced that the *kingdom* of God is 'near' (1:14-15), Mark does not say directly that it has arrived. The repetition of the similar sounding word *king* in this chapter, however, is Mark's way of saying, 'The kingdom of God has now come, in – of all things – the death of the king.' The 'hour' (14:41) has struck.

(1) The second Sanhedrin trial (15:1)

It is now *very early in the morning*, probably dawn on Friday. According to trial procedures, a capital conviction had to be ratified the next day, and it is probably this to which Mark now refers. So, even though the previous session had concluded only a few hours earlier, *the whole Sanhedrin* reconvened. They had probably remained in the high priest's house awaiting the first light of the new day. But their meeting is merely a formality, speedily concluded.

As the result, *they bound Jesus, led him away and handed him over to Pilate.*

Jesus had told his followers that they would be 'handed over to the local councils and flogged in the synagogues' and that 'on account of me you will stand before governors and kings as witnesses to them' (13:9). Mark tells this story to show Jesus is the first 'witness', whom many will follow in the course of history.

Pilate's residence and military headquarters was originally Herod's palace, a great complex located near the present Jaffa gate of old Jerusalem. The prefect's barracks were in the same south-western quarter of the city as the high preist's house, less than half a kilometre away. Note that this is a different location from the traditional site of the Praetorium at the Antonia fortress to the north of the temple. It is likely that Pilate had been told in advance of the probable arrest of the Galilean. When the prisoner is brought to him it is probably no later than 6.00am – quite consistent with the well-established routines of Roman officials, whose working day began before the dawn.

(2) The Roman trial (15:2-5)

It is not Mark's intention to describe in detail the trial procedures adopted by Pilate, any more than he had described the procedures followed by the Sanhedrin. Such technicalities are not Mark's concern. Nonetheless, as with the Sanhedrin trial, he mentions in passing a number of procedures which allow us to recognise the outline of a Roman trial.

Pilate has taken his position at the open-air 'judge's seat' (Greek *bema;* see Matthew 27:19; John 19:13; cf Acts 18:12-13) outside the governor's house. The chief priests, the elders and the teachers of the law (verse 1) then made their accusations to him, with supporting witnesses. Now the prefect-judge will ask his own questions, such as the one which follows. Next, the accused makes his defence, whereupon the judge declares the verdict. If the judge declares the accused guilty, retribution will follow immediately.

Pilate's question, *'Are you the king of the Jews?'* is the Roman version of the high priest's question, 'Are you the Christ?' (14:61). The Romans did not execute for blasphemy (that is, claiming to be 'the Christ'), but they did for high treason (that is, claiming to be the 'king of the Jews'). There was only one *'king* of the Jews' and he was Tiberius, the Roman emperor (cf John 19:15). Any other 'king' was a pretender, to be summarily executed (cf Acts 17:3,7). The high priest had converted the Sanhedrin's conviction of Jesus for blasphemy into a charge of high treason. Indeed, at the Jewish trial the high priest deliberately asked Jesus if he was 'the Christ' in order to accuse him of treason to the prefect, as one who was claiming to be 'king of the Jews'.

Jesus' reply is, literally, 'You say.' Many interpretations of these enigmatic words have been suggested, but the most likely is, 'The words are yours.' Jesus merely acknowledges that he is accused of high treason, without offering further comment.

Then *the chief priests accused him of many things,* probably still including his alleged claim to destroy the temple (see 15:29). The greater the number of charges, the better the chance of making one of them stick. Luke's account of the charges is more comprehensive than Mark's: 'We have found this man subverting our nation. He opposes payment of taxes to Caesar and claims to be Christ, a king ... He stirs up the people all over Judea by his teaching. He started in Galilee and has come all the way here' (Luke 23:2,5).

The accused was entitled to offer a defence against such charges, so *Pilate was amazed* that Jesus *made no reply.* For Jesus not to defend himself was to concede the case to the accusers, and thus to accept the punishment of the judge. Like the Sanhedrin trial, this trial was at heart corrupt. But the silence of Jesus, in the light of earlier prophecies which were now being fulfilled (eg Isaiah 53:7), reveals his sovereignty, as well as his quiet dignity in the face of obvious evil.

(3) The release of Barabbas (15:6-15a)

Because Mark's reference to *the custom at the Feast to release a prisoner whom the people requested* is not confirmed by Josephus, some scholars suggest that Mark has invented it, again to put the Jewish people in a bad light. However, this is an argument from silence; Josephus may have had no need to refer to such a custom. As it happens, the Mishnah says: 'They may slaughter [the Passover] for one ... whom they have promised to bring out of prison' (*Pesahim*, VIII.6).

Mark now tells us about *Barabbas who was in prison with the insurrectionists who had committed murder in the uprising.* Barabbas, a freedom fighter and apparently the leader of a recent uprising against Roman authority, had been imprisoned with a number of others and was awaiting crucifixion during the Passover. Great multitudes were in Jerusalem, and the Romans missed no opportunity to remind the provincials who was master of Israel.

The crowd [who] *came up and asked Pilate to do for them what he usually did* were probably people from Jerusalem, among them supporters and friends of Barabbas. Mark's lack of further comment may be taken to mean that Pilate agreed to their request and released Barabbas.

Pilate goes along with the demands of the Jews, though it is apparent that he does not agree with what he is being asked to do. His question, *'Do you want me to release to you the king of the Jews?'* and Mark's comment that he knew *it was out of envy that the chief priests had handed Jesus over to him* make it clear that the prefect did not regard Jesus as guilty of treason, as charged.

It is regrettable that *Jewish people at large* have been blamed ever since for what happened to Jesus. It is Mark's consistent presentation that the blame lies not with the Jews in general but with an unrepresentative group, the temple authorities, who belonged to the sect of the Sadducees. They are the people who bribe one of Jesus' circle to betray him and who secure Jesus' arrest and conviction at a hastily convened and fundamentally unjust trial. They are the ones who bring the accusation of treason before the governor. And they are the ones who stir up the crowd to have Pilate release Barabbas instead of Jesus.

Equally foolish is any suggestion that Mark blames the Jews and excuses *the Gentiles* for the death of Jesus. Quite simply, Pilate failed to do his job as a judge. His questions, *'What shall I do, then, with the one you call the king of the Jews?'* and, *'What crime has he committed?'* suggest he knew the charge of treason against Jesus was unsupported as well as highly improbable.

Nor, as it is sometimes claimed, did *the people of Jerusalem* treacherously turn against Jesus, acclaiming him with 'Hosannas' on Palm Sunday and clamouring 'Crucify him' on Good Friday. Those who welcomed Jesus into Jerusalem were not Judeans but Jesus' fellow-Galileans. The Judeans could hardly be blamed for preferring Barabbas since he was probably a local, whereas Jesus was from distant Galilee.

Critics of Mark's alleged bias against the Jews also fail to notice the severity of his narrative in relation to *Jesus' own followers,* some of whom were to become the leaders of the early Church. One betrays him. Ten flee into the night and do not reappear in this Gospel. Peter at one point denies any relationship with Jesus at all. No disciple is at hand either to carry his cross or to comfort him in his death. Mark says little about Jews in general, but his account *is* negative in regard to the disciples and to Pilate, as well as to the temple authorities.

Mark also makes a point which is not often noticed — that Jesus is not responsible for the civil disturbances of which he is the centre. At the time Mark wrote, Christians were frequently in the middle of trouble. The Romans may have been asking whether this movement had always created unrest. Perhaps one reason Mark tells his story in the way he does is to show that Jesus was neither a revolutionary, nor a troublemaker.

For his first five years as prefect (AD 26-31), Pilate treated the Jews brutally and provocatively. But in October AD 31, his patron, the Praetorian prefect L. Aelius Sejanus, was executed in Rome, leaving Pilate vulnerable in Judea. The emperor Tiberius took renewed interest in the provinces after the fall of Sejanus, and wrote to the governors not to trouble the Jews. Any complaints to the emperor about the prefect would now lead to his dismissal (John 19:12-13). This explains why Pilate, who had been so ruthless towards the Jews, is now so deferential. Thus, *wanting to satisfy the crowd, [he] released Barabbas to them.*

Pilate then spoke the words of utmost dread to Jesus, *'Ibis in crucem'* — 'You shall mount the cross.'

(4) Pilate hands Jesus over to the soldiers (15:15b-20)

In Roman practice, after the passing of the sentence, the soldiers had unlimited opportunity to torture the prisoner, both in the preliminary beatings and in the freedom to choose the method of impaling the victim. Martin Hengel writes, 'Crucifixion was a punishment in which the caprices and sadism of the executioners were given full rein' (*Crucifixion*, London, 1977, p 25).

Again, Mark is sparing in his details. He mentions that Pilate *had Jesus flogged* by the awful *flagellum* —small pieces

of metal or bone attached to leather whips, which stripped
the victim's flesh from his back.

Jesus is then taken inside the governor's palace, which
also served as the military barracks for the Roman troops
stationed in Jerusalem. It is implied that the soldiers do not
believe the charge against Jesus, for they dress him as an
idiot-king, with *a purple robe* and *a crown of thorns* (or reeds).
In parody of the charge, they mock him in words resembling
the greeting to a Roman emperor — 'Ave, Caesar!' — 'Hail,
king of the Jews!'. Then, *falling on their knees they paid homage
to him.* But viciousness accompanies humiliation: *again and
again they struck him on the head with a staff and spat on him.*
This is Jesus' third beating since the previous evening (cf
14:65; 15:15); but he remains dignified in silence. His
prophetic words are being fulfilled (cf 10:33-34).

The ordeal finished, the soldiers took off his robe and put
his own clothes back on him. *Then,* Mark writes
unemotionally, *they led him out to crucify him.*

(5) To Golgotha (15:21-24)

Because the Praetorium is nowadays considered to be
Herod's former palace at the western wall of the city, it
means that the route to Golgotha is different from the
traditional *via Dolorosa.*

Although it was customary for the man under sentence
to carry his own crossbeam, Jesus, weakened from the
ordeal of the previous hours, was unable to do it (cf John
19:17). So the soldiers forced another man to *carry the cross
– a certain man from Cyrene [in North Africa], Simon,* who was
passing by on his way in from the country. Simon, a Jew of the
diaspora who had settled in Judea, is further identified as
the father of Alexander and Rufus, who were apparently known
to Mark's readers by reputation if not in person. Were they
known on account of their Christian faith (cf Romans

16:13)? External corroboration of this family may be provided by a tomb in the Kidron Valley bearing the inscription, 'Alexander, son of Simon.'

Golgotha, an Aramaic word *which means The Place of the Skull* (presumably because of its skull-like appearance), was probably not more than half a kilometre from the Praetorium to the north. A wall which ran north from the Praetorium, after a short distance turned eastwards for about two hundred metres before turning north again. Thus a right angle was formed outside the city walls (cf John 19:20). Golgotha was located within that right angle, close to or at the position of the Church of the Holy Sepulchre today. Archaeologists suggest that Golgotha may have been part of a quarry for the extensive building work of the city.

This site was doubtless carefully chosen by the Romans because of its proximity to the city walls, from which spectators had a clear view. The terror of crucifixion was given maximum exposure to intimidate potential insurgents. Both the act and the aftermath of crucifixion were horrific: the victims sometimes took several days to die, writhing and screaming in agony. Bodies were usually not buried, but left impaled on the stake to be eaten by birds and wild dogs.

On arrival at Golgotha, as was customary, Jewish women offered the victim *wine mixed with myrrh,* a narcotic to deaden the pain. But Jesus declined — he would not reject the cup the Father had given him to drink (cf 10:38; 14:36).

(6) The crucifixion (15:24-32)

Mark's words *and they crucified him* seem simple and unemotional. Yet to his original readers, familiar as they were with the widespread practice of crucifixion, they would have inspired deep emotion. There was no uniform method: victims might be impaled through their eyes, genitals, hands or feet, with their bodies hanging in a variety of positions. But fundamental to crucifixion was the impaling of the victim by iron spikes to a wooden frame. The pole usually remained in the ground. If the criminal was notorious he would be fixed to a high pole, as was probably the case with Jesus (cf 'come down', 15:30). Otherwise he would be attached to the pole close to the ground.

Some idea of the pain can be discerned by Seneca's words:

> Can anyone be found who would prefer wasting away in pain dying limb by limb, or letting out his life drop by drop, rather than expiring once for all? Can any man be found willing to be fastened to the accursed tree, long sickly already deformed, swelling with ugly weals on shoulders and chest, and drawing the breath of life amid long drawn out agony? He would have many excuses for dying even before mounting the cross. (*Epistle* 101)

Beyond the pain, however, was the victim's powerlessness, his utter helplessness, his humiliation and his degradation. Crucifixion was not practised on Roman citizens, but on slaves, robbers and rebellious provincials as a terrible deterrent against anti-social behaviour. According to Cicero, 'the very word cross should be far removed not only from the person of a Roman citizen but from his thoughts, his eyes and his ears' (*Pro Rabiro*, v.16). With the coming of Christian emperors in the fourth century, crucifixion was gradually replaced by hanging as the means of execution.

Jesus was crucified naked, again as was customary. The soldiers in the execution squad *cast lots* for his clothes to see what each would get (cf John 19:23-24). Thus, at the moment when the forces of evil seemed to be omnipotent, an Old Testament scripture ('They divide my garments among them and cast lots for my clothing' — Psalm 22:18) was being fulfilled; despite all appearances God was, in fact, present in this dreadful event.

Mark notes that *it was the third hour when they crucified* Jesus, that is 9.00am. In this detail, however, Mark is not followed by Matthew or Luke (who do not state the hour) and is, in effect, contradicted by John (John 19:14). Nonetheless, there is no good reason to reject Mark's version.

Attached to each criminal's pole was a notice (the *titulus*) setting out his crime. The charge against Jesus read: *THE KING OF THE JEWS.* Whatever misgivings the governor may have had (15:9,12), he succumbed to the demands of the temple authorities and executed Jesus of Nazareth on their terms. The finger of accusation points symbolically at them for what they did. Jesus is innocent of the charge.

It is no accident that Mark places in adjoining verses *crucified* and *the king of the Jews.* On the surface his words accurately reflect the legalities of the situation: the Romans have crucified a self-styled king for high treason. More profoundly, however, Mark is allowing his readers see that this man is not a self-styled king, but God's King, his Messiah who is crucified.

By his entry to Jerusalem, Jesus revealed himself as 'king of the Jews', challenging the temple authorities and the people to receive him. But his demands were too great; they rejected him. Now the king must die. The one being crucified is the Christ of God who drinks 'the cup', undergoes 'the baptism', in obedience to the Father's will (8:29,31; 10:38; 14:36). This is the 'hour' of God's kingdom, the 'time' for the king to mount his throne. Thus *Christ crucified* will become the central message of the apostles (1 Corinthians 2:2; 15:3-5; Galatians 3:1; Colossians 2:13-14; 1 Peter 1:19; Revelation 5:5-6).

Passover was the opportune time and Golgotha a suitably public place (cf verse 29 — *those who passed by*) for the Romans to crucify also those held in custody for the recent uprising (15:7). The two criminals between whom Jesus was crucified were in reality not *robbers* (as in the NIV) but 'revolutionaries' (Greek *lestai*, a word often used by Josephus for Jewish freedom fighters.) How deeply ironical that Jesus, who had repudiated the way of violence and introduced the ethic of forgiving the enemy (11:25; Matthew 5:43-48), should be crucified between men committed to violence and vengeance, and be depicted as the king who exemplified their nationalistic cause. But in letting us see that Jesus died the death Barabbas should have died (cf Acts 3:14), Mark is teaching us that Jesus died in the place of others.

It is the author's remarkable achievement that his bare narrative of the events also serves as their interpretation. Some of Mark's most important theological statements about Jesus now follow. It is a tribute to his skills that such profound statements are found in the mouths of those who deride the crucified man.

First, *those who passed by*, on what would have been a popular route, *hurled insults at him ... 'So! You who are going to destroy the temple and build it in three days, come down from the cross and save yourself!'* This half-truth about the temple's destruction had been thrown at Jesus the previous night at the Sanhedrin trial, and by now had gained currency among the wider population. Mark would have us understand that the temple will be destroyed – though not directly by Jesus – and replaced after three days by a temple of Jesus' own making (cf 11:22; 13:27; John 2:19).

Next, *the chief priests and the teachers of the law mocked him among themselves*, saying, *'He saved others but he can't save himself!'* Once more we are presented with profound insights, uttered ironically from the lips of Jesus' enemies. By his death, Jesus would indeed *save others* at the cost of his own life (10:45; 14:24). But as the obedient Son of God (cf

14:36), who had displayed great power to heal others (eg 9:17-29), he is now powerless to *save himself,* helpless and vulnerable. The power of God is at work in the powerless Christ to save others (cf 1 Corinthians 1:21-25).

The chief priests continue, *'Let this Christ, this King of Israel, come down from the cross, that we may see and believe.'* Once more they unintentionally declare the truth about Jesus. What do they want to *see and believe?* If they were to see Jesus *come down from the cross,* they say they would believe that he is the Christ. But the Christ, the King of Israel, is reigning from the cross, bringing in the kingdom; he cannot come down. It is not God's will that he save himself; he must save others. Mark's profundity is expressed in simplicity and naivety.

Finally, *those crucified with him also heaped insults on him,* but their words are not recorded. Here is evidence that Jesus was not a revolutionary like them, that the conviction 'king of the Jews' was legally ridiculous.

(7) The death of Jesus (15:33-40)

Mark now narrates the final three hours of Jesus' life, from the sixth hour (noon) to the ninth hour (3.00pm) on the day of preparation for the Sabbath (Friday).

From the beginning of his story Mark has been preparing us with a series of events: the rapidly approaching kingdom of God (1:14-15); the Holy One's struggle with and destruction of Satan and the demons (1:24; 3:26-27); the 'cup' and 'baptism' which Jesus must endure when he comes to Jerusalem (10:38; 14:36); and Jesus' death which will be the 'ransom for many' and 'the [new] covenant' (10:45; 14:24). Now Mark wants us to understand that all these events are but different aspects of one event: the death of Jesus. His death achieves every task which has been signalled earlier within the narrative.

Mark describes four *signs* which occur during these three hours, each one telling us that the 'hour' of God has at last struck, that God's time has finally come, that transactions of cosmic and eternal importance are taking place.

First, *at the sixth hour darkness came over the whole land until the ninth hour.* Since it was midday, at the time of a full moon, astronomically this could not have been an eclipse of the sun. (There is evidence from a Samaritan contemporary, the historian Thallus, which may confirm the historicity of this period of darkness in Palestine – see Julius Africanus, *Extant Writings,* xviii.1). It must have been a miraculous and cosmic sign. But of what? At one level the darkness was God's sign of his profound disapproval of the cruel acts against a good and innocent man. At a deeper level, however, the darkness must be interpreted by Jesus' cry of abandonment (verse 34) as the sign of Jesus' 'baptism' in cosmic evil. In this last ordeal with Satan and the demons, the Son of God is overcome by the hosts of darkness. Yet Jesus absorbs the evil within himself and forever breaks its power.

Second, *at the ninth hour Jesus cried out in a loud voice, 'Eloi, Eloi, lama sabachthani?'* — Aramaic words which Mark translates for his Greek readers as, *'My God, my God, why have you forsaken me?'* These are the opening words of Psalm 22. It is likely that Jesus was meditating on this Psalm during his final moments of life.

The 'saints of the Most High', the Twelve, have failed the test of loyalty to the Son of Man. Among God's people Jesus alone is found to be obedient to God, alone worthy to suffer for others. But what is the nature of his suffering? Not primarily crucifixion, awful as that was: many have suffered this or worse. Jesus' suffering is a 'cup' to be drunk, a 'baptism' to be undergone, which only he can endure. It is the suffering of the separation of the Son from the Father with whom he had enjoyed unhindered fellowship, on account of sins — not his own, but those of 'the many' whom he had come to rescue (10:45). At the Jordan River the Father had declared his pleasure in his beloved Son (1:11), but at Golgotha the Son declares himself to be forsaken by his Father. Now he is engulfed in sins, of which the darkness over the land is a sign. In Paul's words, the Holy One of God 'became sin' (2 Corinthians 5:21). This is a mystery equalled only by the incarnation.

Bystanders mistook Jesus' words, *'Eloi, Eloi,'* as a cry to Elijah the prophet, who was taken up to heaven in a chariot (2 Kings 2:11). Perhaps to them the unnatural darkness was a sign that he would appear to rescue the crucified man. The offering of *wine vinegar* and the request, *'Now leave him alone,'* were intended to keep Jesus alive till the spectacular apocalyptic appearance of the fiery prophet. It was another version of the earlier plea for 'a sign from heaven' (cf 8:11-12).

As then, Jesus rejects the request, not with words on this occasion, but with action — his death: *With a loud cry Jesus breathed his last.* In Mark's account, Jesus' life is not taken from him. He had been sovereign in rejection and suffering; now he is king even in death, choosing his own moment of dying. When the work of salvation was complete, as symbolised by the darkness, Jesus released his own life.

The death of Jesus is followed by the third sign, namely that *the curtain of the temple was torn in two from top to bottom.* This sign points to the destruction of the temple as prophesied by Jesus. The prophecy, which his enemies interpreted in a distorted way, was one of the two main reasons the Sanhedrin had handed Jesus over to the Romans for execution. The curtain in question was probably the one visible from the outer court, rather than the curtain to the Holy of Holies, beyond which only the high priest could pass.

The symbolism is powerful. At the death of Jesus, the curtain is torn from the *top* — that is, by God — signifying the divine foreclosure of the temple. But the death of Jesus will be followed after three days by his resurrection, and with it, the resurrection of the temple. It will, however, be a new temple of praying believers in Christian congregations (see comment on 11:22-25; John 2:19-21). The destruction of Herod's temple and the rise of Christian congregations are direct consequences of the death of Jesus.

The fourth sign is the utterance of the Roman *centurion*, the duty officer of the crucifixion squad. It is possible this was the man who had taken Jesus into custody when the temple authorities handed him over to Pilate. It also is possible that he was present at the torture session inside the Praetorium after the prefect had given his verdict. This would mean that he had had the opportunity to observe the demeanour of Jesus for much of that day. At any rate, the man was deeply impressed with him. When he heard Jesus' cry and saw how he died, he said, *'Surely this man was the Son of God!'*

This signals the climax of Mark's narrative. The centurion's utterance here at Golgotha, coming near the end of the story, is presented as heaven-inspired, matching the words which God himself had directed to his beloved Son at the Jordan, near the beginning of the story (1:11). Mark positions the readers in front of the crucified man; we stand with the centurion and confess with him, *'Surely this man was the Son of God.'*

Once more the meaning of Mark's narrative is directly apparent and needs little elaboration. That a *Roman*, for whom crucixion was an unmentionable obscenity, declares a crucified Jew to be the *Son of God* is astonishing. Romans only applied that title to the Roman emperor, who was associated with power and triumph. But this soldier applies the title to Jesus – a poor, humiliated, crucified man.

This represents an inconceivable reversal in values. This Gentile is the first man to see Jesus as God sees him, as the

Son of God (cf 1:11). He sees what the disciples have not yet seen. This man is the forerunner of many 'Romans' who over the next centuries will declare the crucified one to be the Son of God. Indeed, historically speaking, this man is the first Christian confessor.

It appears that no disciples are present to comfort Jesus in death, except 'the disciple whom he loved' (see John 19:26-27). But there are many *women,* including some from Galiee who *had followed him and cared for his needs* (cf Luke 8:2-3), and others *who had come up with him to Jerusalem.* They *were watching from a distance* — in silence, as the Romans did not permit mourning for executed criminals. Among them are *Mary Magdalene, Mary the mother of James the younger and of Joses, and Salome.* Mary Magdalene (that is, Mary from the fishing village Magdala to the south of Capernaum) had been healed of severe demon possession by Jesus (Luke 8:2). Nothing is known of the other Mary or of her son James the younger, but Salome may have been the mother of James and John Zebedee cf (Matthew 27:56).

It is a fact of great significance that these women, not the Twelve, were witnesses to Jesus' death (verse 40), his burial (verse 47) and the empty tomb (16:1,8). The Gospel of John also tells us that the first appearance of the risen Lord was to Mary Magdalene (John 20:10-18). And these events — the death, the burial, the discovery of the empty tomb, the appearance of the risen Jesus — are the leading elements in the gospel proclamation (cf 1 Corinthians 15:3-5). It is well known that the legal testimony of women was unacceptable among the Jews (Mishnah, *Rosh Ha Shanah,* 1.8), and this may be the reason the oral tradition of resurrection sightings quoted in 1 Corinthians 15:5-8 mentions only men. But according to the gospel writers, those who were on hand to witness these major events, and who therefore must have been the source of the information used in the gospels and indeed in 1 Corinthians 15:3-5, were women.

(8) The burial of Jesus (15:42-47)

The women who witnessed the death of Jesus were faced
with further agony. According to Jewish Law, if the corpse
of someone executed for a capital offence is left hanging
overnight, the land is defiled (Deuteronomy 21:23; cf John
19:32). Yet, as the women probably knew, the Romans
denied burial to anyone who had been crucified for high
treason. Meanwhile, it was now late in the afternoon and
Preparation Day (Greek *prosabbaton*) would end at nightfall.
Once the Sabbath had begun nothing further could be done
for the corpse of Jesus hanging on the cross. Defilement
seemed inevitable.

Yet, *as evening approached, Joseph of Arimathea* [30
kilometres north-west of Jerusalem], *a prominent member of
the Council* [= Sanhedrin] ... *went boldly to Pilate and asked for
Jesus' body.* Mark tells us that Joseph *was himself waiting for
the kingdom of God,* a secret disciple of Jesus (cf John 19:38).
Perhaps he had heard Jesus debating in the temple courts
in the days leading up to his arrest. Nonetheless,
considerable courage is implied by his approach to the
prefect; his discipleship was now out in the open.

As we have noted, Jesus released his own life when the
three hours of darkness had passed (15:37), but victims of
crucifixion usually suffered for days. So *Pilate was surprised
to hear that he was already dead* (cf John 19:31) and asked the
centurion *if Jesus had already died.* The centurion confirmed
it, then, for reasons not given, Pilate exercised his discretion
as a Roman magistrate and released the body of the man
executed for high treason for burial.

Then Joseph (with Nicodemus, cf John 19:39), having
purchased *some linen,* returned to Golgotha and *took down
the body* of Jesus from the pole and crosspiece. By now it was
quite late, with the Sabbath very near (John 19:31,42).
Moreover, the site prescribed for the burial of criminals was

some distance from Jerusalem. However, there was a newly hewn *tomb* close to the place of crucifixion (John 19:41) — according to Matthew, it was Joseph's own tomb (Matthew 27:60) — and it was decided to place the body of Jesus there. Finally, as was customary, *a stone* was rolled against *the entrance of the tomb* to afford protection from grave-robbers and wild animals. And just as the Galilean women, *Mary Magdalene and Mary the mother of Joses,* had witnessed Jesus' death, so now they witness his burial, noting the place *where he was laid.*

QUESTIONS ON MARK 15:1-47

1.   What is your verdict on the accusation that Jesus was 'king of the Jews'?
2.   How does Mark bring out the irony that the 'king of the Jews' was crucified?
3.   Who does Mark blame for the death of Jesus?
4.   Why was crucifixion so horrific? Why does Mark give so few details?
5.   How was Jesus different from the other two men who were crucified (15:27)?
6.   What profound truths are unintentionally stated by those who mocked Jesus (15:31-32)?
7.   Which four signs accompany the death of Jesus (15:33-40)?
8.   Why does Mark show so much interest in the burial of Jesus (15:42-47)?

24

The empty
tomb   16:1-8

Mark's story began with the mysterious appearance of a
powerful but enigmatic stranger (1:1); now the narrative
ends just as mysteriously. The tomb where Jesus was buried
is empty and he is gone. The end of the story focuses on
three women and is told in four brief scenes.

(1) Saturday night (16:1)

When the Sabbath was over, on the Saturday evening, the
three Galilean women – *Mary Magdalene, Mary mother of
James, and Salome – bought spices ... to anoint Jesus' body.*
Presumably they are unaware that it has already been done
(John 19:40). They anxiously wait for the night to pass so as
to come to the tomb at the first opportunity.

(2) Sunday morning: Back to the tomb (16:2-4)

In the New Testament, Easter day is referred to in two
ways. Mark and John (John 20:1) both speak of *the first day
of the week* (Greek *te mia ton sabbaton*). Thus, the resurrection
of Jesus apparently influenced believers to meet together
regularly on the first day, Sunday (Acts 20:7; I Corinthians
16:2; cf John 20:19,26). On the other hand (and equally

correct), in the oral tradition quoted by Paul, Jesus was raised on 'the third day' (1 Corinthians 15:4). This tradition appears to go back to the pre-resurrection statements of Jesus (cf Mark 8:31; 9:31; 10:34; Matthew 12:40-41; Luke 13:32; John 2:19), being passed on by the Jerusalem apostles to Paul (1 Corinthians 15:1-2).

On that day, *very early ... just after sunrise,* as the women *were on their way to the tomb ... they asked each other, 'Who will roll the stone away from the entrance of the tomb?'* Although the women knew the disciples' whereabouts (verse 7), the men had not reappeared in public, fearing arrest by the authorities.

(3) Sunday morning: In the tomb (16:5-7)

When the women *looked up, they saw that the stone, which was very large, had been rolled away.* It was typical of tombs to have an outer and an inner chamber, separated by a small opening. When the women entered the inner *burial chamber* (Greek *mnemeion*) they were *alarmed* to see *a young man dressed in a white robe sitting on the right side.* The man's youthful appearance and the whiteness of his robe suggest an angelic messenger, appropriate to an act of divine revelation as well as pointing forward to the second advent of Jesus (8:38; 13:26-27).

'Don't be alarmed,' he said, reacting to the women's alarm. This short passage contains a number of words expressing 'fear' (verses 5,6,8) which are all appropriate to this eschatological moment, signified both by the presence of the angel and by the absence of the body of Jesus. The tomb was indeed empty; the body of Jesus was not there. The angel speaks, but in reality it is God who addresses the women: *'You are looking for Jesus the Nazarene, who was crucified. He has risen! He is not here. See the place where they laid him.'*

In this divine oracle we hear the central truths of the death, burial and resurrection which are later set out in the gospel tradition formulated at Jerusalem and passed on to Paul (1 Corinthians 15:1-8). Jesus had told the disciples often enough that he would rise from the dead 'after three days' (8:31; 9:31; 10:34), though they had difficulty understanding what he meant (9:10).

Finally, the angel instructs the women, *'Go, tell his disciples and Peter, "He is going ahead of you into Galilee. There you will see him, just as he told you."'* Here we see the great mercy of Jesus in rehabilitating his disciples, who have been so blind to him throughout his ministry. They abandoned him in Gethsemane and Peter denied him at the high priest's palace. At this point there was no longer a flock. But, with Peter singled out as a sign of his kindness, Jesus has said that he is going ahead of them (in the manner of a shepherd; see comments on 10:32; 14:28) to Galilee. There he will reconstitute them as his flock. We can imagine the thankfulness of the disciples when the women gave them this message.

(4) Sunday morning: Fleeing from the tomb (16:8)

After the burial of Jesus (15:46) the reader does not meet him again. God, through the words of an angel, tells us what happens to him. The 'disappearance' of Jesus here at the end of the Gospel matches his mysterious appearance at the beginning.

In earlier times Christians were frustrated that Mark's Gospel ended on the note of the women's fear, without any reference to the appearances of the risen Lord. A more appropriate ending was composed which is sometimes printed in the margin of our translations, but it is clearly from another hand and from a later time.

305

Yet Mark's ending as it stands makes good sense. The women who come to the tomb are *alarmed.* The same word (Greek *ekthambeisthai*) is used for the overwhelming wonder of those who saw Jesus after he descended the mount of transfiguration (9:15), and for Jesus' own deep distress in Gethsemane at the prospect of his suffering (14:33). Other words for terror appear as the story closes: *trembling and bewildered* [Greek *tromos kai phobos*], *the women went out and fled from the tomb;* so terrified were they that *they said nothing to anyone, because they were afraid.* This word *afraid,* with which the gospel ends, has often been used earlier to signify people's amazement, terror and fear in the face of Jesus' miracles (4:41; 5:15,33,36; 6:50; 9:32; 11:18,32), wherever the supernatural intrudes among them.

The absence of the risen Jesus — a tomb that is empty — combined with the presence of an angel who speaks for God, symbolises the universal and unrestricted lordship of Jesus in his resurrection persona, the Son of Man who will appear in the glory of his Father with the holy angels (8:38). The women were terrified because they were standing at the edge of this eschatological abyss. In the emptiness of the tomb, eternity yawned wide before them. And that future belongs to God.

QUESTIONS ON MARK 16:1-8

1. Would you have preferred Mark to describe some of the resurrection appearances of Jesus? Explain your answer.
2. Does the ending suffer for the lack of any Great Commission (see 8:35; 10:29-30; 13:10; 14:9)?
3. What does this passage say about Jesus' relationship with the disciples?
4. What does the women's terror really tell us?

Notes

Other titles in the
Reading the Bible Today series

Apocalypse Now and Then – Reading Revelation Today
Paul Barnett

Kingdoms in Conflict – Reading Daniel Today
Andrew Reid

Dust to Destiny – Reading Romans Today
David Seccombe

The Majestic Son – Reading Hebrews Today
Peter Adam

The Tree of Life – Reading Proverbs Today
Graeme Goldsworthy

Order copies directly from
**Aquila Press: PO Box A287, Sydney South, NSW 1235
Ph: (02) 8268 3344 Fax: (02) 9283 3987**
or contact your local Christian bookshop.